THE THOUGHT OF MAO TSE-TUNG

Also in the series:

Mao Tse-tung in the Scales of History (1977) *edited by Dick Wilson*

Shanghai: Revolution and Development in an Asian Metropolis (1980) *edited by Christopher Howe*

Mao Zedong and the Political Economy of the Border Region: A Translation of Mao's *Economic and Financial Problems* (1980) *edited and translated by Andrew Watson*

The Politics of Marriage in Contemporary China (1981) *by Elisabeth Croll*

Food Grain Procurement and Consumption in China (1984) *by Kenneth R. Walker*

Class and Social Stratification in Post-Revolution China (1984) *edited by James L. Watson*

Warlord Soldiers. Chinese Common Soldiers, 1911–1937 (1985) *by Diana Lary*

Centre and Province in the People's Republic of China: Sichuan and Guizhou, 1955–1965 (1986) *by David S. G. Goodman*

Economic Development in Provincial China: The Central Shaanxi since 1930 (1988) *by Eduard B. Vermeer*

THE THOUGHT
OF MAO TSE-TUNG

STUART SCHRAM

Professor of Politics
School of Oriental and African Studies
University of London

Generously Donated to

The Frederick Douglass Institute

By Professor Jesse Moore

Fall 2000

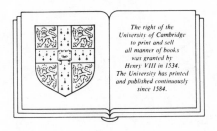

The right of the
University of Cambridge
to print and sell
all manner of books
was granted by
Henry VIII in 1534.
The University has printed
and published continuously
since 1584.

CAMBRIDGE UNIVERSITY PRESS

Cambridge   New York   Port Chester
Melbourne   Sydney

Published by the Press Syndicate of the University of Cambridge
The Pitt Building, Trumpington Street, Cambridge CB2 1RP
32 East 57th Street, New York, NY 10022, USA
10 Stamford Road, Oakleigh, Melbourne 3166, Australia

First published 1989

Printed in Great Britain at the
University Press, Cambridge

British Library cataloguing in publication data
Schram, Stuart R.
The thought of Mao Tse-Tung.
1. Mao, Zedong 2 China – Politics and
government – 1912–1949 3. China – Politics
and government – 1949– 4. China –
History – 1900–
I. Title
951.05'092'4   DS778.M3

Library of Congress cataloguing in publication data
Schram, Stuart R.
The thought of Mao Tse-Tung / Stuart Schram.
p.   cm.
Bibliography.
Includes index.
ISBN 0 521 32549 8   ISBN 0 521 31062 8 (pbk)
1. Mao Tse-tung. 1893–1976 – Political and social views.
2. Communism – China – History.   3. China – History – 20th century.
I. Title.
DS778.M3S34   1988
951.05'092'4 – dc19
87-24617
CIP

ISBN 0 521 32549 8 hard covers
ISBN 0 521 31062 8 paperback

CONTENTS

PREFACE

The body of this book consists of my chapter on Mao Tse-tung's thought down to 1949, already published in Volume 13 of the *Cambridge History of China*, and my chapter on Mao's thought from 1949 to 1976, which will appear in due course in Volume 15 of the *Cambridge History*. Some minor editorial changes have been made, but it has not been possible, because of technical constraints, to modify the text at will, especially in the first half of this book. As a result, the account of Mao Tse-tung's thought which follows remains very largely a summary and analysis of his ideas. Though I sought wherever possible to relate these succinctly to the circumstances in which they were elaborated, it would not have been appropriate, in the original context, to deal at any length with historical facts covered in other chapters of the larger work, even in the case of events which decisively influenced Mao's own intellectual development.

It is the purpose of the Introduction and Conclusion, which have been written specifically for this book, to compensate for these omissions, and to situate the development of Mao's thought in a wider framework. The Introduction takes up, first of all, the problem of the nature of the process of revolutionary change in China in the twentieth century which Mao Tse-tung sought to master, and the factors which enabled him to play the role he did. It then examines the relation between phases in Mao's life, and turning points in his thinking. As for the Conclusion, its purpose is not to sum up yet again the main tenets of Mao Tse-tung's thought, but rather to assess its continuing significance in China, and its likely future place in a system, and a society, which some people argue has been undergoing 'de-Maoization'.

While I do not regard this book as an adequate, still less as a definitive account of Mao Tse-tung's intellectual development, it builds on work which I have done over the past quarter century. Whether or not it takes my interpretation a step further will be for others to judge. The fact that I have conducted research on Mao's thought for a number of years does mean, in any case, that I have accumulated many debts, and it is my very pleasant duty here to acknowledge these.

In so doing, it is appropriate to go back to the beginning. My earliest published monograph in this field, a translation and analysis of Mao's 1917 article 'A study of physical culture', benefited from the encouragement and criticism of Etienne Balazs, whose seminar I had the privilege of attending in Paris in the early 1960s. Thereafter, a year spent at the East Asian Research Center of Harvard University, supported by a Rockefeller Foundation fellowship, provided the opportunity to produce my first attempt at an overview of Mao's thought.

In the course of this work, I received assistance from many people and institutions, as noted in detail in the Acknowledgements to *The political thought of Mao Tse-tung*. Among them, three were pre-eminent. John Fairbank, the then Director of the Center, presided over the activities of those working there with his characteristic mixture of discipline and cordiality. Benjamin Schwartz provided, in the course of a year during which we shared the same suite of offices, exceptional intellectual stimulation and judicious comments on my ideas. Eugene Wu, as Curator of the East Asian Collections of the Hoover Institution, facilitated my initial encounter with the materials of the Yenan period, thus helping me to open the door to research on Mao Tse-tung's intellectual itinerary based on the pre-1949 texts of his writings.

In the summer of 1962, as I read *Chieh-fang jih-pao* in the Hoover Library, I could not have imagined that I would subsequently become acquainted with leading members of its editorial staff such as Yü Kuang-yuan, Li Jui, Liao Kai-lung and Wen Chi-tse. This fact symbolizes the political changes which have subsequently taken place in the world, and the intellectual changes they have brought in their wake. Already in 1963 I was indebted not only to European and American, but to Japanese scholars and libraries for materials and for valuable exchanges of views. The role of Japan in research on Mao Tse-tung's thought was vastly increased by the compilation, in the early 1970s, of the ten-volume *Mao Tse-tung chi*, edited by Takeuchi Minoru. Very many materials were, however, simply not available outside China itself, and without the extensive publication of these since 1978, both in openly available and in internal editions, our knowledge of Mao's thought would be far more fragmentary and incomplete than is today the case. Indeed, the supplement to the Tokyo edition, comprising nine volumes of texts plus an index, published in the early 1980s, was derived in substantial measure from *nei-pu* collections produced in China.

Apart from the opportunity to consult printed documents, I have, as already suggested, obtained an entirely new perspective on Mao's life and thought thanks to the six visits which I have been privileged to make to the Chinese Academy of Social Sciences, where I was received by the Institute of Marxism-Leninism and Mao Tse-tung Thought in June–July 1980,

April–May 1982, September 1982, March–April 1984, and March–April 1986, and by the Institute of Philosophy in December–January 1987–88. The list of Chinese scholars and political figures with whom I have discussed such questions is too long to reproduce here. Some indications regarding particular points of fact or interpretation are contained in the notes to the body of this book.

Particular thanks are due to the successive Directors of the Institute of Marxism-Leninism, Yü Kuang-yuan (until May 1982), and Su Shao-chih (from then until 1987), and also to Liao Kai-lung and Feng Lan-jui, Deputy Directors until May 1982, as well as to the Director of the Institute of Philosophy, Hsing Fen-ssu. They and their colleagues have devoted many hours of valuable time to talking with me about issues relating to Mao Tse-tung's thought, to commenting on my own interpretation (including drafts of various portions of this volume), to organizing seminars, and to arranging meetings and access to materials. I have also benefited greatly from a number of conversations with Kung Yü-chih and his colleagues of the Research Centre on Party Literature under the Central Committee. Needless to say, none of those mentioned here bears any responsibility whatever for the views expressed in this work, but without these exchanges my interpretation would have been the poorer.

My gratitude for these opportunities also extends, as a matter of course, to the institutions which have provided the resources for my visits to China: the British Academy, and the Economic and Social Research Council, which have nominated me under their joint exchange scheme with the Chinese Academy of Social Sciences and financed my travel, and the Chinese Academy itself, which has provided generous hospitality and assistance during the periods I have spent in China. The National Endowment for the Humanities likewise contributed to the cost of my participation in the 'North American Delegation to Investigate Problems of the Chinese Revolution' in the summer of 1980, which marked the crucial first step in my contacts with Chinese scholars. I have also received financial assistance from the School of Oriental and African Studies for several brief visits to Japan, and to American libraries, to pursue my research for this volume.

Valuable as access to China has been during the past decade, the kindness I have been shown there, and the lessons I have learned there do not make me forget the constantly accumulating obligations I owe to friends and colleagues outside China, from whom I have continued to receive both stimulation and help in locating sources.

As regards materials, particular thanks are due in two quarters. On the one hand, Takeuchi Minoru, Nakamura Kimiyoshi, and the Japanese scholars associated with the *Mao Tse-tung chi* have given me copies of many important documentary collections on Mao's thought after, as well as before, 1949. On the other, the Harvard-Yenching Institute, which has recently collected many volumes of internal editions of Mao's writings, has allowed me to consult these, and to xerox some key texts. The unrevised text of Mao's speech of 27 February 1957 on contradictions among the people, as originally delivered, and his talks at the Pei-tai-ho Conference of August 1958, which (as will be seen below) play a central role in my interpretation of Mao's thought of the 1957–8 period, have been taken from this source. A volume of translations drawn from the same collection, accompanied by interpretative articles, will be published by Harvard University under the title *The secret speeches of Chairman Mao*. As the present book goes to press, I have not yet seen this collective assessment of Mao's thought of the Great Leap period, but I am grateful, once again, to Eugene Wu, now the Librarian of the Yenching Institute, for giving me the opportunity to incorporate these important materials into my own analysis.

My debt to the editors of the *Cambridge History of China*, for which the chapters making up the bulk of this book were originally written, is likewise considerable. Roderick MacFarquhar, joint editor of Volumes 14 and 15, has subjected my discussion of Mao's thought since 1949 to very careful scrutiny and criticism, and has made many helpful suggestions for improving it. John Fairbank, the general editor, sent me ten pages of witty, incisive and judicious comments on the chapter for Volume 13 before it was published, and has contributed substantially to the form and substance of the post-1949 half of the book as well.

Finally, I wish to express my gratitude to the organizers of, and participants in, the many seminars and other meetings at which my interpretation of various aspects and periods in Mao Tse-tung's thought has been subjected to criticism, often searching but always useful as a spur to further reflection. Over the years, such occasions have taken place in Europe (from London, Edinburgh and Aberystwyth to Paris, Venice and Naples), in Asia (from Delhi, Beijing, Changsha and Hsiang-t'an to Tokyo and Kyoto), and in many parts of North America (from Berkeley, Stanford and San Diego to Boston and New York, and from Vancouver to Mexico City). The institutions and individuals involved are far too numerous to mention. Some of my interlocutors may regret that I do not appear to have learned as much as I might have from their observations. The fault for this must, of course, rest entirely with me, as does the responsibility for errors and shortcomings in general.

INTRODUCTION

This book is about revolution in China in the twentieth century, and Mao Tse-tung's role in shaping that revolution. Mao's influence was exerted in various guises, including the taking of decisions which determined the course of events, and also the cultivation of myths centred on his own person, especially in his later years. The most general, and probably the most lasting expression of his contribution to the Chinese revolution was, however, Mao Tse-tung's thought. My purpose is to elucidate the development of that thought, and in so doing to shed light on other aspects of Mao and of his times.

'Ideas grow out of history; they also shape history,' I wrote at the beginning of my first attempt at an overview of the thought of Mao Tse-tung.[1] That proposition, while undoubtedly true, conveys far too simple and schematic a view of the problems with which we are dealing. It suggests (especially as I elaborated it two decades ago) that ideas are put together by drawing on a variety of sources, and that, having been formulated, they are then applied in order to achieve certain goals. In reality, both the content of Mao's ideas and their function were constantly changing in the course of their implementation, although there were major elements of continuity, grounded both in Mao's own nature and in China's predicament.

The stages in this process, the substance of Mao's thought during each stage, and the influences which led to significant changes and innovations, form the main burden of this work as a whole. This Introduction offers some preliminary considerations on the Chinese revolution, and Mao's role in it.

Thus far, I have used the term 'revolution' without specifying what I meant by it. No precise and rigorous definition can be given except on the basis of a theory of revolution, and it is not my intention to add one more such theory or paradigm to those which have already been put forward. For present purposes, it will suffice to stipulate that by revolution, as distinguished from other forms of change, I refer to a transformation which is far-

---

[1] S. Schram, *The political thought of Mao Tse-tung*, hereafter *PTMT*, p. 15. (The first edition of 1963 began with the same sentence.)

I

reaching, rapid, and involves an element of rupture or discontinuity with the past. All three of these characteristics are, of course, somewhat ambiguous. Not only are the scope and speed of change matters of degree, but the boundary between continuity and discontinuity implies a judgement as to which aspects of reality are decisive in determining the nature or quality of the thing in question. Taken together, however, these three indications should suffice to evoke the type of phenomenon under discussion.

Can one speak of *the* Chinese revolution of the twentieth century? Has there been a continuous revolutionary process since the beginning of the century, or even since the early nineteenth century, a process in which each phase was the logical and ineluctable sequel to what preceded it? Or have there been a series of discrete revolutionary changes, not necessarily linked together by some inexorable chain of causality?

It is useful in examining this question to distinguish not only between successive phases, but also between various dimensions or aspects of revolution: political revolution, national revolution, cultural revolution, social revolution, economic revolution, technological revolution. Mao himself referred many times over the years to all six of these types of revolution. Like Lenin, he regarded politics as the 'leading thread', and the conquest of political power as the key to all other dimensions of change. At the same time, he saw national, cultural and social revolution as the indispensable complement of political revolution if it were to be carried to completion.

A first political revolution (regarded in China as 'bourgeois' in nature) had already taken place before Mao began to play even a minor role in Chinese history. The 1911 revolution was, to be sure, a diffuse and inconclusive event. It was not organized, controlled and carried through by a clearly defined political force, like the victory of 1949, or even Chiang Kai-shek's establishment of a National government in 1927. Sun Yat-sen, Huang Hsing, and the organizations they led had contributed to creating the conditions for the overthrow of the monarchy, but they had neither brought about the uprising of 10 October 1911, nor succeeded in determining its consequences. None the less, by discrediting once and for all the imperial idea, the 1911 Revolution opened the door not only to further political change, but to other forms of revolution as well.

However significant the change of regime which took place in 1911, the collapse of the Ch'ing dynasty was the culmination of a process which had been under way since early in the nineteenth century. Nor was it simply the result of the Western impact, in the period following the Opium War. The root causes were in large measure internal: the population explosion of the late eighteenth and early nineteenth centuries, and the emergence of other economic and social forces with which the old order was unable to cope. The foreigners did, all the same, hasten the end of the dynasty even as they supported it, as well as adding by their presence new elements to the revolutionary equation.

Nationalist ferment was increasingly in evidence in China from 1840 onwards. Foreign penetration and encroachment on Chinese rights, on the part of the Europeans, the Americans and the Japanese, soon reached a level which aroused not only xenophobic reactions among the peasantry, but the sentiment, in nearly all categories of the Chinese political and intellectual elite, that the situation must be redressed. In the 1850s, Marx and Engels had referred to the Taiping Rebellion as a 'formidable revolution', and as a 'popular war for the maintenance of Chinese nationality' (today we would say a 'war of national liberation').[2] There was, in any case, an impulse to national revolution, which soon took more modern forms than had been the case with the Taipings, or with the Boxers.

This nationalist sentiment had, of course, contributed to the political revolution of 1911 because, quite apart from hostility to the Manchu rulers of the Ch'ing dynasty as an alien race, they appeared to be doing their job badly, and hence, in traditional terms, to have lost the Mandate. Anguish before the prospect of *wang kuo mieh chung* – the loss of the state (or nation) and the extinction of the race – led increasing numbers of Chinese to move from the camp of reform to the camp of revolution.

Such a rejection of the imperial idea constituted a revolution in Chinese political culture, but it was also the consequence of the cultural changes which had been under way since the middle of the nineteenth century. First the piecemeal, and then the wholesale introduction of Western ideas, and the drastic re-shaping of China's own tradition under these influences, had led to new trends in thought which can only be called revolutionary, even before the advent of the May Fourth movement. Thus national revolution and cultural revolution nourished one another.

In the political revolution which followed the Wuhan uprising, Mao Tse-tung, as a soldier in the revolutionary army, had been only a bit player. In the accelerating cultural revolution of the May Fourth period, and the increasingly forceful and organized manifestations of nationalism, from the aftermath of the Twenty-one Demands of 1915 to the May Thirtieth Movement of 1925 and the events of 1926–7, he was a significant, though not yet a dominant actor. Of the social revolution which emerged in the 1920s in the form of peasant militancy in the countryside, Mao was, if not the initiator (that honour belongs to P'eng P'ai), the most successful

[2] K. Marx, 'Revolution in China and in Europe', 20 May 1853; F. Engels, 'Persia and China', 22 May 1857. For extracts, see H. Carrère d'Encausse and S. Schram, *Marxism and Asia*, pp. 119–21, 123–4.

exponent, and the one who channelled it in the form of guerrilla warfare from rural bases.

Does this mean that Mao Tse-tung was, as many writers have claimed over the decades, a 'peasant revolutionary'? Some have argued this view simply on the grounds that he perceived the revolutionary potential inherent in the peasantry, and made revolution in the countryside. Others have gone much farther, insisting that, in 1927, Mao did not merely turn his back on the cities for the time being, but utterly rejected all notions of working-class leadership or of any role for the urban intellectual elite, and made himself the servant of utopian aspirations immanent among the peasantry.

That Mao Tse-tung mobilized the peasants to make revolution is indisputably true; that he blindly followed the ideas of the peasants instead of leading them is patently absurd. The evidence for his commitment to the Leninist conception of the vanguard party, in theory and in practice, is overwhelming. The thesis of a total rupture between the Chinese revolution before 1927, dominated by the urban intellectual elite, and the Chinese revolution under Mao's leadership thereafter, in which the urban elite played no part, cannot be sustained. It remains true that Mao's awareness of the centrality of the peasants in Chinese society, and the influence of certain agrarian ideals on his mind, persisted for half a century, from the mid-1920s to 1976, and wove a complex contrapuntal pattern with the explicitly Marxist and 'orthodox' elements in his thought.

On the other hand, Mao's view of revolution was remarkable for the importance he attached not only to those educated individuals who served as the theorists and organizers of the party, but to intellectuals in general. 'The whole of the Chinese revolutionary movement found its origin in the action of young students and intellectuals who had been awakened,' Mao declared in 1939 in a passage subsequently removed from his speech on the anniversary of the May Fourth movement.[3] He added, to be sure, that this movement, launched by the intellectuals, could achieve its goal of defeating 'imperialism' and 'feudalism' only if it united with the 'main force', made up of the workers and peasants. The categorical statement that the initial impetus came from young students and intellectuals none the less reflects one facet of Mao's Tse-tung's own personal vision of the Chinese revolution of the twentieth century.

It was a vision which remained remarkably consistent from the time of the May Fourth movement onwards. 'The world is ours, the nation is ours, society is ours,' he wrote in August 1919. 'If we do not speak, who will speak? If we do not act, who will act?'[4] There is implied here, not merely the

[3] Schram, *PTMT* 354–5; *Mao Tse-tung chi*, hereafter *MTTC*, 6.332.
[4] Mao Tse-tung, 'The great union of the popular masses', tr. S. Schram, *The China Quarterly*, hereafter *CQ*, 49 (Jan.–March 1972) 84.

claim that the destinies of China are in the hands of his generation, but a certain view, expressed more clearly in the text of 1939 just quoted, about the relation between the various aspects of the revolutionary process which I have been discussing. Many years later, in his reading notes of 1959–60 on a Soviet textbook of political economy, he was to put these insights together in an explicitly-formulated theory of historical causality:

All revolutionary history shows that the full development of new productive forces is not the prerequisite for the transformation of backward production relations. Our revolution began with Marxist-Leninist propaganda, which served to create new public opinion in society, and thereby to push forward the revolution. Only after the backward superstructure had been overthrown in the course of revolution was it possible to destroy the old production relations. After the old production relations had been destroyed, and new ones established, the way was cleared for the development of new social productive forces . . .

It is a gëneral rule that you cannot solve the problem of ownership, and go on to develop the productive forces in a big way, until you have created public opinion and seized political power.[5]

Manifestly, the view expressed here that, while change may be triggered off by an incremental development of the productive forces, fundamental changes can only follow political revolution, itself prepared and made possible by the mobilization of public opinion, is in harmony with Mao's consistent stress on the importance of conscious activity, subjective forces and the superstructure. It should be noted also, however, that the schema outlined in this passage fits both the pattern of Mao's own life, and the broader context of Chinese history and culture.

The industrialization launched by Chang Chih-tung (which he more than once designated as the starting point for the Chinese revolution as a whole)[6] having initiated a process of change, Mao Tse-tung and other, at the time more eminent participants in the May Fourth movement were able to carry through the cultural revolution which ultimately opened the door to political revolution, and then to socialist transformation after 1949. That is how Mao saw it, and that is how it was. But in forging a general theory of revolution from this experience, Mao was also following a deeply-ingrained Chinese bent. Not only had intellectuals played a crucial role in the Chinese political system for more than two thousand years, but in a society ruled in accordance with the written word, 'creating public opinion' necessarily required the participation of the wielders of brush and pen, as was the case in 1919. Mao Tse-tung regarded this as a matter of course; it is doubtful if he was even aware of the differences between China and other cultures, not based on a written tradition, in this respect. In other words, he was not so

---

[5] *Mao Tse-tung ssu-siang wan-sui* (1969), 334, 347; Mao Tsetung, *A critique of Soviet economics* (tr. Moss Roberts), 51, 66–7. [6] See below, p. 131.

much a 'peasant revolutionary' as an intellectual of peasant origins engaged in revolution, as he might, in a different age, have practised the art of government.

I said above that the May Fourth movement had contributed to the victory of 1949, and it is widely accepted that this was the case. The relative importance of these two events is, however, a more controversial issue. Until recently, the official Chinese view has been that the May Fourth movement constituted the dividing line between 'modern' and 'contemporary' history, and thus, by implication, marked a more fundamental change than 1949. In the early 1980s, preference was given to the view that contemporary history begins, in fact, with the conquest of power in 1949, because it is this which opened the way to a change in the mode of production, from capitalism to socialism. In an authoritative article on this subject, Li Hsin reveals that in 1956, when 1919 was officially adopted as the starting point for contemporary history, he had argued in favour of 1949, on the grounds that the mode of production was the proper criterion for a Marxist periodization of history, but that the majority disagreed.[7] It seems safe to assume that this majority, which saw the May Fourth movement as the beginning of the contemporary era, enjoyed Mao's support.

Li Hsin accepted that 1919 marked, as Mao had proclaimed in 1939, the beginning of the 'new democratic' phase of the bourgeois revolution, but underscored that, concretely, there was no change in the political system, which continued to be dominated by warlord power.[8] Mao Tse-tung was naturally aware of the importance of socialist transformation and the creation of a new mode of production. But, at the same time, Mao plainly regarded the May Fourth movement, in which he had himself participated, as an epoch-making event.[9]

Whatever the relative symbolic importance attributed to 1919 and 1949, the three decades which separate these dates saw the emergence, development and ultimate triumph of the Chinese Communist Party. It can be argued that the Communists achieved victory because, in vigorously promoting social as well as national revolution, they responded to the felt needs of the Chinese people, and to the structural requirements of China's national and international situation. Given the extremes of wealth and poverty within Chinese rural society, and the progressive breakdown of the old Confucian moral order and its replacement by relations of naked exploitation, the partisans of social revolution must, at the very least, have had a distinct tactical advantage over its adversaries.

[7] Li Hsin, 'Kuan-yü Chung-kuo chin-hsien-tai li-shih fen-ch'i wen-t'i' (On problems of periodization of Chinese modern and contemporary history), *Li-shih yen-chiu* 4 (1983) 3–6.
[8] Li Hsin, p. 4.   [9] See below, pp. 77–9.

And yet, however favourable the objective circumstances, both the fact that the Communists triumphed in 1949, and the use which they made of their victory, were not simply phenomena of 'the Chinese revolution' in general. They reflected the peculiar circumstances of the struggle for power, and they also reflected, in no small measure, the influence of one man. For better or for worse, Mao Tse-tung placed his stamp on the Chinese revolution of the twentieth century. At no point was he able to impose his own position absolutely, and since his death many of his ideas have been criticized or qualified, and some repudiated altogether. The fact remains that the influence of his thought and his leadership was so deep and all-embracing as to justify characterizing the People's Republic of China as 'the China of Mao Tse-tung'. Though his imprint has crumbled or been effaced here and there since his death, it is still unmistakably present.

Why was Mao able to dominate the scene to such a degree, for the better part of four decades? In a word, I would argue, because he was in so many ways representative of China in his day, and yet in certain crucial ways exceptional. He was born a peasant, and therefore knew (even though he forgot it for a time, during his school days) that the centre of gravity of Chinese society was in the countryside. During Mao's childhood and adolescence, his father made the transition from poor peasant to rich peasant and grain merchant, thus giving Mao a view of the inequalities of Chinese rural society from both ends of the scale. Geographically, too, he came from an intermediate position. He was not a native of the great coastal cities which, however important, were in some degree alien to rural China. But neither did he come from the remote hinterland, insulated from foreign influences and political ferment. From the time when T'an Ssu-t'ung founded the Southern Study Society there in 1897, Mao's native province of Hunan was aware of, and responsive to, new intellectual and political trends.

There were, however, millions of young Chinese of Mao's generation who likewise came from the country's geographical and social centre of gravity. What were the personal traits that set Mao apart from the others? One which should be noted at the outset is his overwhelming confidence in his own capacity for leadership. Not only did he admire strong rulers East and West, from the founders of the Ch'in and Han dynasties to Peter the Great and Napoleon, but he was plainly convinced, from early manhood, of his ability to emulate them. Such supreme self-confidence does not in itself guarantee that the possessor will play a significant political role, but it is very difficult to be an effective political leader without it.[10]

---

[10] For an extended discussion of Mao Tse-tung's leadership qualities and leadership role, see my article 'Party leader or true ruler? Foundations and significance of Mao Zedong's personal power', in S. Schram, *Foundations and limits of state power in China*, 203–56.

Another point, closely linked to this one, is Mao Tse-tung's very strong sense of identification with China and her fate. This gave rise, not only to a fierce and uncompromising nationalism, but to an insistence on the need to adapt theories of foreign origin, including Marxism, to Chinese conditions and to Chinese culture. Indeed, two of Mao's best-known theoretical contributions, contained respectively in the essays 'On practice' and 'On contradiction', can be traced back, before they were developed in Marxist terms, to very ancient Chinese ideas: that of 'seeking the truth from facts' (*shih-shih ch'iu-shih*), and the old *yin-yang* dialectics.

Peasant virtue and the vocation of the intellectuals, revolutionary theory and Chinese tradition – no doubt it was because Mao Tse-tung resonated with, and incarnated so well, *all* of these elements that he was able to play the role he did in the history of China in the twentieth century. The form in which these dispositions manifested themselves changed and developed with the years, under the influence of various historical circumstances, including the cumulative effects of his own actions. The stages in Mao Tse-tung's life and thought, and the reasons for the emergence of new ideas at particular times, are discussed one after the other in the body of this book. Here it seems appropriate to look in broad outline at the pattern as a whole.

Considering the matter from the inside, as it were, from the standpoint of Mao Tse-tung's personality and motivation, one might suggest that his attitude towards his own thought changed over the years. In his youth, Mao was primarily concerned to find a way out of China's problems, and to persuade others of the correctness of his analysis. In middle age, while continuing to seek understanding, he became concerned also with laying down a doctrine, which would be binding on his followers. In his later years, with the further unfolding of this trend, doctrine became dogma, or even ritual incantation. And yet, to the very end, he sought as well to mobilize knowledge of the past in order to chart a course to the future.

For Chinese intellectuals and political leaders, the context of the revolutionary struggle is naturally the first factor taken into consideration in interpreting Mao's thought. At the same time, they recognize that the decisive break points may be different for different dimensions of reality. Thus, in a conversation of May 1982, Liao Kai-lung suggested a separate periodization for Mao Tse-tung's life and thought, against the background of the periodization of the Chinese revolution as a whole.[11] Other authors have proposed not only a periodization for the development of Mao's thought, different from that for the history of the party, but even a separate

[11] Liao Kai-lung, 'Kuan-yü Mao Tse-tung kung-kuo p'ing-chia ho she-hui-chu-i kao-tu min-chu – tui Shih-la-mu chiao-shou lun Mao Tse-tung ti chi p'ien wen-chang ti p'ing-shu' (Regarding the evaluation of Mao Tse-tung's merits and faults, and high-level socialist democracy – a commentary and evaluation on several articles by Professor Schram on Mao Tse-tung), in Liao Kai-lung, *Ch'üan-mien chien-she she-hui-chu-i ti tao-lu* (The road to building socialism in an all-round way), 321.

framework for a particular aspect of his thought, such as his doctrine of party-building, while stressing that all of these domains are interrelated.[12]

To distinguish periods or phases in Mao's life and thought, and the crucial turning points that led from one to another, is not for us, as it is for the Chinese, a delicate and weighty political task. It may, however, prove a useful analytical device. In broad outline, the development of Mao's thought falls into six periods of approximately a decade:

1917–1927: Mao goes through a variety of learning experiences, both in his final years at school and in revolutionary organizations, from the New People's Study Society to trade unions, the Chinese Communist Party, and the Socialist Youth League. His itinerary leads from liberalism and pragmatism to Leninism, and from an urban-centred to a rural-centred perspective, culminating in his work with the peasant associations from 1925 to 1927.

1927–1936: This period opens with Mao's enunciation, at the 7 August Emergency Meeting, of the axiom 'Political power grows out of the barrel of a gun'. It is marked by wide swings in Mao's place in the Chinese Communist Party, from a side-current, to one line (and perhaps one faction) in the leadership struggles of the Kiangsi Soviet period, and then, following the Tsun-yi Conference of January 1935, to the early stages in his rise to supreme and unchallenged power in the party. Throughout, however, the military dimension of the revolution remains central. During these years, the strategy of encircling the cities from the countryside gradually takes shape, both in theory and in practice, though the formula of a 'protracted war' is enunciated only in 1938. Similarly, the ideas and methods corresponding to the 'mass line' begin to make their appearance, though this concept is formulated systematically only during the ensuing decade.

1936-1947: During this period, Mao writes all his principal theoretical works of the pre-1949 era, beginning in late 1936 with *Problems of strategy in China's revolutionary war*, and continuing in 1937 with the lecture notes on dialectical materialism from which 'On practice' and 'On contradiction' were later extracted. He also makes his entry on the international stage in a big way, with the publication of Edgar Snow's *Red star over China*, containing his autobiography as recounted to Snow in July 1936. Mao launches the idea of the 'sinification of Marxism', and carries through the rectification campaign of 1942-3, which both promotes this goal, and enhances his own standing in the party. In March 1943, he becomes chairman of the Politburo and of the Secretariat, and is formally set above all his peers in the leadership. At the Seventh Congress in April 1945 his thought becomes the guide to all the party's work. Finally, after the collapse of attempts at

---

[12] Cheng Chih-piao, 'Mao Tse-tung chien-tang hsüeh-shuo ti li-shih fen-ch'i' (The historical periodization of Mao Tse-tung's doctrine of party-building), *Mao Tse-tung ssu-hsiang yen-chiu* (Chengtu), 2 (1985) 72–6, 93.

mediation by Marshall and others, Mao turns his attention to the prosecution of the civil war, and to a new upsurge in land reform. By the end of 1947, both of these matters are well in hand, and victory is in sight.

1947–1957: While playing an important role in leading the civil war to a victorious conclusion, Mao begins, in 1947–9, to think also of the tasks awaiting the Chinese Communist Party after the conquest of power. At the outset, he stresses the need to follow the Leninist and Soviet model, giving primacy to the role of the cities and of heavy industry. He also advocates gradualism and moderation, especially in the countryside, where the rich peasants are to be left alone in order to foster the restoration of agricultural production. And while economic policies suddenly become much more radical in 1955, with the big push toward the collectivization of agriculture launched by Mao in July, Mao advocates in early 1956 an extremely conciliatory set of policies toward the intellectuals. His speech 'On the ten great relationships', which he later viewed as the first attempt at a systematic formulation of a road to socialism different from that of the Soviets, comprises in particular, as revised on 2 May 1956 for delivery to a non-party audience, a section advocating the slogan: 'Let a hundred flowers bloom, let a hundred schools of thought contend!' In the original version of his speech of 27 February 1957 on the handling of contradictions among the people, Mao denounces Stalin's leftist errors and his propensity to liquidate anyone who disagreed with him, and declares that class struggle in China has 'basically' come to an end. Then, in one of the most celebrated, dramatic and decisive turning points in the history of the Chinese People's Republic, this phase of relative pluralism is succeeded by a new upsurge of leftism, both in Mao's thinking and in the political climate.

1957–1966: The 'Anti-Rightist Campaign' of autumn 1957 leads to the first of Mao Tse-tung's great radical inventions, the Great Leap Forward of 1958–60. When this experiment results in chaos and mass starvation, Mao retires to the 'second line' and lets Liu Shao-ch'i, Chou En-lai, Teng Hsiao-p'ing and others take the lead in devising policies of retrenchment and rationalization, but he becomes more and more exasperated at the abandonment of the utopian and egalitarian vision of the Great Leap. This reaction incites him to put forward, at the tenth plenum in the autumn of 1962, the slogan 'Never forget the class struggle!', and from that time onward he prepares the ground for the counter-offensive against the so-called 'capitalist roaders' in the party known as the 'Great Proletarian Cultural Revolution'.[13]

---

[13] On the inexorable chain of causality leading from the radical policies of 1957–8 to the 'Cultural Revolution', see (apart from the relevant section of this book) my article 'The limits of cataclysmic change: reflections on the place of the "Great Proletarian Cultural Revolution" in the political development of the People's Republic of China', *CQ* 108 (Dec. 1986) 613–24.

1966–1976: Mao's last decade begins with widespread and savage violence, directed above all at his adversaries in the party, and at all those he regards as retrograde in their thinking or bureaucratic in their behaviour. The first phase of the Cultural Revolution, in 1966–8, is also marked by a certain amount of hope and enthusiasm, at least among the young. Soon, however, the Red Guard movement degenerates into an orgy of bloody factional fighting, and Mao is obliged to order Lin Piao and the People's Liberation Army to intervene. While violence is to some extent contained as a result, no real political or social order is ever restored in Mao's lifetime. His last years are marked by increasing bafflement and frustration, as he becomes more and more desperate to resolve China's problems while he is still in command, and less and less capable of doing so. At the end, he is scarcely able to think, let alone to speak, and has become indeed, as he complained of being in 1966, a dead ancestor at his own funeral, or at the burial of his hopes.

How can one characterize the six phases marked by the events and tendencies summarily enunciated above? Perhaps somewhat along the following lines:

1. *The formative years.* In lectures delivered in Hong Kong in April 1982, I called the period down to 1927 'The apprenticeship of a revolutionary', but when they were published, I changed this to 'The formative years'. In so doing, I was influenced by Liao Kai-lung, who argued that by the mid-1920s Mao could by no means be regarded as a simple apprentice.[14] Apart from this very sound point, there is another, and perhaps even stronger reason for not using the word 'apprenticeship'. However loosely employed, this term implies in some way an initiation by a master into a trade or professional specialty having quite clear and definite standards, qualifications and requirements. The fact is that, in the 1920s, there were no 'masters of revolution' to whom Mao could have been apprenticed. From Sun Yat-sen to Li Ta-chao and Ch'en Tu-hsiu, there were leaders senior to Mao in age and experience, but none of them really knew how to make revolution successfully in a country such as China. Stalin thought he knew, and from 1925 or thereabouts was in a position to order the Chinese Communists to do his bidding, but events were to show that he was not a reliable master either. Mao Tse-tung learned something from all those I have just mentioned, during the years 1917–27, but in many fundamental respects he was self-taught.

2. *Forging the weapons.* Even though he was not, in 1927, fully trained in the art of revolution, Mao Tse-tung was plunged from that time forward into

---

[14] See the Preface to S. Schram, *Mao Zedong: a preliminary reassessment* xii–xiv, and also the Chinese text of our conversations cited in note 11.

the midst of the revolutionary struggle, and obliged to solve the problems that confronted him if he was to survive. During the years 1927–36 he, Chu Te, P'eng Te-huai and others created the army, and devised the strategy, which would enable the Chinese communists, after narrowly escaping annihilation before and during the Long March, to expand their influence during the more favourable circumstances created by the Anti-Japanese War.

3. *Defining and pursuing the 'Chinese road' to the conquest of power.* During the 'Yenan period', Mao Tse-tung summarized the lessons of the previous decade regarding the simultaneous pursuit of national revolution and social revolution through armed struggle in the countryside, and applied them so successfully that, by 1947, the Chinese Communists were on the brink of final victory.

4. *From the 'Chinese road to power' to the 'Chinese road to socialism'.* From 1947 to 1957, Mao Tse-tung and his comrades gathered in the fruits of victory over the Kuomintang, and turned their attention to the new task of building a socialist society and a socialist economy. By early 1957, the prospects for success in this enterprise were seen by many, both in China and outside, as very fair indeed.

5. *The Great Leap into the unknown.* In 1958, Mao Tse-tung declared war on nature, in alliance with the masses. When victory eluded him in the Great Leap Forward, he declared war in the early 1960s on those in the party who had shown insufficient enthusiasm for his policies, and had participated in dismantling them. Then, in the mid-1960s, he declared war on human nature itself.

6. *The 'Cultural Revolution' decade.* Under the slogan 'Fight self, criticize revisionism', Mao sought to root out the egoism which had its source, he had come to believe, not simply in the unequal distribution of rewards according to a hierarchical salary structure, but in the heart of man. He also continued his efforts to overthrow those who had opposed him. This latter goal he achieved in significant degree, though by no means completely. As for the goal of changing human nature, it would appear, in the light of developments during the years since his death, that the sea change which many people believed had occurred a decade ago was very largely illusory.

The fact that the cataclysm of the Cultural Revolution did not, as Mao had hoped and intended, effect an irreversible qualitative change in the Chinese people, does not, of course, imply that the twenty-seven years of his rule were merely a passing and ephemeral phase in China's long history. On the contrary, the influence of Mao Tse-tung, of Mao Tse-tung's thought, and of the revolutionary experience he led, both before and after 1949, remains profound, even today. I shall attempt to assess it in the Conclusion.

MAO TSE-TUNG'S THOUGHT
TO 1949

Mao Tse-tung's thought, as it had found expression prior to the establishment of the Chinese People's Republic, was at once the synthesis of his experience down to 1949, and the matrix out of which many of his later policies were to grow. Part 1 seeks to document and interpret the development of Mao's thought during the first three decades of his active political life. It also tries to prepare the reader better to understand what came after the conquest of power. While stressing those concerns which were uppermost in Mao's own mind in the earlier years, it also devotes attention to ideas of which the implications were fully spelled out only in the 1950s and 1960s.

As regards the context in which Mao's ideas evolved, the period from 1912 (when Mao, at the age of $18\frac{1}{2}$, returned to his studies after half a year as a soldier in the revolutionary army) to 1949 (when he became the titular and effective ruler of a united China) was one of ceaseless and far-reaching political, social and cultural change. Mao lived, in effect, through several distinct eras in the history of his country during the first half-century of his life, and the experience which shaped his perception of China's problems, and his ideas of what to do about them, therefore varied radically not only from decade to decade, but in many cases from year to year. The present effort to bring some order and clarity to the very complex record of Mao's thought and action adopts an approach partly chronological and partly thematic. It begins by looking at the development of Mao Tse-tung's political conceptions from early manhood down to 1927, when he first embarked on a revolutionary struggle of a distinctive stamp in the countryside.

FROM THE STUDENT MOVEMENT TO THE PEASANT MOVEMENT
1917–1927

In terms both of age and of experience, Mao Tse-tung was a member of the May Fourth generation. An avid reader of *New Youth* (*Hsin ch'ing-nien*) from the time of its first appearance in 1915, he served his apprenticeship in political organization and in the study of politics under the influence of the 'new thought' tide, and his career as a revolutionary effectively began in the wake of the May Fourth demonstrations.

Although he had many strongly marked individual traits, Mao shared certain attributes characteristic of this group as a whole. One of the most important was that it was a transitional generation. Of course all generations are 'transitional', since the world is constantly changing, but Mao's life and that of his contemporaries spanned not merely different phases but different eras in China's development. The process of adaptation to the Western impact had begun in the mid-nineteenth century and was to continue into the mid-twentieth century and beyond, but the May Fourth period marked a great climacteric after which nothing would ever be the same again. In a word, the members of the May Fourth generation were aware of the certainties regarding the enduring superiority of the Chinese Way which had comforted their elders, but they were never able to share this simple faith. Some of them, including Mao, soon espoused Westernizing ideologies to which they remained committed for the rest of their lives, but most remained deeply marked both by faith in the intrinsic capacities of the Chinese people, and by the traditional modes of thought which they had repudiated. Thus they were fated to live in circumstances of permanent political and cultural ambiguity and instability.

Mao Tse-tung's political views prior to his early twenties are known only from odd fragments of contemporary documentation, and from his own recollections and those of others many years afterwards.[1] He first emerges clearly into our field of vision with an article written when he was approximately 23, and published in the April 1917 issue of *New Youth*.

Although this, Mao's first article, was written long before he was exposed to any significant Marxist influences, it reveals many personality traits, and many strands of thought, which can be followed through subsequently. The overriding concern – one might almost say obsession – which penetrates the whole article is anxiety lest the Chinese people should suffer the catastrophe of *wang-kuo*, that is, of losing their state and

---

[1] The fullest account of Mao's life and thought in the early years is to be found in the biography of the young Mao by Li Jui, first published in 1957 under the title *Mao Tse-tung t'ung-chih ti ch'u-ch'i ko-ming huo-tung*. This version has been translated into English by Anthony W. Sariti as *The early revolutionary activities of Comrade Mao Tse-tung*, ed. James C. Hsiung, with introduction by Stuart R. Schram. Li Jui has now published a very substantially revised and expanded second edition, *Mao Tse-tung ti tsao-ch'i ko-ming huo-tung*. This version incorporates a considerable amount of new material, including a whole chapter on Mao's thought before and after the May Fourth period, originally published in *Li-shih yen-chiu*, hereafter *LSYC*, 1 (1979) 33–51. It should henceforth be regarded as the standard. In some cases, for the convenience of non-Sinologist readers, I also cite the translation.

becoming 'slaves without a country'. This theme, so widespread in China in the late nineteenth and early twentieth centuries, is vigorously stated in the opening sentences:

Our nation is wanting in strength. The military spirit has not been encouraged. The physical condition of the population deteriorates daily. This is an extremely disturbing phenomenon....If this state continues, our weakness will increase further....If our bodies are not strong, we will be afraid as soon as we see enemy soldiers, and then how can we attain our goals and make ourselves respected?[2]

Mao thus evoked at one stroke two basic themes of his thought and action throughout the whole of his subsequent career: nationalism, or patriotism, and admiration for the martial spirit. But if he is clearly preoccupied here with what might loosely be called nationalist goals, was his nationalism at this time conservative or revolutionary? An obvious touchstone for deciding this point is whether or not he saw the aim of *fu-ch'iang* (increasing the wealth and power of the state) as in any way tied to a social and cultural revolution perceived as a necessary precondition for strengthening the nation. In fact, the article shows us a Mao concerned with China's fate, but almost totally uninterested in reform, let alone revolution.

Of the twenty-odd textual quotations, or explicit allusions to particular passages from classical writings contained in the article, there are a dozen to the Confucian canon; one to the Confucian 'realist' Hsun-tzu, a precursor of the Legalists, and two to the Sung idealist interpreter of Confucianism, Chu Hsi, as well as one to his late Ming critic, Yen Yuan. There are also three references to Mao's favourite Taoist classic, the *Chuang-tzu*. The range of his knowledge at this time was clearly very wide, for he refers in passing to obscure biographical details regarding a number of minor writers of various periods. (It is all the more noteworthy that eleven out of twelve references to the Confucian classics should be to the basic core of the *Four books*).

And yet, though there are no explicit references to social change, nor even any suggestion that it is necessary, the article does contain many traces of modern and non-conformist thinking, of both Chinese and

---

[2] 'Erh-shih-pa hua sheng' (Mao Tse-tung), 'T'i-yü chih yen-chiu' (A study of physical education), *New Youth*, 3.2 (April 1917) (separately paginated) 1; translated in *PTMT*, 153. This book contains only extracts from Mao's 1917 article. I have also published a complete translation in my monograph *Mao Ze-dong. Une étude de l'éducation physique*. In 1975, M. Henri Day translated the whole text into English in his Stockholm thesis *Máo Zédong 1917–1927: documents*, 21–31. This very valuable work, which contains translations of all of Mao's writings included in volume 1 of the Tokyo edition of the Chinese text (Takeuchi Minoru, ed., *MTTC*), together with provocative and original, though occasionally unconvincing commentaries, is an important contribution to our knowledge of the young Mao and his thought.

Western origin. To begin with, there is the emphasis on the value of the martial spirit, expressed in the opening sentences quoted above, and summed up in the statement: 'The principal aim of physical education is military heroism.'[3] To justify this view, Mao hails the example of many heroes of ancient times, and quotes from Yen Yuan, who had denounced Chu Hsi for 'emphasizing civil affairs and neglecting military affairs' (*chung-wen ch'ing wu*), thus creating a harmful tradition contrary to the teachings of Confucius.[4]

The dual matrix out of which Mao's thinking at this time had evolved is explicitly evoked in a letter he wrote in 1916, at about the time when he was working on the article for *New Youth*:

In ancient times, what were called the three great virtues of knowledge, benevolence, and courage were promoted simultaneously. Today's educationalists are of the view that we should combine virtue, knowledge, and [a sound] body. But in reality, virtue and knowledge depend on nothing outside the body, and knowledge, benevolence, and [a sound] body are of no use without courage.[5]

Thus Mao not only underscored at the outset the crucial importance of the body, i.e., of material reality, but also exalted the ancient Chinese virtue of courage (*yung*). Mao did not of course derive this strain in his thought primarily from books. Like many other Chinese in the early twentieth century, he developed his ideas in response to circumstances similar to those which prevailed at the end of the Ming, when the unity and integrity of the Chinese nation was threatened as a result of military weakness.

If this enthusiasm for things military remained a permanent trait of Mao's thinking, an even more basic theme of the 1917 article, and one which revealed more unmistakably modern influences, was that of the importance of self-awareness (*tzu-chueh*) and individual initiative (*tzu-tung*). He put the point forcefully in the opening paragraph of his article: 'Strength depends on drill, and drill depends on self-awareness....If we wish to make physical education effective we must influence people's subjective attitudes and stimulate them to become conscious of physical education.'[6]

The source for the idea that the key to effective action lies in first transforming the hearts of men lies, of course, partly in the Confucian tradition. But the main inspiration for passages such as this is to be found

[3] *Ibid.* 5; PTMT 157.
[4] Yen Yuan, 'Ts'un hsueh', book 2 in Yen Yuan, *Ssu ts'un pien*, 63.
[5] 'Kei Li Chin-hsi ti hsin' (Letter to Li Chin-hsi), MTTC, *pu chüan*, 1, 17–18. Li Chin-hsi was a former teacher at the Normal School in Changsha who had moved to Peking. (See Li Jui, 28 for a brief biography.) The contemporary 'educationalists' referred to by Mao who spoke of virtue, knowledge and a sound body included in particular, as Benjamin Schwartz has pointed out, Herbert Spencer, whom Mao had certainly read in Yen Fu's translation.
[6] Mao Tse-tung, 'T'i-yü', 1; PTMT 153.

no doubt in the eclectic, and yet basically Westernizing ideas Mao had absorbed from his reading of *New Youth* and from the lessons of his ethics teacher and future father-in-law, Yang Ch'ang-chi.

Yang, who was a disciple of Chu Hsi as well as of Kant and Samuel Smiles, taught a moral philosophy which combined the emphasis of Western liberalism on self-reliance and individual responsibility with a strong sense of man's duty to society.[7] To this end, he had compiled a volume of extracts from the Confucian *Analects*, with accompanying commentaries, to illustrate his own interpretation of 'self-cultivation'. The first chapter of this book took its title from the concept of 'establishing the will' (*li chih*), and contains the statement: 'If one has an unbreakable will, there is nothing that cannot be accomplished.'[8]

Like Yang Ch'ang-chi, Mao laid particular stress on the role of the will. 'Physical education,' he wrote in his 1917 article, 'strengthens the will....*The will is the antecedent of a man's career.*'[9] This belief in the importance of the will and of subjective forces was a central and characteristic element of his outlook. In a letter he wrote to Miyazaki Toten in March 1917, with the aim of inviting him to give a speech at the First Normal School in memory of Huang Hsing, Mao described himself as a student who had 'to some extent established [his] will (*p'o li chih-ch'i*)'.[10]

But at the same time, in very Chinese fashion, he regarded an authentic will as impossible without understanding or enlightenment. In a letter of 23 August 1917 he wrote: 'truly to establish the will is not so easy; one must first study philosophy and ethics, in order to establish a standard for one's own words and actions, and set this up as a goal for the future'. But it was not merely a matter of subjective attitudes; action and commitment were required:

Then one must choose a cause compatible with this goal, and devote all one's efforts to pursuing it; only if one achieves this goal, is it possible to speak of having [a firm] will. Only such a will is a true will, not the will which consists in blind obedience....A simple inclination to seek the good, the true or the beautiful is nothing but an impulse of passion, and not an authentic will....If, for a decade, one does not obtain the truth, then for a decade, one will be without a will...[11]

[7] Edgar Snow, *Red star over China*, 143.
[8] Li Jui, *Mao Tse-tung ti tsao-ch'i*, 30; translation, 18.
[9] Mao Tse-tung, 'T'i-yü', 5–6; *PTMT* 157–8.
[10] Or, as Jerome Ch'en translates, 'disciplined [his] aspirations' (*Mao papers*, 3). Text in *MTTC* 1.33. For the circumstances in which this letter was written, see Day, *Máo Zédōng*, 18–20.
[11] In one Cultural Revolution collection (*Tzu-liao hsüan-pien*, 10–11) this is identified as having been written to Yang Huai-chung (Yang Ch'ang-chi) himself, but it was in fact addressed to Li Chin-hsi. For the full text, see *MTTC, pu chüan*, 1, 19–23; the passage quoted here is on pp. 20–1.

Some idea of Mao's overall political position at this time is furnished by the fact that he says only three people in China have had, in recent years, ideas about how to rule the country as a whole (*chih t'ien-hsia*): Yuan Shih-k'ai, Sun Yat-sen and K'ang Yu-wei. Of these, only K'ang really had something like basic principles (*pen-yuan*), and even his ideas were mainly rhetoric. The sole figure of the modern age he truly admired, wrote Mao, was Tseng Kuo-fan, whom he called (as in the *New Youth* article) by his posthumous title, Tseng Wen-cheng.[12]

Despite this, the pattern of Mao's thinking of 1917 was by no means purely traditional. The goal he wished to pursue was, of course, the strengthening and renewal of China. The realm (*t'ien-hsia*), he wrote, was vast, the organization of society complicated, and the knowledge of the people limited. In order to get things moving, it was necessary to move people's hearts. The first requirement for this was to have some great basic principles (*ta pen-yüan*). At present the reformers were beginning with details, such as assemblies, constitutions, presidents, cabinets, military affairs, industry, education and so on. The value of all this should not be underestimated, but all these partial measures would be ineffectual if they were not founded in principle. Such principles should embrace the truth about the universe, and about man as a part of the universe. And, Mao went on:

Today, if we appeal (*hao-chao*) to the hearts of all under heaven on the basis of great principles can any of them fail to be moved? And if all the hearts in the realm are moved, is there anything which cannot be achieved? And...how, then, can the state fail to be rich, powerful, and happy?

In Mao's view, the place to start was with philosophy and ethics, and with changing the thinking (*ssu-hsiang*) of the whole country. China's thinking, he wrote, was extremely old, and her morals extremely bad. Thought ruled men's hearts, and morals ruled their actions; thus both must be changed.[13]

But though Mao saw China's ancient and rigid thought-patterns as an obstacle to progress, he did not propose wholesale Westernization as a remedy. Commenting on the view, attributed by Yang Ch'ang-chi to 'a certain Japanese', that Eastern thought entirely failed to 'correspond to real life', Mao observed: 'In my opinion, Western thought is not necessarily all correct either; very many parts of it should be transformed at the same time as Oriental thought.'[14]

[12] *Ibid.* 19–20.   [13] *Ibid.* 20.

[14] *Ibid.* 20–1. In his view that China, too, had something to contribute to the world, Mao was following the basic orientation of his teacher, Yang Ch'ang-chi, who had taken the style 'Huai-chung' (literally, 'yearning for China') during his long period of study abroad, to express his patriotic sentiments. On this, see Li Jui, 'Hsueh-sheng shih-tai ti Mao Tse-tung' (Mao Tse-tung during his student years), *Shih-tai ti pao-kao*, 12 (December 1983); reprinted in *Hsin-hua wen-chai*, 1 (1984) 178.

Having said this, however, Mao embarks on a notably untraditional discussion of the importance, in the enterprise of uniting the hearts of the people on the basis of thought and morals, of the little people (*hsiao-jen*), as compared to the 'superior men' (*chün-tzu*). To be sure, it is the latter who have a high level of knowledge and virtue, but they exist only on the basis of political institutions and economic activities mainly established by ordinary people, the mass of whom constitute the source of the 'superior men' (*hsiao-jen lei chün-tzu*). Thus, the 'superior men' must not only be benevolent toward the little people, but must educate and transform them in order to attain the goal of 'Great Harmony' (*ta-t'ung*). Already at this time Mao proposed to set up a private school (*ssu-shu*), combining traditional and modern methods, to prepare people for study abroad.[15]

As for the theme of practice, which was to play so large a part in Mao's subsequent thinking, he asserted in his 1917 article that hitherto there had been all too much talk about physical education: 'The important thing is not words, but putting them into practice.'[16] Mao's stress on linking theory and practice has often been traced back to Wang Yang-ming, but this is mere speculation; there is not the slightest mention of Wang in any of Mao's known writings, and no evidence that he was influenced by him. More relevant, in any case, to Mao's development during the May Fourth period are the Westernizing ideas he assimilated in 1917-18.

Mao's thinking evolved very rapidly during his last two years at the First Normal School in Changsha. Perhaps the most important single element which makes its appearance at this time is an explicit and strongly-marked individualism. For example, in marginal annotations to a textbook on ethics by the German neo-Kantian, Friedrich Paulsen, Mao wrote:

The goal of the human race lies in the realization of the self, and that is all. What I mean by the realization of the self consists in developing our physical and mental capacities to the highest degree.…Wherever there is repression of the individual, wherever there is a violation of individuality, there can be no greater crime. That is why our country's 'three bonds' must go, and why they constitute, with the churches, capitalists, and autocracy, the four evil demons of the realm….[17]

Like older and more eminent intellectuals of the time, such as Ch'en Tu-hsiu, Li Ta-chao or Lu Hsun, Mao had seized on the notion of the absolute value of the individual as a weapon to 'break out of the nets' of the old culture and the old society. He was by no means unaware of the social framework necessary to the realization of the individual,

---

[15] *MTTC, pu chüan*, 1, 22-3.

[16] Mao Tse-tung, 'T'i-yü', 7; translated in *Mao Ze-dong. Une étude de l'education physique*, 52; and Day, 27.

[17] Quoted by Li Jui, 110. The full text of Mao's annotations on Paulsen has been reproduced in *MTTC, pu chüan*, 9, 19-47.

describing how groups were formed from individuals, societies were formed from groups, and states were formed from societies. In this complex interrelationship between the individual and the state, or civil society (*kuo-min*), Mao stressed that the individual was primary; Paulsen's contrary emphasis reflected, he said, the influence of 'statism' in Germany.[18]

A dialectical approach to the relations between opposites is, indeed, one of the hallmarks of Mao's thought from this time forward. Among the pairs which he treated as in some sense identical were concept and reality, finite and infinite, high and low, *yin* and *yang*, as well as two which would be criticized by the Soviets decades later: life and death, and male and female. Man he saw as the unity of matter and spirit, and morality as arising from the interaction of conscience and desire. (The view that moral law had been laid down by a command of the spirits he stigmatized as a 'slave mentality'.) Moreover, because matter was indestructible, man and society were likewise indestructible, though constantly changing and renewing themselves through reform and revolution. For this reason, he no longer feared, as he had done, that China would perish; she would survive by reform of the political system, and transformation of the nature of the people. Such reform was possible only under the guidance of new knowledge, and knowledge would be effective if it was first built into belief, and then applied. 'Knowledge, belief, and action,' he wrote, 'are the three steps in our intellectual activity.' The medium of action could only be 'various social and political organizations'.[19]

Thus the stress of the April 1917 article on practice was strongly reasserted, and a new theme, that of organizing for reform, emerged. Both of these were to be central to the very important essay entitled 'The great union of the popular masses', which Mao published in July and August 1919.

The most startling passage of Mao's 1919 article[20] is no doubt that contrasting Marx and Kropotkin:

As to the actions which should be undertaken once we have united, there is one extremely violent party, which uses the method 'Do unto others as they do unto you' to struggle desperately to the end with the aristocrats and capitalists. The leader of this party is a man named Marx who was born in Germany. There is another party more moderate than that of Marx. It does not expect rapid results,

---

[18] *MTTC, pu-chüan*, 9, 21, 40–1.

[19] *Ibid.* 28–34, 37–9, 42, 45–6. Most but not all of these passages are included in Li Jui, 114–16; translation, 40.

[20] I have published a full translation in *CQ*, together with an analysis. Mao Tse-tung, 'The great union of the popular masses', followed by S. Schram, 'From the "Great union of the popular masses" to the "Great alliance"', *CQ* 49 (Jan.–March 1972) 76–105. See also Day, 85–100. The Chinese text is available in *MTTC* 1.57–69.

but begins by understanding the common people. Men should all have a morality of mutual aid, and work voluntarily....The ideas of this party are broader and more far-reaching. They want to unite the whole globe into a single country, unite the human race into a single family.... The leader of this party is a man called Kropotkin, who was born in Russia.[21]

Quoting this passage verbatim, Li Jui comments that, although at this time Mao could not clearly distinguish between Marxism and anarchism, 'The great union of the popular masses' and other articles he wrote for the journal he edited in Hunan, the *Hsiang River Review* (*Hsiang-chiang p'ing-lun*), already displayed glimmerings of class analysis, and constituted the earliest building blocks of the future great edifice of Mao Tse-tung's Thought.[22] But while Mao was unquestionably, in the summer of 1919, learning rapidly about the theory and practice of revolution, it is very difficult to find in his writings of the period serious elements of Marxist analysis. Concepts such as class struggle, dialectics, or the materialist view of history are not even mentioned, and the very term 'class' is used only once, and then in a totally un-Marxist sense (the 'classes' of the wise and the ignorant, the rich and the poor, and the strong and the weak).[23] If the article has a discernible philosophical bias, this is to be found neither in Marx nor in Kropotkin, but in the ideas of Western liberals as transmitted – and transmuted – by certain Chinese writers of the late nineteenth and early twentieth century. Among these were Yen Fu and Liang Ch'i-ch'ao, the Hunanese revolutionary thinker and martyr T'an Ssu-t'ung, as well as Mao's teacher Yang Ch'ang-chi, all of whom developed in one way or another the view that spontaneous action by members of society, unfettered by the old hierarchical bonds, would maximize the energy of society as a whole.

Another important influence on Mao's thought during the May Fourth period was that of Hu Shih. It has often been pointed out that Mao's articles of 1919 were enthusiastically hailed following their publication by the Peking journal *Weekly Review* (*Mei-chou p'ing-lun*). Summarizing the contents of the first few issues of Mao's *Hsiang River Review* one commentator said: 'The strong point of *Hsiang River Review* lies in discussion. The long article "The great union of the popular masses" published in the second, third and fourth issues...exhibits exceedingly

[21] *CQ* 49. 78–9. Understandably, this paragraph was not included in the extracts from this article reproduced in 1957 by Li Jui, since it would hardly have supported the view he put forward there to the effect that 'The great union of the popular masses' was 'one of the most important writings' in which Mao 'began to combine a Marxist-Leninist viewpoint with the reality of the Chinese revolution'. (*Ibid.* 1st ed., 106; translation, 115.) As noted below, his approach in the revised edition of 1980 is radically different.
[22] *Ibid.* 213.   [23] *CQ* 49. 77–8.

far-reaching vision, and exceedingly well-chosen and effective arguments. Truly it is one of the important articles which have appeared recently.'[24] The author of these words was in fact none other than Hu Shih himself.

This appears less surprising when we note that, in his editorial for the first issue of the *Hsiang River Review*, Mao said, after enumerating the progress in various domains which had been achieved by humanity since the Renaissance (for example, from a dead classical literature for the aristocracy to a modern, living literature for the common people, and from the politics of dictatorship to the politics of parliamentarianism), that in the field of thought or philosophy (*ssu-hsiang*) 'we have moved forward to pragmatism'.[25] I do not mean to suggest, in noting this point, that Mao was a disciple of Hu Shih or John Dewey. His favourable evaluation of pragmatism in 1919 did reflect, however, an attitude he was to maintain *almost* until the end of his life, to the effect that one should not spin theories without linking them to concrete experience.

If Mao's ideas in 1919, like those of older and more learned men at the time, were a mosaic of many influences, his article 'The great union of the popular masses' had one remarkable peculiarity: it represented one of the few attempts to put forward a general programme on the basis of concrete experience of the revolutionary mass movements of the May Fourth period. It is true that Mao's hierarchy of social categories in the total picture as he saw it was quite un-Marxist: he attributed maximum importance to the student movement, and relatively little to the peasants, not to mention the workers. He also, characteristically, devotes considerable attention to women, and to school teachers. Looked at as a whole, his vision of the revolutionary alliance he is striving to create is not unlike that of the 'New Left' in the United States and elsewhere in the 1960s. The central theme of the articles is that China's renewal will come above all from the rebellion of young people, and especially of students, against the old order. The instrument and motive force of change lies in democratic organizations spontaneously building up from the grass roots. The goal of the whole process will be, in Mao's view (and here he

---

[24] *Mei-chou p'ing-lun*, 36 (24 August 1919), 4.

[25] *MTTC* 1.53–4, translated in Day, 81. (For the reasons for translating *shih-yen chu-i* as 'pragmatism' see Day, 83, n. 2.) Hu Shih's influence on Mao at this time (which had earlier been acknowledged by Mao himself in his autobiography as told to Edgar Snow) was, of course, unmentionable in China until recently. (For some brief but pithy observations on the subject by a Western scholar, see Day, 47–8.) It is a reflection of the remarkable revolution which has taken place since 1978 in the climate of intellectual inquiry in China that an article published in 1980 should not only call attention to Hu's praise of Mao and to Mao's regard for pragmatism as the 'leading ideology' (*chih-tao ssu-hsiang*) of the time, but should explicitly state that in 1919 differences of principle had not yet emerged between them. See Wang Shu-pai and Chang Shen-heng, 'Ch'ing-nien Mao Tse-tung shih-chieh-kuan ti chuan-pien' (The transformation in the world view of the young Mao Tse-tung), *LSYC* 5 (1980) 83.

reveals himself as a true disciple of Yen Fu), not merely the liberation of the individual from the shackles of the old society, but also, and by that very fact, the strengthening and renewal of the Chinese nation as a whole. In a supremely eloquent peroration, Mao addressed his compatriots thus:

in every domain we demand liberation. Ideological liberation, political liberation, economic liberation, liberation [in the relations between] men and women, educational liberation, are all going to burst from the deep inferno where they have been confined, and demand to look at the blue sky. Our Chinese people possesses great inherent capacities! The more profound the oppression, the greater its resistance; since [this] has been accumulating for a long time, it will surely burst forth quickly. I venture to make a singular assertion: one day, the reform of the Chinese people will be more profound than that of any other people, and the society of the Chinese people will be more radiant than that of any other people. The great union of the Chinese people will be achieved earlier than that of any other place or people. Gentlemen! Gentlemen! We must all exert ourselves! We must all advance with the utmost strength! Our golden age, our age of glory and splendour, lies before us![26]

There is more than one echo here of Mao's 1917 article, in the emphasis on persistent efforts and a firm resolve as the keys to national resurgence. In the intervening two years, he had learned much, both from books and from experience, about the way to tap and mobilize the energies which he perceived to be latent in the Chinese people. He had, however, a great deal still to learn before he could even begin to devise a complete and effective strategy for making revolution in a country such as China.

Although Mao showed little understanding of Marxism at this time, his imagination had been caught by the victory of the Russian Revolution. He listed the establishment of a soviet government of workers and peasants first among the worldwide exploits of what he called the 'army of the red flag', and went on to mention the Hungarian Revolution, and the wave of strikes in America and in various European countries.[27] Other articles by Mao in the *Hsiang River Review* evoke themes which were later to become classic in his thought, such as the need of politicians to 'wash their brains' and 'go to the factories to work and the countryside to cultivate the land, together with the common people' (*p'ing min*), or the idea that 'the true liberation of humanity' would come on the day when thousands and tens of thousands of people in America shouted together in the face of injustice and the despotism of the trusts, 'This must not be!' (*pu-hsu*). But Mao also expressed very strong support for the Germans, who are presented as an oppressed people dictated to by the Entente.[28]

[26] *CQ* 49.87.   [27] *CQ* 49.84.
[28] On going to the factories, see [Mao] Tse-tung, 'Cha-tan pao-chü' (A brutal bomb attack), *Hsiang River Review*, 1 (14 July 1919), 3. On shouting in unison, Tse-tung, 'Pu-hsu shih-yeh chuan-chih'

The idea of China as a proletarian nation, which should show solidarity with other oppressed peoples, was of course commonly put forward in the years immediately after the May Fourth period by Li Ta-chao, Ts'ai Ho-sen and others. Mao, too, was naturally drawn in this direction.

A phase in Mao's subsequent apprenticeship, which provides a highly suggestive complement to his analysis, in 1919, of the role of grass-roots organizations in social change, was his participation in the Hunanese autonomy movement in the following year. This hitherto obscure episode has only recently been illuminated by the publication of important documents.[29] The record of this episode throws a revealing light not only on Mao's intense Hunanese patriotism, but on his attitude to political work generally. In an article published on 26 September 1920, Mao wrote:

In any matter whatsoever, if there is a 'theory', but no 'movement' to carry it through, the aim of this theory cannot be realized....I believe that there are two kinds of real movements: one involves getting inside of things (*ju yü ch'i chung*) to engage in concrete construction; the other is set up outside, in order to promote [the cause].

Both types of movement, he added, were and would remain important and necessary. At the same time, he stressed that an effective movement must have its origin in the 'people' (*min*). 'If this present Hunanese autonomist movement were to be successfully established, but if its source were to reside not in the "people", but outside the "people", then I venture to assert that such a movement could not last long.'[30]

As for the broader context in which these statements were made, Mao and the co-authors of the proposal of 7 October 1920 for a constitutional convention summed up their views about the relation between political developments at the provincial and national levels as follows:

The self-government law the Hunanese need now is like that of an American state constitution....China is now divided into many pieces, and we do not know when a national constitution will be produced; in fact, we are afraid that first

(No to the despotism of industry and commerce), *ibid.* 1.3. On the oppression of Germany see (among many articles, some by other authors) Tse-tung, 'Wei Te ju hu ti Fa-lan' (France fears Germany as if it were a tiger), *ibid.* 3 (28 July 1919), 2. Giorgio Mantici has published a complete Italian translation of the available issues of the *Hsiang River Review* under the title *Pensieri del fiume Xiang*. The articles just mentioned appear on 76–8 and 164–5. I wish to thank Mr Mantici for kindly giving me a copy of the Chinese text of these materials. All of these texts have now been published in *MTTC*, *pu chüan*, 1.

[29] These materials – four articles by Mao, and a proposal for a constitutional convention drafted jointly with two others, were discovered by Angus McDonald in the course of research on his doctoral dissertation 'The urban origins of rural revolution' (University of California, Berkeley, 1974), also published in book form under the same title. McDonald has published the Chinese texts in *Hōgaku kenkyū*, 46.2 (1972) 99–107, with a commentary in Japanese, and has also discussed them in English in *Rōnin* (Tokyo), 14 (December 1973), 37–47, and in *CQ* 68 (December 1976), 751–77.   [30] *MTTC*, *pu chüan*, 1.229–30.

every province will have to produce its own constitution, and only later will we have a national constitution. This is just like the route from separation to unification followed by America and [Bismarckian] Germany.[31]

This dimension of Mao's 1920 writings reflects the circumstances of the times, and by no means corresponds to his long-term view, which consistently stressed, from 1917 to the end of his life, the importance of national unity and a strong state. In other respects, however, the ideas put forward in the passages quoted above are altogether typical of Mao Tse-tung's political approach throughout his subsequent career as a revolutionary. On the one hand he called for 'getting inside things' to engage in concrete construction, by which he meant obviously that revolutionaries, or reformers, should immerse themselves in social reality. But at the same time, he perceived the need for a movement set up outside, in order to promote the cause. In other words, although political activists should respond to the objective demands of the 'people', and should immerse themselves in the people, in order to mobilize them, another organization, standing outside the people, was also required. It could be said that the Leninist-type Communist Party which Mao joined in the following year was precisely such an organization which did not allow itself to be confounded with the masses but stood outside them. But at the same time Mao never hesitated, throughout his political career, to enter boldly into things, and to participate in concrete organizational work.

The other question raised by Mao's writings during the Hunanese autonomist movement concerns the 'people' on whose behalf these activities were to be carried out, and from whom the initial impulse and inspiration for the movement were to come. By putting the term in quotation marks, Mao himself underscored its ambiguity. Were these the 'popular masses' (*min-chung*) of his 1919 article? Or were they the 'Chinese people' or 'Chinese nation' (*Chung-hua min-tsu*), who were never far from the centre of his concerns? It is perhaps a characteristic trait of Mao's thought that these two entities are indissolubly linked. He was never, at any time after 1918 or 1919, a nationalist solely, or primarily, interested in China's 'wealth and power'. But neither was he a 'proletarian' revolutionary like M. N. Roy, who never thought in terms of the nation.

In the course of the year 1920, Mao Tse-tung's attitude toward the problem of learning from the West how to transform Chinese society underwent a significant change. This shift is symbolized by the changing views regarding the narrower problem of study abroad expressed by Mao Tse-tung in a letter of 14 March 1920 to Chou Shih-chao, and another of 25 November 1920 to Hsiang Ching-yü. In the first, he declared that,

[31] *Ibid.* 242.

although a lot of people had a kind of superstitious reverence for the benefits of foreign study, in fact only a very few of the tens or hundreds of thousands of Chinese who had gone abroad had really learned anything of value. In any case, he wrote, the two currents of Eastern and Western culture each occupied half the world, and Eastern culture 'could be said to be Chinese culture' (*k'o-i shuo chiu shih Chung-kuo wen-ming*); he would master that first, before proceeding abroad, though he was not opposed in principle to all study abroad.[32]

Half a year later, Mao wrote, on the contrary, to Hsiang Ching-yü in France complaining that there was very little progressive education for women (or for men either) in Hunan, and urging her to lure as many women comrades as possible abroad, adding: 'One more person lured [abroad] is one more person saved (*yin i jen, chi to chiu i jen*).'[33]

The shift in Mao's basic attitude toward ideologies of Western origin was not so dramatic as suggested by these contrasting passages. One of his reasons, in March, for preferring to remain in China was, according to his letter to Chou Shih-chao, that a person could absorb foreign knowledge more rapidly by reading translations. His ideological orientation remained unsettled, however, as he said himself: 'To be frank, among all the ideologies and doctrines, I have at present still not found any relatively clear concept.' Mao's aim was to put together such a 'clear concept' (*ming-liao kai-nien*) from the essence of culture Chinese and Western, ancient and modern. In his plans for creating a 'new life' in Changsha within three years or so, Mao said that the individual was primary, and the group secondary. He went out of his way to stress his links with Hu Shih, and even noted that Hu had coined the name 'Self-Study University' (*tzu-hsiu ta-hsueh*) for an institution Mao proposed to set up in Changsha. But in this university, said Mao, 'we will live a communist life' (*kung-ch'an ti sheng-huo*), and he also declared that 'Russia is the number one civilized country in the world'.[34]

By the end of November 1920, Mao still advocated, in his letter to Hsiang Ching-yü, that Hunan should set itself up as an independent country (*tzu li wei kuo*), in order to detach itself from the backward northern provinces, and 'join hands directly with the nations of the world endowed with consciousness'. But at the same time he expressed great disillusionment with the absence of ideals and of far-sighted plans even among the educated elite of Hunan, and with the corruption of political

---

[32] *Hsin-min hsueh-hui tzu-liao*, hereafter HMHHTL (*Materials on the New People's Study Society*), 62–5. (*Chung-kuo hsien-tai ko-ming-shih tzu-liao ts'ung-k'an*). Reprinted in *MTTC, pu chüan*, 1.191–4.
[33] HMHHTL 75–6. *MTTC, pu chüan*, 1.261–2.
[34] HMHHTL 63–5. *MTTC, pu chüan*, 1.192–4.

circles, which made reform wholly illusory. It was necessary, he said, to 'open a new road'.[35]

An important influence in Mao's search for such a road was the group of Hunanese students, members of the New People's Study Society, then studying in France, and above all his intimate friend (who was also Hsiang Ching-yü's lover), Ts'ai Ho-sen. This was, incidentally, the case not only in the explicitly political realm, but in the attitude of iconoclasm and rebellion against established customs which was so prominent a feature of the May Fourth era and its aftermath. Having learned, in a letter of May 1920 from Ts'ai, that he and Ching-yü had established 'a kind of union based on love', Mao responded with enthusiasm, denouncing all those who lived under the institution of marriage as the 'rape brigade' (*ch'iang-chien t'uan*), and swearing that he would never be one of them.[36]

A year earlier, in the context of his campaign against arranged marriages, following the suicide of a young girl in Changsha forced by her father to marry against her will,[37] Mao had called rather for the reform (*kai-ko*) of the marriage system, to replace 'capitalist' marriages by love matches. Already in 1919 he had concluded that among the various human desires, for food, sex, amusement, fame, and power, hunger and sexual desire were the most important. Then he had written that members of the older generation were interested only in food, and hence in exploiting their daughters-in-law as slaves, and not, like the young, in love and sexual desire, which involved 'not only the satisfaction of the biological urge of fleshly desire, but the satisfaction of spiritual desires, and desires for social intercourse of a high order'. Thus they were the natural allies of capitalism against the fulfilment of the desires of young people.[38] Now he had decided that marriage as such was the 'foundation of capitalism', because it involved the prohibition of 'that most reasonable thing, free love' (*chin-chih tsui ho-li ti tzu-yu lien-ai*).[39]

Just as the strongly patriotic Li Ta-chao went in 1920 through an internationalist phase, in which he proclaimed that all the members of humanity were brothers,[40] Mao Tse-tung, as he embraced Ts'ai Ho-sen's

---

[35] *HMHHTL* 75–6. *MTTC, pu chüan*, 1.261.

[36] *HMHHTL* 127 (Ts'ai's letter of 28 May 1920) and 121 (Mao's letter of 25 November 1920 to Lo Hsueh-tsan). The latter is also in *MTTC, pu chüan*, 1.275–7.

[37] Mao wrote in all nine articles on this theme. For a brief summary, see Li Jui, translation, 119–21. Extracts are translated in *PTMT* 334–7. For the full texts of all nine articles, published in the Changsha *Ta-kung-pao* between 16 and 28 November 1919, see *MTTC, pu chüan*, 1.143–72.

[38] See, especially, 'Lien-ai wen-t'i – shao-nien-jen yü lao-nien-jen' (The question of love – young people and old people), *ibid.* 161–3. Also 'Kai-ko hun-chih wen-t'i' (The problem of the reform of the marriage system), *ibid.* 149.   [39] *Ibid.* 276.

[40] Li Ta-chao, 'Ya-hsi-ya ch'ing-nien ti kuang-ming yun-tung' (The luminous Asiatic youth movement), *Li Ta-chao hsuan-chi*, 327–9; extracts in Carrère d'Encausse and Schram, *Marxism and Asia*, 208–10.

vision of a revolution like that of the Russians, also accepted Ts'ai's view that all socialism must necessarily be internationalist, and should not have a 'patriotic colouration'. Those born in China should work primarily (though not exclusively) in 'this place, China', because that was where they could work most effectively, and because China, being both 'more puerile and more corrupt' than other places in the world, was most in need of change, but this did not mean that they should love only China and not other places. But in the same letter of 1 December to Ts'ai Ho-sen, and in discussions at a meeting of the New People's Study Society in Changsha on 1–3 January 1921, Mao insisted that the goal of the society should be formulated as 'transforming China and the world'. Others argued that, since China was part of the world, it was not necessary to mention it separately. For Mao it was important.[41]

As for the goals of political change, and the methods to be used in pursuing them, Mao replied on 1 December to several communications he had received from Ts'ai Ho-sen, Hsiao Hsü-tung (Siao Yü) and others detailing their own views and the debates among members of the society in France about these matters. Ts'ai and Hsiao had formed, with Mao, during their years at the Normal School in Hunan, a trio who called themselves the 'three worthies' (san-ko hao-chieh), but following their exposure to Western influences they had moved in opposite directions, Ts'ai toward Bolshevism and Hsiao toward a more moderate vision of revolution vaguely anarchist in character. Mao agreed unequivocally with Ts'ai's view that China's road must be the Russian road. But at the same time, in the process of refuting the arguments of Hsiao, and of Bertrand Russell, who had just been lecturing in Changsha along similar lines, in favour of non-violent revolution, without dictatorship, he showed only the vaguest understanding of Marxist categories. Thus he divided the world's total population of one and a half billion into 500 million 'capitalists' (tzu pen chia) and a billion 'proletarians' (wu-ch'an chieh-chi).[42]

Plainly, Mao's usage here reflects an understanding of the term wu-ch'an chieh-chi closer to its literal meaning of 'propertyless class' than to the Marxist concept of the urban, or even of the urban and rural proletariat. In the course of the next few years he came to know better intellectually, though it is a moot point whether, in terms of instinctive reactions, the Chinese expression did not continue to signify for him something more like 'the wretched of the earth'.

[41] HMHHTL 146, and 15–41, especially 20–3.

[42] HMHHTL 144–52; MTTC, pu chüan, 1, 289–96; extracts translated in PTMT 196–8 (there misdated, following the then available source, November 1920). For the letters of August 1920 from Ts'ai and Hsiao, see HMHHTL 128–43. The problem of Ts'ai's influence on Mao at this time is discussed by R. Scalapino in 'The evolution of a young revolutionary – Mao Zedong in 1919–1921', Journal of Asian Studies 42.1 (Nov. 1982) 29–61.

Nevertheless, although his understanding of Marxist categories was as yet somewhat uncertain, Mao was definitely moving, during the winter of 1920–1, toward an interpretation of politics more in harmony with that of Lenin. Above all, he had grasped a Leninist axiom which was to remain at the centre of his thinking for the rest of his life, namely the decisive importance of political power. Replying on 21 January 1921 to a letter of 16 September 1920 from Ts'ai, declaring that the only method for China was 'that of the proletarian dictatorship as applied now in Russia',[43] Mao wrote:

The materialist view of history is our party's philosophical basis....In the past, I had not studied the problem, but at present I do not believe that the principles of anarchism can be substantiated.

The political organization of a factory (the management of production, distribution etc. in the factory) differs from the political organization of a country or of the world only in size, and not in nature (*chih yu ta-hsiao pu t'ung, mei yu hsing-chih pu-t'ung*). The view of syndicalism (*kung-t'uan chu-i*) according to which the political organization of a country and the political organization of a factory are different in nature, and the claim that these are two different matters which should be in the hands of different kinds of people...only proves that they are confused and do not understand the principles of things. Moreover, if we do not obtain political power, we cannot promote (*fa-tung*) revolution, we cannot maintain the revolution, and we cannot carry the revolution to completion....What you say in your letter [to the effect that China needs a proletarian dictatorship exactly like that in Russia] is extremely correct, there is not a single word with which I disagree.[44]

Mao Tse-tung's experience during the six years after the First Congress of the Chinese Communist Party in July 1921 falls neatly into three segments. During the first two years he was engaged in organizing the labour movement in Hunan, and this could be called his workers' period. Thereafter, in 1923 and 1924, he served as a member of the Chinese Communist Party's Central Committee, and of the Shanghai Executive Bureau of the Kuomintang, in Canton and Shanghai, and this could be called his period as an 'organization man'. Finally, as everyone knows, he devoted himself in 1925–7 largely to organizing the peasant movement, and this could be called his peasant period.

The most striking thing about the first of these periods is that it appears, on the basis of all the available primary and secondary sources, to have been, in comparison with what came before and after, intellectually sterile. In any case, Mao's writings from this workers' period are few in number,

[43] *HMHHTL* 153–62.
[44] *HMHHTL* 162–3. This and the previous letter, as well as Ts'ai's letters of 28 May and 13 August, and Mao's letter of 1 December 1920 to Ts'ai and Hsiao, are reproduced in a more widely available openly published source: *Ts'ai Ho-sen wen-chi* (*Collected writings of Ts'ai Ho-sen*), 37–40, 49–73. Mao's letters of December 1920 and January 1921 to Ts'ai are the first two items in *Mao Tse-tung shu-hsin hsuan-chi* (Selected letters of Mao Tse-tung), 1–16. Hereafter *Selected letters*.

and largely lacking in the fire and eloquence which, on other occasions, he showed himself so capable of manifesting. To be sure, Mao, like everyone else in the party, was overwhelmingly busy with organizational tasks during these first two years. The main explanation lies, however, in the fact that Mao himself had never really lived the life of a worker, as he had lived both the life of a peasant and the life of a student and city-based intellectual. He had, to be sure, organized a night-school for workers when he was a student at the Normal School in Changsha, and befriended individual workers on many occasions. His instinctive understanding of their problems was not, however, quite the same. Thus, although Mao's work in organizing strikes in a variety of industries undoubtedly influenced his intellectual and political development in the long run, at the time the harvest was meagre.

It is suggestive that the only item by Mao dating from the period mid-1921 to mid-1923 available in complete form outside China until very recently (thanks to the fortuitous circumstance that a widely-circulated magazine reprinted it in 1923) belongs in fact rather to the tail end of Mao's May Fourth period activities. It is the 'Declaration on the inauguration of the Hunan Self-Study University' which Mao wrote in August 1921 when he finally set up that intriguing institution.[45]

This text places, as Mao had done since 1917, the emphasis on individual initiative and self-expression in the learning process; it also echoes the articles Mao had written a year earlier on the mission of the Hunanese. But though Mao denounces vigorously the fact that 'learning is monopolized by a small "scholar clique" and becomes widely separated from the society of the ordinary man, thus giving rise to that strange phenomenon of the intellectual class enslaving the class of ordinary people', he shows as vague an understanding of what is meant by the 'so-called proletariat' as he had in his letter to Ts'ai of the previous December.

The writings of Mao's 'workers' period' relating specifically to the workers' movement are few and far between. Li Jui, whose biography of the young Mao is the principal source for texts of this period, is able to find only one item worthy of quoting at any length. This dates from December 1922, a time when Mao was engaged in leading the strike of the Changsha printing workers, and constitutes his reply to an attack by the editor of the Changsha Ta-kung-pao on the workers for getting involved in politics and lending themselves to other people's experiments. In a few characteristic sentences, Mao wrote:

What we workers need is knowledge; that is entirely correct. We workers are more than willing that people with knowledge should come forward and be our

[45] MTTC, 1.81–4; Day, Máo Zédōng, 140–3. This appeared in Tung-fang tsa-chih, 20.6 (1 March 1923).

real friends....Sir, you must never again stand on the sidelines....We acknowledge as good friends only those who are capable of sacrificing their own positions, and of enduring hunger and hardship in order to work on behalf of the interests of us workers, who constitute the great majority [of society]....Please, take off your long robe in a hurry![46]

We find here once again the recurrent theme that those who seek to reform society (as the *Ta-kung-pao* editor claimed he also wanted to do) should 'enter into the midst of things', and not remain on the sidelines as observers, or believe themselves superior to ordinary people. There is nothing here, however, about the role of the workers in the revolution, not to mention working-class hegemony. The *Ta-kung-pao* was not, perhaps, the place to advance such ideas, but Li Jui cites nothing at all from Mao's period as a labour organizer on this theme.

The explanation may well lie in the line of the Chinese Communist Party at the time. In 1922 the Comintern envoy Maring (Sneevliet) had pushed his Chinese comrades into the singular organizational form for a united front with the Nationalists known as the 'bloc within', under which the Chinese Communists joined the Kuomintang as individuals. This idea was originally put forward in March 1922 by Maring on the basis of his experience in the Dutch East Indies, where left-wing socialists had cooperated in a similar way with Sarekat Islam, a nationalist organization with (as the name implies) a pronounced religious colouration. Ch'en Tu-hsiu and a majority of the other leading members of the Chinese party having rejected this idea out of hand, Maring travelled to Moscow, put his case to the Executive Committee of the International, and obtained a formal mandate from the Comintern endorsing his policy. Armed with this, he was able, following his return to China in August 1922, to ram the 'bloc within' down the throats of his Chinese comrades.[47]

This pattern of collaboration has been the object of intense controversy

---

[46] Li Jui, 428–30; translation, 251–2. The editors of the supplement to the Tokyo edition of Mao's works, who have cast their net very widely indeed, have also come up with only two or three very brief texts, in addition to this one, relating to the workers' movement. See *MTTC*, *pu-chüan*, 2.89–107.

[47] He lied, therefore, when he told Harold Isaacs that he had persuaded the Chinese to accept the proposal simply on the basis of his personal authority, and had 'no document in his hand' from Moscow to back him up. (*CQ* 45 (January–March 1971) 106.) The view summarized in the text is shared by both Soviet and Chinese scholars. See V. I. Glunin, 'The Comintern and the rise of the communist movement in China (1920–1927)', in R. A. Ulyanovsky, ed. *The Comintern and the East*, 280–344, and Hsiao Sheng and Chiang Hua-hsuan, 'Ti-i-tz'u Kuo-Kung ho-tso t'ung-i chan-hsien ti hsing-ch'eng' (The formation of the first Kuomintang-Communist United Front), *LSYC* 2 (1981) 51–68. Important new documentation is presented in a forthcoming volume edited by Tony Saich, *The origins of the First United Front in China: the role of Sneevliet alias Maring*, which contains the whole of the Sneevliet Archives as they relate to China, with an extended introduction.

ever since its inception. So far as is known, Mao Tse-tung played no significant part either in devising it, or in securing its adoption. He was, however, one of the first to participate actively in implementing it. In the summer of 1922, Mao was involved in the organization of the Socialist Youth League in Hunan, and wrote to the Central Committee of the league in his capacity as secretary of the Changsha branch. Fifteen months later, in September 1923, he was already active in establishing Kuomintang organizations in the same localities, and wrote to the Central Office of the Kuomintang asking that he be formally appointed a member of the Preparatory Committee for this purpose, in order to facilitate contacts on all sides.[48]

From that time onwards, Mao Tse-tung was to play an important role in 'united front work'. Broadly speaking, once Ch'en Tu-hsiu and the other Chinese Communist leaders had accepted the 'bloc within', there was a tendency on their part to conclude that this implied accepting the leadership of the Nationalists, as the 'party of the bourgeoisie', at least for the time being. Such was Ch'en's position in 1923, and Mao for his part went very far in that direction during his period as an 'organization man'.

This is clearly apparent in the article entitled 'The foreign powers, the militarists, and the revolution' which Mao published in April 1923, on the eve of the crucial Third Congress, which formally adopted the 'bloc within'. Within China, he declared, only three factions (*p'ai*) were to be found: the revolutionary democratic faction, the non-revolutionary democratic faction (*fei ko-ming ti min-chu p'ai*), and the reactionary faction. Regarding the first of these, he wrote: 'The main body (*chu-t'i*) of the revolutionary faction is, of course, the Kuomintang; the newly-arisen (*hsin-hsing*) Communist faction (*kung-ch'an p'ai*) is cooperating with the Kuomintang.'

The non-revolutionary democratic faction included on the one hand the Research Clique and the 'faction of the newly-arisen intellectual class' (*hsin-hsing ti chih-shih chieh-chi p'ai*) of Hu Shih, Huang Yen-p'ei and others; and on the other hand the newly-arisen merchant faction. The reactionaries were, of course, the three main cliques of militarists.

The division of the totality of social forces into three was, and would remain, highly characteristic of Mao's approach to politics and to revolution. Another trait very much in evidence here is what might be called the dialectics of disorder and oppression, on which Mao had laid

---

[48] See his letter of 20 June 1922, 'Chih Shih Fu-liang ping She-hui-chu-i ch'ing-nien-t'uan chung-yang' (To Shih Fu-liang and the Central Committee of the Socialist Youth League), and his letter of 28 September 1923, 'Chih Lin Po-ch'ü, P'eng Su-min' (To Lin Po-chü and P'eng Su-min), *Selected letters*, 21–4.

great stress in his 1919 article 'The great union of the popular masses'. Because of the power of the militarists, and because the union of China under a democratic government would be contrary to the interests of the imperialists, there can be, Mao argues, neither peace nor unity for another eight or ten years. But the more reactionary and confused the political situation, the more this will stimulate the revolutionary sentiments and organizational capacity of the people of the whole country, so that in the end democracy and national independence will triumph over the militarists.[49]

The merchants, who were to have a share in the victory of the democratic forces, revolutionary and non-revolutionary, were featured more prominently in an article of July 1923 entitled 'The Peking coup d'état and the merchants', which has been the subject of considerable controversy. In this text, Mao stated in part:

The present political problem in China is none other than the problem of a national revolution (*kuo-min ko-ming*). To use the strength of the citizens [*kuo-min,* literally the people of the country] to overthrow the militarists, and also to overthrow the foreign imperialists with whom the militarists are in collusion to accomplish their treasonable acts, is the historic mission of the Chinese people. This revolution is the task of the people as a whole, and the merchants, workers, peasants, students and teachers should all come forward to take on the responsibility for a portion of the revolutionary work. Both historical necessity and present realities prescribe, however, that the work for which the merchants must take responsibility in the national revolution is both more urgent and more important than the work that the rest of the people should take upon themselves....
The broader the organization of merchants, the greater will be their...ability to lead the people of the whole country, and the more rapid the success of the revolution![50]

It has been suggested that Mao's July 1923 article is not about the role of the merchants in the Chinese revolution at all, but rather about the nature of the tasks in the present 'bourgeois-democratic' stage of the revolution.[51] This view not only flies in the face of the evidence, but completely fails to note the epoch-making shift in Mao's outlook between 1923 and 1925–6, from an urban-oriented perspective to one turned toward the countryside. In another passage of his July 1923 article, Mao wrote:

---

[49] 'Wai li, chün-fa yü ko-ming' (The foreign powers, the militarists, and the revolution), *MTCC*, *pu-chüan*, 2.109–111.
[50] *The Guide Weekly*, 31/32 (11 July 1923), 233–4; translated in *PTMT* 106–9.
[51] Lynda Shaffer, 'Mao Ze-dong and the October 1922 Changsha construction workers' strike', *Modern China*, 4.4 (Oct. 1978) 380, 416–71. The same argument is repeated in L. Shaffer, *Mao and the workers: the Hunan labor movement, 1920–1923*, 1–2, 222–3.

We know that the politics of semi-colonial China is characterized by the fact that the militarists and foreign powers have banded together to impose a twofold oppression on the people of the whole country. The people of the whole country obviously suffer profoundly under this kind of twofold oppression. Nevertheless, it must be acknowledged that the merchants are the ones who feel these sufferings most acutely and most urgently.

In other words, Mao regarded the merchants, and more broadly the city-dwellers directly exposed to imperialist oppression, as most capable of playing a leading role in the national revolution because they suffered the most. This whole sociological analysis was turned right around three years later, after Mao had discovered the revolutionary potential inherent in the peasantry. Before we consider these developments, another persistent trait in Mao's July 1923 article deserves to be noted. The conclusion reads as follows:

Everyone must believe that the only way to save both himself and the nation (*kuo-chia*) is through the national revolution (*kuo-min ko-ming*). . . . Circumstances call upon us to perform an historic task. . . . To open a new era by revolutionary methods, and to build a new nation – such is the historic mission of the Chinese people (*Chung-hua min-tsu*). We must never forget it!

Here once again, we can see how clearly people in the political sense (*kuo-min* or citizens) and people in the biological sense (*min-tsu* or nation) were linked in Mao Tse-tung's thought.

Few substantial texts by Mao are available outside China for the period of nearly two and a half years from the appearance of this and two briefer articles in the Chinese Communist Party organ *Hsiang-tao* (The guide) until Mao took up the editorship of the Kuomintang organ *Cheng-chih chou-pao* (The political weekly) in December 1925. He spoke briefly at the First KMT Congress in January 1924, and drafted some resolutions for submission to the KMT Central Executive Committee (of which he was a member) in February 1924. Even in this formal context, some of Mao's utterances illustrate the persistent traits of his work style and political strategy. Thus, at the first KMT Congress, he opposed a proposal for setting up a 'research department' on the grounds that this would have as its consequence 'the separation of research from application – something which our party, as a revolutionary party, cannot do'.[52]

Following his sojourn in Shanghai as a member of the Shanghai Executive Bureau of the KMT, Mao returned in early 1925 to Hunan for a rest, and began his practical apprenticeship in organizing the peasants. He came back to Canton in the autumn of 1925 to take de facto charge

[52] *Chung-kuo Kuo-min-tang ch'üan-kuo tai-piao ta-hui hui-i-lu* (Minutes of the National Congress of the Kuomintang of China), 47.

of the Kuomintang Propaganda Department, edit *Cheng-chih chou-pao*, begin lecturing at the Peasant Movement Training Institute (which he was to head from May to October 1926), and participate in the Second Congress of the KMT. By this time he had come to hold the view, from which he was never afterwards to waver, that the centre of gravity of China's revolution lay with the peasants in the countryside.

Enumerating the weak points of Kuomintang propaganda in his report on the subject to the Second Congress in January 1926, Mao noted: 'We have concentrated too much on the cities and ignored the peasants.'[53] To some extent, this shift in Mao's outlook merely reflected the changing pattern of the revolution itself: the increasing militancy of the peasantry, and the activity of P'eng P'ai and many others, as well as of Mao, in mobilizing the peasants. Only by tapping this potential, Mao had concluded, would the revolutionary party (or parties) be able to create the force necessary to the achievement of their anti-imperialist goals – which Mao continued to proclaim in all his writings of the 'peasant period', 1925–7. But though the Chinese Communist Party, or a substantial fraction of it, turned its attention to the peasantry in the mid-1920s, the case of Mao Tse-tung is unique, not only in the obvious sense that he subsequently assumed the leadership of a revolution which effectively encircled the cities from the countryside, but because he formulated as early as 1926 theoretical propositions foreshadowing the future course of the Chinese revolution.

The emergence of Mao's ideas regarding a peasant-based revolution has probably been the subject of more discussion than any other single topic in the history of the Chinese Communist movement. Many historical and theoretical questions have been clarified in the course of this scholarly debate, but some points have until very recently remained obscure for lack of adequate documentation. In his interviews of 1936 with Edgar Snow, Mao declared that he had become aware of the revolutionary potential to be found in the Chinese peasantry only after the May Thirtieth incident of 1925 and the subsequent upsurge of patriotic sentiment in the countryside as well as in the city. The available evidence tends to confirm Mao's statement, and indeed suggests that he truly shifted his attention to the problem of rural revolution only toward the end of 1925. In order to bring out the over-arching continuity in Mao's thinking, despite such shifts of focus, however, it is appropriate to say a few words about his attitude toward the peasantry on the eve of the foundation of the Chinese Communist Party, before analysing the ideas he put forward in 1926–7.

In the latter part of 1919, Mao had drawn up an extensive plan for

[53] Day, 232; *MTTC* 1.151.

promoting 'new villages' along the lines earlier advocated in Japan, and a chapter from this was published in Changsha in December. Apart from the 'new village' slogan itself, this article called for young Chinese to follow the example of Russian youth in entering the villages to preach socialism.[54] In both these respects, the ideas advocated by Mao on this occasion reflected Li Ta-chao's influence.[55] Other elements, however, such as the discussion of the concept of 'work and study' in the United States, of which 'our Chinese students in America have taken advantage' seem to come rather from Dewey and Hu Shih.

More important, however, than these intellectual influences was Mao's own experience of peasant life, upon which he drew in developing his ideas in the early 1920s. In a lecture of September 1922, at the Self-Study University, Mao expounded views on the class structure of the Chinese countryside contained in an article published in a party organ in December 1920. Although Mao most probably had not written this article, he implicitly endorsed the analysis put forward there by taking it as his text. Refuting those who said that the life of the Chinese peasants was not so very hard, and the distribution of land not so very unequal, Mao divided the 'classes making up the peasantry' into four categories:

1. Those who own a lot of land but do not till it themselves (either employing people to till it, or renting it out for cultivation) and sit at home collecting rent. Such people do not really count as peasants, and where I come from we call them local moneybags (*t'u ts'ai-chu*).

2. Those who till their own land and are able to keep their whole family on the produce. They may also rent other people's land and till it, in addition to their own. These are the middle peasants.

3. Those who do have a bit of land, but are quite unable to keep their whole family on what it produces, and who thus have no alternative but to rely on tilling other people's land and being allotted a measure of what is produced in order to support themselves. These can be called lower (*hsia-chi*) peasants.

4. There are the paupers (*ch'iung kuang-tan*), who have not even a piece of land big enough to stick a needle into it, and rely exclusively on other people's land to keep body and soul together. These are the poorest of all the peasants.

The third and fourth categories, said Mao, made up the overwhelming majority of the peasantry, and moreover those in the third category were constantly being obliged by debt to sell their land to the 'rural money-bags' or the middle peasants, and descend into the fourth category.[56]

---

54 Mao Tse-tung, 'Hsüeh-sheng chih kung-tso' (The work of the students), *Hunan chiao-yü* (Hunan education), 1.2 (Dec. 1919), quoted in Wang Shu-pai and Chang Shen-heng, *LSYC* 5 (1980) 59–60.
55 See Maurice Meisner, *Li Ta-chao and the origins of Chinese Marxism*, esp. 55–6 and 80–9.
56 'Kao Chung-kuo ti nung-min' (Address to China's peasants) was originally published in *Kung-ch'an-tang* 3 (23 December 1920); it is reproduced in *I-ta ch'ien-hou* (Before and after the First Congress), 207–14. The fact that Mao gave a lecture using this text is noted in Li Jui, 455. The attribution of authorship to Mao in *Tzu-liao hsuan-pien*, 24, appears to be wrong.

Although the analysis is far more rudimentary, one can detect a faint resemblance between the text I have just summarized and Mao's two articles of January and February 1926, analysing respectively the class structure of the Chinese countryside and of Chinese society as a whole.[57] When, after analysing class relations in the countryside, and discussing the exploitation of the tenants by extortionate rents, and the tendency toward the concentration of land ownership, Mao went on to draw the political consequences, he adopted a categorically egalitarian position. 'We members of the human race,' he declares, 'are all equal as we come from our mother's womb; all of us should, in the same way, have food to eat and clothes to wear, and we should all work in the same way.' Formerly, everyone had used the land in common; the private property which allowed a minority to live in idleness, eating meat and wearing satin, was based on nothing else but the theft of what should rightfully belong to the peasants, and the peasants should arise and take it back. As soon as they arose, communism (which meant food and work for all) would come to their aid.[58] No doubt this rhetoric was designed to appeal to the peasants' mentality, but it also reflected the fact that, even in 1922, neither Mao nor the Chinese Communist Party as a whole had a coherent and realistic strategy for rural revolution. Four years later Mao had gone a long way toward the elaboration of such a strategy.

The general level of Mao's understanding of Marxist theory in 1925–6 was by no means high. Toward the beginning of his article of February 1926, he declared: 'In any country, wherever it be under the heavens, there are three categories of people; upper, middle, and lower.'[59] In this general framework, he classified the big landlords as part of the big bourgeoisie, and the small landlords as part of the bourgeoisie, and defined sub-groups in classes, both urban and rural, as much by their levels of wealth or poverty as by their relation to the means of production. In thus stressing whether or not peasant households could 'make ends meet', rather than the more orthodox Marxist criteria of land ownership or the hiring of labourers as the standard for defining strata in Chinese rural society, Mao adopted a framework quite different from that employed in 1923 by Ch'en Tu-hsiu.[60]

---

[57] 'Analysis of the various classes of the Chinese peasantry and their attitudes toward revolution' (January 1926) and 'Analysis of all the classes in Chinese society' (February 1926), in *MTTC* 1.153–73; extracts from the article on the peasantry analogous to the passages quoted above are translated in *PTMT* 241–6.   [58] *I-ta ch'ien-hou*, 212–14.

[59] Mao Tse-tung, 'Chung-kuo she-hui ko chieh-chi ti fen-hsi' (Analysis of all the classes in Chinese society), *MTTC* I, 161–74. The sentence quoted is translated in *PTMT* 211.

[60] I have compared Mao's analysis of class relations in the countryside and that of Ch'en Tu-hsiu in my article 'Mao Zedong and the role of the various classes in the Chinese revolution 1923–1927', in *Chūgoku no seiji to keizai* (The polity and economy of China – the late Professor Yuji Muramatsu commemoration volume), 227–39.

It is therefore entirely wrong to argue[61] that Mao's categories and those of Ch'en were basically the same. But it is true that the main difference between the two men, and Mao's essential originality, lay elsewhere, namely in his resolve to make rural revolution on the basis of his own experience, and in his propensity to interpret, or even mould analysis to fit tactical goals.

Mao's analysis of social forces in China and their attitudes toward revolution in fact took shape in late 1925. One of five articles he contributed to the first five issues of *Cheng-chih chou-pao* under the pseudonym 'Tzu Jen' outlined essentially the same scheme he was to use in early 1926, minus the division of the peasant proprietors and other 'petty bourgeois' elements into those with a surplus, those who could just make ends meet, and those who did not have enough to live on.[62] In this piece, published in January, but corresponding probably to the substance of a speech he delivered in October 1925 to the First Kwangtung Provincial Congress of the KMT, Mao discussed, basically in the same terms he was to use in his famous article 'Analysis of all the classes in Chinese society' of February 1926, the implications of social divisions for political behaviour, and more particularly for factionalism within the Kuomintang. Here the apparently unorthodox division of society into 'upper', 'middle' and 'lower' came into its own, for having put the upper classes (big bourgeoisie and big landlords) firmly in the camp of the counter-revolution, and the lower classes (petty-bourgeoisie, semi-proletariat, urban and rural, and proletariat) in the camp of revolution, Mao proceeded to consider how the 'bourgeoisie' (national bourgeois and small landlords) would be pulled asunder and forced to choose, in the wake of the polarization which had developed following the emergence of the 'Western Hills' faction. As he did in 1926, and was consistently to do thereafter, Mao placed the overwhelming majority of the Chinese people (395 out of 400 million) on the side of revolution, leaving only one million hard-core reactionaries,

---

[61] As Philip Huang has done in his article 'Mao Tse-tung and the middle peasants, 1925–1928', *Modern China*, 1.3 (July 1975), 279–80.

[62] These articles were first attributed to Mao Tse-tung by John Fitzgerald in his article 'Mao in mufti: newly identified works by Mao Zedong', *The Australian Journal of Chinese Affairs*, 9 (January 1983) 1–16. Fitzgerald's arguments are altogether convincing in themselves, but the fact of Mao's authorship was also confirmed by Hu Hua, head of the Department of Party History of People's University, in a conversation with me on 10 September 1982. For a complete translation of Mao's article entitled 'The reasons underlying the secession of the GMD rightist faction and its ramifications for the future of the revolution', *Cheng-chih chou-pao*, 4 (10 January 1926) 10–12, see Fitzgerald, 9–15. Mao had, in fact, taken the name Tzu-jen as an alternative style as early as 1910, when he was a student at the Tungshan Higher Primary School. He did so out of respect for Liang Ch'i-ch'ao, whose influence on Mao at that time has already been noted. Liang's honorific name being Liang Jen-kung, 'Tzu-jen' had the meaning 'son of Jen'. See Li Jui, 'Hsueh-sheng shih-tai ti Mao Tse-tung', 176.

corresponding to the 'upper' category, and four million of those wavering people in the middle, who were torn both ways.[63]

As for the problem of leadership, Mao, in early 1926, while stressing the numerical importance of the peasantry and the degree of privation – and therefore of sympathy for the revolution – prevailing in the countryside, also characterized the urban proletariat as the 'main force' in the revolution.[64] Thus, even though the concept of 'proletarian hegemony' was inserted in this text only in 1951, he did recognize in early 1926 the Marxist axiom that the workers would play the central role in the revolutionary process. In September 1926 he allowed himself to be carried away by enthusiasm for the revolutionary forces which had been unleashed in the countryside to such a point that he turned the axiom of working-class leadership explicitly on its head.[65]

Mao's article, 'The national revolution and the peasant movement', published at this time, begins with the statement: 'The peasant question is the central (*chung-hsin*) question in the national revolution.' This in itself was not at all remarkable, for the upsurge of revolutionary activity in the country, since the middle of 1925, had forced itself on the attention even of the most urban-oriented, to such an extent that a bow in the direction of the peasant movement had become a cliché automatically included in almost every utterance of a Communist and/or Kuomintang spokesman. Mao's argument demonstrating the importance of the peasantry in terms of the structure of Chinese society was, on the other hand, very remarkable indeed. 'The greatest adversary of revolution in an economically backward semi-colony,' he wrote, 'is the feudal-patriarchal class (the landlord class) in the villages.' It was on this 'feudal landlord class' that the foreign imperialists relied to support their exploitation of the peasantry; the warlords were merely the chieftains of this class. Thus, as the example of Hai-feng showed, the domination of the imperialists and the warlords could be overthrown only by mobilizing the peasantry to destroy the foundations of their rule. 'The Chinese revolution,' he wrote, 'has only this form, and no other.'[66]

Not only did Mao Tse-tung assert the importance of the rural forces

---

[63] For the argument to the effect that the article by Tzu Jen corresponded to Mao's speech of 1 October see Fitzgerald, 5 and 9. The identical figures used in this article and in that of February 1926 for various categories of the population are clearly presented in the table in Fitzgerald, 4. The parallel passages in the two articles stressing that 395 millions support the revolution are translated in Fitzgerald, 14–15, and *PTMT* 213–14.

[64] Mao Tse-tung, 'Analysis of all the classes', *MTTC* 1.170; *PTMT* 247.

[65] Mao Tse-tung, 'Kuo-min ko-ming yü nung-min yun-tung' (The national revolution and the peasant movement), *MTTC* 1.175–9; for a more detailed discussion, with extracts in translation, see my article 'Mao Zedong and the role of the various classes'.

[66] *MTTC* 1.175–6.

of reaction in the old society, and of the rural revolutionary forces in overthrowing them – he went on to argue against the importance of the cities:

There are those who say that the rampant savagery exercised by the compradors in the cities is altogether comparable to the rampant savagery of the landlord class in the countryside, and that the two should be put on the same plane. It is true that there is rampant savagery, but it is not true that it is of the same order. In the whole country, the areas where the compradors are concentrated include only a certain number of places such as Hong Kong, Canton, Shanghai, Hankow, Tientsin, Dairen, etc., on the sea coast and the rivers. It is not comparable to the domain of the landlord class, which extends to every province, every *hsien*, and every village of the whole country. In political terms, the various warlords, big and small, are all the chieftains chosen by the landlord class....This gang of feudal landlord chieftains...use the comprador class in the cities in order to dally with the imperialists; both in name and in fact the warlords are the hosts, and the comprador class are their followers. Financially, 90 per cent of the hundreds of millions of dollars the warlord governments spend each year is taken directly, or indirectly, from the peasants who live under the domination of the landlord class...Hence, although we are aware that the workers, students, and big and small merchants in the cities should arise and strike fiercely at the comprador class, and directly resist imperialism, and although we know that the progressive working class, especially, is the leader of all the revolutionary classes, yet if the peasants do not arise and fight in the villages, to overthrow the privileges of the feudal-patriarchal landlord class, the power of the warlords and of imperialism can never be hurled down root and branch.

Despite the ritual reference to the 'leading role' of the working class, the implication of this passage is clearly that the real centre of power of the old society is to be found in the countryside, and the real blows must therefore be struck in the countryside. This is spelled out explicitly, in startlingly bald terms, in the concluding paragraph of the article:

The peasant movement in China is a movement of class struggle which combines political and economic struggle. Its peculiarities are manifested especially in the political aspect. In this respect it is somewhat different in nature from the workers' movement in the cities. At present, the political objectives of the urban working class are merely to seek complete freedom of assembly and of association; this class does not yet seek to destroy immediately the political position of the bourgeoisie. As for the peasants in the countryside, on the other hand, as soon as they arise they run into the political power of those village bullies, bad gentry, and landlords who have been crushing the peasants for several thousand years...and if they do not overthrow this political power which is crushing them, there can be no status for the peasants. This is a very important peculiarity of the peasant movement in China today.[67]

In other words, the workers ('at present' – but for how long?) are merely

[67] *Ibid.* 176–7.

reformists, pursuing limited benefits for themselves; they are animated, it could be said, by 'trade union consciousness'. The peasants, on the other hand, not only occupy a decisive position in society, so that they cannot achieve their aims without overthrowing the whole edifice of the old order; they are aware of the situation, and are deliberately waging a broad struggle, political as well as economic.

Never afterwards was Mao to go so far in explicitly putting the peasants in the place of the workers as the conscious vanguard of the revolution. His Hunan peasant report of February 1927 attributed to the poor peasants the leading role in the struggle in the countryside; it did not downgrade the importance of the cities, and of the classes based in the cities, in the same graphic terms, though there are indications suggesting that he had not abandoned his position of the previous September. The famous phrase attributing 70 per cent of the achievements of the revolution to date to the peasants[68] might be interpreted as relating to force rather than to leadership, and as merely describing a temporary condition. Another passage summarizes in capsule form the analysis developed in the September article to the effect that the 'patriarchal feudal class of local tyrants, evil gentry and lawless landlords has formed the basis of autocratic government for thousands of years and is the cornerstone of imperialism, warlordism, and corrupt officialdom', and adds: 'To overthrow these feudal forces is the real objective of the national revolution.'[69]

That the peasantry, though it is an important revolutionary force, must follow the leadership either of the workers or of the bourgeoisie, and cannot play an autonomous political role, is one of the most basic political axioms of Marxism, going back to Marx himself. Mao's theoretical contribution, during the ensuing half century, consisted not in replacing this axiom by its opposite, but in weaving together the principle of working-class leadership and his conviction that the fate of the Chinese revolution ultimately depended on what happened in the countryside.

In September 1926 Mao said, in effect, that the peasants could not emancipate themselves without emancipating the whole of Chinese society. He seemed to be investing them with a mission not unlike that which Marx attributed to the urban proletariat in the capitalist societies of the West. At the same time, as we have seen, he recognized that the workers were the 'leaders of all the revolutionary classes'. These two statements can be reconciled if we take the one as relating to the form of the revolutionary struggle in the immediate future, and the other as defining the long-term pattern of events, though the synthesis implied by such an interpretation would attribute to the peasants a degree of initiative scarcely

[68] *MTTC* 1.211–12; *PTMT* 252.   [69] Mao Tse-tung, *Selected works*, hereafter Mao, *SW*, 1.27.

compatible with Marxist orthodoxy. In any case, if this was Mao's understanding of the matter, the second half of his approach to the peasant problem would come into play only after the conquest of power, in fixing the pattern for the revolutionary transformation of society. And before that moment arrived, both Mao and the Chinese Communist movement had a long road to travel.

PARTY, ARMY AND MASSES 1927–1937

As noted in the previous section above, Mao Tse-tung, though he played no part in devising the singular organizational framework of the 'bloc within', worked forcefully to implement it from 1923 onwards. Manifestly, he was able to work effectively in such a context because he attached primary importance to national unification and China's struggle to throw off the domination of the imperialists, and accepted that, for the moment, the Kuomintang and its army were the best instrument for achieving this.

Mao therefore did his utmost, in particular during the eight-month period from October 1925 to May 1926, when he effectively ran the Propaganda Department of the Kuomintang Central Executive Committee, to consolidate the overwhelming majority of the Nationalist Party and its supporters on positions which were radical, but in no sense Communist or Marxist. Indeed, he devoted a large part of his introductory editorial for the Kuomintang organ *The Political Weekly* (*Cheng-chih chou-pao*) to refuting the accusations that Kwangtung was being 'communized'. The true goals of the revolution, he wrote, were 'to liberate the Chinese nation...to bring about the rule of the people...to see that the people attain economic prosperity'.[70] In other words, the goal was to implement the 'Three People's Principles'.

In his article of January 1926, 'The reasons underlying the secession of the KMT rightist faction and its ramifications for the future of the revolution', Mao argued that the emergence of a new rightist faction was not the result of the machinations of the KMT left, but the natural outcome of the interaction between the development of the revolution and the class basis of the KMT. 'The real force for revolution,' he wrote, was the alliance of petty-bourgeoisie, semi-proletariat, and proletariat. Landlord and big-bourgeois elements who had supported the anti-Manchu Revolution of 1911 could not accept the demand for 'people's rights' and 'people's livelihood'. 'Hence, as the revolution has developed and the

70 *MTTC* 1.109–11; translated in Day, 205–6.

KMT has progressed, the old and the new rightist factions have split off one by one like bamboo shoots from their stem.'[71]

At this time, in early 1926, as I noted above in discussing Mao's approach to peasant revolution, he still believed that 395 million of China's 400 million people were on the side of the revolution. Thus he was able to accept Stalin's view that the Kuomintang was the only vehicle for reaching the vast masses, particularly in the countryside.

Following his investigation of the peasant movement in Hunan in early 1927, Mao's views on this and other matters changed fundamentally. He expressed his new insights more forthrightly in a separate report, dated 16 February 1927, to the Central Committee of the Chinese Communist Party than he did in the well-known document openly published at the time. Dividing the course of events in the countryside into three periods – that of organizing the peasant associations, that of the rural revolution, and that of setting up a united front – he stressed very strongly that a genuine revolutionary catharsis was indispensable between the first and third stages. The united front would not produce the desired results unless it was preceded by a period of 'fierce struggle to overthrow the power and prestige of the feudal landlords'. To be sure, he said that conflicts which arose in the countryside should, insofar as possible, be dealt with through the KMT apparatus rather than directly by the Communist Party under its own banner, but Mao clearly saw this as a temporary tactic. The masses, he said, were moving toward the left, and were eager for another revolution; the Communist Party must not shrink back from leading them in that direction.[72] Later in 1927, in any case, having lost all hope that Chiang Kai-shek or even the so-called 'Left Kuomintang' would support action by the peasants which went dead against their own class interests, Mao Tse-tung was one of the very first to call for a radical break with these former allies, and for the raising of the red flag in the countryside.

The twenty-two years from the Autumn Harvest uprising to the proclamation of the Chinese People's Republic were spent by Mao Tse-tung almost wholly in a rural environment, and witnessed the emergence and triumph of a strategy of 'surrounding the cities from the countryside'. In this sense, they marked the continuation and fulfilment of his earlier ideas regarding the role of the peasants in the revolution. But they were also years of unremitting military struggle, and to that extent constituted a fundamental rupture with the past. Mao Tse-tung had, of course, known

---

[71] *MTTC, pu chüan*, 2; translated in Fitzgerald, 9–15.

[72] 'Shih-ch'a Hunan nung-yun kei chung-yang ti pao-kao' (Report to the Central Committee on an inspection of the peasant movement in Hunan), *MTTC, pu-chüan*, 2.255–7.

intermittent fighting throughout the greater part of his life, and had been a soldier at the age of 18. He had also shown a keen insight, in 1925–7, into the political opportunities offered by the civil war between the Kuomintang and the northern warlords. It was, however, quite another matter for the Communists to organize their own independent armed forces, and to rely on these as a primary instrument in the revolutionary struggle.

The imprint of this dimension of Mao's experience on his theoretical contributions, beginning in 1927, was many-faceted. To begin with, he developed progressively more elaborate conceptions of the strategy and tactics of guerrilla warfare, which must be regarded as an integral part of his thought as a whole. The matrix of guerrilla warfare which shaped the Chinese Communist movement in Ching-kang-shan, Kiangsi and Yenan days did not, however, merely incite Mao to write about military problems; it also influenced deeply both his ideas as to how revolutionary leadership should be organized, and the spirit which pervaded his outlook. The last point, though very important, should not be exaggerated. Mao's stress on the role of armed force in the Chinese revolution did not make of him, as Wittfogel and others have argued, a thug or fascist who delighted in naked military force for its own sake. It did, however, unquestionably strengthen the emphasis on courage, firmness of heart, and the martial spirit which is visible in his first published article, and never left him until the end of his life.

Of more lasting significance were the patterns of organization and political work adopted by the Chinese Communists at the time, and to some extent conserved by them later, even when circumstances had changed. In a word, a guerrilla army mobilizing peasant masses is a thing quite different from a Communist Party mobilizing the urban workers, and neither the relation between the revolutionary elite and its supporters, nor the ideology which defines and justifies the nature of the whole enterprise, can be entirely the same.

The contrast between the Chinese revolution and its Russian and European predecessors was not, of course, so stark as the preceding one-sentence summary suggests. Even in Kiangsi, if not on the Ching-kang-shan, there was some small-scale industry and therefore some workers; and throughout the whole period 1927–49, there existed a Chinese Communist Party to which the Red Army was theoretically subordinate. Therefore, it was not a question of the army leading the peasants, but of party and army leading 'masses', rural and urban. The fact remains that, throughout the greater part of these twenty-two years, the party existed in significant measure as a soul or parasite in the body of the army. Even to the extent that the Chinese Communist Party appeared on the stage as an actor in its own right, it owed its very survival to the protecting shield of the Red Army, rather than to the solidity of its working-class basis. And though neither party nor army could have endured without the support of a large proportion of the population, the relation of such a Communist movement to the people was different from any which had been known before.

As Mao himself pointed out in later years, the differences between the patterns of the Chinese and Soviet revolutions lay not merely in the fact that the Chinese Communists had engaged in armed struggle, and armed struggle in the countryside. They also flowed from the exercise, by Mao and his comrades, of effective political control over varying but often considerable areas and populations, long before the actual conquest of power. Because of this the Chinese Communist movement stood in a threefold relationship to the people: that of a revolutionary army, seeking to draw from the 'ocean' of the masses the sustenance necessary to the conduct of its operations; that of the 'vanguard party', seeking to guide the proletariat in the accomplishment of its historical mission; and that of government, or state within a state, in which capacity it established with the population under its control a complex network of interactions on many levels.

Mao Tse-tung was one of those most closely attuned to the singular realities of the Chinese revolution, and these various dimensions of the relationship between leaders and masses all find expression in his thought. The over-arching concept which, in principle, infused all of these relationships was that of the 'mass line'.

The mass-line approach to leadership represents a very important element in the political and ideological heritage of the Chinese Communist Party, which sets off Chinese communism from that of the Soviet Union. Although it was fully elaborated by Mao in theoretical terms only in the early 1940s, the key concepts and methods emerged progressively during the previous decade and a half, when the sheer necessity of survival required that the Chinese Communists establish the closest kind of relationship with the populations among whom they worked.

To work with the people did not, however, mean for Mao to lose oneself in them, in some great orgy of populist spontaneity. Nor should the Yenan heritage be romanticized, or sentimentalized, to make of Mao a believer in some kind of 'extended democracy' with overtones of anarchism. The classic directive of 1 June 1943 itself, in which Mao first formulated systematically his ideas on the mass line, reflected, to be sure, his concern that policy-makers should listen to those below and learn from experience at the grass roots. His injunction to 'link the nucleus of leadership closely with the broad masses', and to 'sum up the experience of mass struggles' was seriously meant. But in the end the aim was to take the 'scattered and unsystematic ideas of the masses', turn them into 'concentrated and systematic ideas', and then 'go to the masses and propagate and explain these ideas *until the masses embrace them as their own* (*hua wei ch'ün-chung ti i-chien*)...'[73]

In other words, the people were to be made to interiorize ideas which they were quite incapable of elaborating for themselves. There is a remarkable parallel between this last phrase and Lenin's view that class consciousness could only be imported into the proletariat from outside. And yet there were significant differences between Mao's approach to leadership and that of Lenin, as well as in the revolutions they led. Let us now look at the development of Mao's ideas regarding these matters, from 1927 onwards, beginning first with the role of the army.

In August 1927, when the Central Committee criticized his strategy for the Autumn Harvest uprising, accusing him of attaching undue importance to military force, lacking faith in the strength of the masses, and turning this action into a 'mere military adventure', he replied bluntly that the Central Committee was practising 'a contradictory policy consisting in neglecting military affairs and at the same time desiring an armed insurrection of the popular masses'.[74] In fact, Mao had already answered such criticisms in his remarks at the 7 August emergency conference, where he said:

In the past, we criticized Sun Yat-sen for running a purely military movement, and we did just the opposite, not engaging in any military movement but concentrating on the mass movement....Now we have begun to pay attention to this, but we have not grasped the issue resolutely. For example, the Autumn Harvest uprising will be impossible without attention to military matters, and the present meeting must attach due importance to this question....We must be aware that political power grows out of the barrel of a gun.

This appears to be the first occasion on which Mao used this famous aphorism. He repeated it ten days later at a meeting of the Hunan Provincial Party Committee, adding that in the existing circumstances 60 per cent of the party's energies should be devoted to the military movement.[75] Only armies, Mao was persuaded, or in any case organized

[73] *PTMT* 316–17. (Italics added.)
[74] For the text of letters dated 20 and 30 August 1927, and presumed to have been written by Mao, see *MTTC* 2.11–14. Extracts from this correspondence are translated and its implications analysed in my article, 'On the nature of Mao Tse-tung's "deviation" in 1927', *CQ* 27 (April-June 1964), 55–66.
[75] *MTTC, pu-chüan*, 2.297–8, 299–300.

and disciplined guerrilla units, could fight armies; the masses could not fight the white armies bare-handed.

For a moment, in the autumn of 1927, the Central Committee, in the context of the chiliastic vision of uninterrupted revolution which had seized the Ch'ü Ch'iu-pai leadership, was persuaded that they could, but these hopes and illusions soon evaporated. For his part, Mao never wavered, after the Autumn Harvest uprising, from the conviction that a Red Army was indispensable to the survival of the revolution.

Until the collapse of the Li Li-san line in the late summer of 1930, Mao Tse-tung was inclined to believe that the central role of the army was merely a temporary phenomenon; thereafter, he came to see the encirclement of the cities from the countryside as the long-term pattern of the Chinese revolution. (I shall return subsequently to the strategic aspect of Mao's thinking.) But despite these changes in his ideas regarding the time-scale of the revolution, his view of the relations between the army and the masses, so long as the form of the struggle was primarily military, remained constant. In essence, they were summed up in the metaphor of the fish and the ocean, which he put forward in the 1930s. Clearly, this formulation does not underestimate the importance of the population, for without the 'ocean' of mass sympathy and support, the 'fish' of the revolutionary army would die helplessly. The Communists must therefore cultivate carefully the sources of popular support, so that the ocean which sustains them does not dry up. But, at the same time, Mao's metaphor makes perfectly clear that the military struggle will be waged by the Red Army on behalf of the masses, and not by the masses themselves.

A detailed analysis of every aspect of Mao Tse-tung's thought from the 1920s to the 1940s would involve extensive discussion of the changing circumstances. What follows is a succinct summary of the main traits of Mao's ideas regarding the aims and tactics of the revolution, by broad periods.

As early as 1928, on the Ching-kang-shan, Mao discovered the importance not only (as already noted) of regularly constituted guerrilla units, but of base areas, in which the Red Army could rest and recuperate, and where it could develop the contacts with the population without which its campaigns would become mere military adventures. Mao did not, however, at that stage, have a clear idea of the relation between the actions in which he was engaging in a remote mountainous area, and the nationwide 'revolutionary high tide' which not only Li Li-san, but Mao himself, was confidently expecting. In his report of 25 November 1928 on the struggles on the Ching-kang-shan, Mao declared that the activities of his forces did not amount to an insurrection, but merely to 'contending for the country' (*ta chiang-shan*), and would remain so as long as there was no revolutionary high tide in the country as a whole. But very rapidly the idea began to germinate in his mind that the rapid expansion of the territory held by the Red Army could significantly contribute to the rising of the tide. Thus, replying on 5 April 1929 to a letter from the Central Committee advising him and Chu Te to scale down their efforts to small-scale guerrilla activities aimed at arousing the masses, Mao replied that the assessment of the situation on which this advice was founded was excessively pessimistic. It was perfectly feasible, taking advantage of the conflict between Chiang Kai-shek and the Kwangsi clique, to conquer all of Kiangsi, as well as western Fukien and western Chekiang, within one year. He also defended the orthodox character of his struggle in the countryside by asserting that it took place under the leadership of the workers, adding that bases for proletarian struggle could likewise be created in Shanghai and other cities.[76]

For its part, the Comintern, though it frequently could not make up its mind as to how fast the high tide was approaching, and consequently whether it should tell the Chinese Communists to advance or consolidate their positions, had a perfectly clear and coherent theoretical position on these matters. In essence, Moscow's view was that the activities of the Red Army and the establishment of base areas in the countryside were important, but could lead to the victory of the revolution only if these activities were carried out side by side with effective work in the cities, to make the urban proletariat once more a force to be reckoned with. Thus, in February 1928, the Executive Committee of the International declared in a Resolution:

In leading spontaneous [*sic*] demonstrations by peasant partisans in the different provinces, the party must bear in mind that these demonstrations can become a starting point for a victorious national uprising only on condition that they are linked with the new upsurge of the tide of revolution in the proletarian centres. Here too, the party must see its main task as the organization of general and coordinated demonstrations in the country and in the *towns, in a number of neighbouring provinces*, and of other uprisings on a *wide* scale.[77]

A Comintern letter of December 1929 gave a decisive impetus to Li Li-san's plans for immediate revolutionary action, by telling the Chinese Communist Party that a new upsurge was beginning, and steps must therefore be taken to set up a peasants' and workers' dictatorship as soon as the tide had risen high enough. The Comintern further explained: 'One distinctive characteristic of the national crisis and the revolutionary upsurge in China is the peasant war.' But although the movement in the

---

[76] For the relevant passage from the report of November 1928, see *MTTC* 2.59. Mao's letter of 5 April 1929 is now available in *MTTC*, *pu-chüan*, 3.37–45; see also *PTMT* 259–60.
[77] Translated in Carrère d'Encausse and Schram, 243. (Italics in Russian original.)

countryside (in which the Comintern lumped together the soviets under Mao's leadership and the activities of traditionalistic organizations such as the 'Red Spears') was 'in the process of becoming one of the courses along which the mighty upsurge of the all-Chinese revolution will continue to develop', the 'truest and most substantial indication of the swelling upsurge' was 'the animation of the workers' movement, which has emerged from its depressed state following the heavy defeat of 1927'.[78]

In other words, guerrilla warfare in the countryside was a legitimate and valuable part of the revolutionary effort, under Chinese conditions, but the more conventional and less exotic activities of the workers in the cities were not only more fundamental, but in the last instance would be more decisive. For his part, Li Li-san was initially far more sceptical than the Comintern regarding the significance of anything which took place in the countryside. In early 1930, however, as he began to lay his plans for a great offensive the following summer, it struck him that the Red Army could provide an extremely useful auxiliary force to distract the attention of the Kuomintang from the workers' movement, and ultimately to permit victory through a two-pronged attack from the cities and from the countryside.

On the issue of the relative weight of the cities and the countryside in the Chinese revolution, Mao Tse-tung and Li Li-san stood at opposite extremes, with Moscow occupying a centrist position. On the two other points, of the time-scale of the revolution and of the central role of China in the world revolution, Mao and Li stood in many respects close to one another, and in opposition to Moscow.

The divergences between Li Li-san and Moscow about the immanence of the revolutionary high tide are somewhat obscured by the fact that communications between China and the Soviet Union were poor, so that letters often took several months to reach their destination. As a result, the two protagonists were often responding to positions which had long since been abandoned. To take only one example, the Comintern letter of June 1930 (commonly dated 23 July in Chinese sources because that is when it was received in Shanghai) was drafted in Moscow in May in response to what was known there of decisions adopted by the Chinese Communist Party in February.[79] Even if the sequence of argument and

---

[78] *Ibid.* 243–4.

[79] These matters have been clarified by recent Soviet publications, which, though strongly biased in their interpretations, are probably accurate regarding many such factual details, drawn from the Comintern archives. Perhaps the most conveniently available of these is A. M. Grigoriev, 'The Comintern and the revolutionary movement in China under the slogan of the soviets (1927–1931)', in Ulyanovsky, ed., 345–88. The correct date of the June 1930 directive was given in Soviet publications of the 1930s, and there is no excuse whatsoever for continuing to refer to it as the '23 July directive'.

counter-argument is thus obscured, however, this does not prevent us from grasping the broad differences in perspective between Stalin and Li Li-san, though it does complicate the historian's task of assigning responsibility for specific decisions, and in particular for costly blunders, during the first half of 1930.

Thus in June 1930, the Comintern, while noting that there was still not an objective revolutionary situation in the whole country, because the 'waves of the workers' movement and the peasants' movement' had still not merged into one, predicted that the revolutionary situation would shortly encompass 'if not the whole of Chinese territory, then at least the territory of a number of key provinces'.[80] None the less, though the Comintern expected the decisive battles in China to take place in the near future, they did not agree with Li Li-san that the time for an offensive had already come. Moscow therefore explicitly refused to sanction Li's decision to order an attack on Wuhan, Changsha, etc. and for co-ordinated uprisings in those cities, arguing that both the Red Army and the workers' movement should first be further strengthened.[81]

For his part, Mao Tse-tung was initially reluctant to throw his forces against such Kuomintang strongpoints, thus risking both the future of the revolution and the foundations of his own power. To this extent he was in agreement with Moscow. But by early 1930, he had in fact become extremely sanguine regarding the prospects for rapid victory. In a letter of January 1930 to Lin Piao, he criticized Lin for his undue pessimism about the coming of the high tide, and declared that though the time limit of one year he himself had set in April 1929 for the conquest of all of Kiangsi had been 'mechanical', such an achievement was not far off.[82]

Mao Tse-tung's attitude toward the Li Li-san line in 1930 has recently been the subject of a wide-ranging debate among Chinese scholars, enjoying access to the relevant sources. Although some of these authors still adhere to the view laid down in the resolution of 1945 on party history according to which Mao never agreed with Li's plan to attack the cities, and only implemented it because discipline required obedience to orders, others argue that Mao Tse-tung was won over to this strategy by the spring of 1930, and some even go so far as to suggest that from early 1930 he followed it spontaneously and enthusiastically. In any case, there is clear evidence that as late as October 1930 Mao Tse-tung continued to profess a radical line. A resolution adopted in Chi-an on 7 October, when Mao's forces were holding the town, noted the existence of 'a revolutionary situation in the whole world, in the whole country, in all

---

[80] Carrère d'Encausse and Schram, 244.   [81] Grigoriev, 369–73.
[82] MTTC 2.139.

provinces', and concluded: 'In the course of this revolutionary "high tide"...soviet power must undoubtedly burst upon the scene in the whole country and in the whole world.' And a letter by Mao dated 19 October called for the rejection of pessimism, and for an immediate attack on Nanchang and Chiu-chiang to annihilate the enemy, in the context of the existing 'high tide'.[83]

If there is still room for some disagreement as to the extent of Mao's chiliastic expectation of an immediate and all-encompassing revolutionary tide in the autumn of 1930, since some of the above statements might be interpreted as telling the Central Committee what he thought it wanted to hear, there can be no argument at all about Mao's conviction that the Chinese revolution was a central and decisive factor in the world revolution. And in this respect, he was altogether in agreement with Li Li-san, and aligned with Li against Moscow.[84]

On one point in particular Mao's agreement with Li was complete: they both held that foreigners did not, and could not, understand the Chinese revolution. At the 'trial' to which he was summoned in Moscow in the winter of 1930–1, Li Li-san was quoted by a Comintern inquisitor as saying: 'The Chinese revolution has so many peculiarities that the International has great difficulty in understanding it, and hardly understands it at all, and hence cannot in reality lead the Chinese Communist Party.' In consequence, he was denounced by Manuilsky as an 'extreme localist'. For his part, Mao declared, three decades afterwards:

Speaking generally, it is we Chinese who have achieved understanding of the objective world of China, not the comrades concerned with Chinese questions in the Communist International. These comrades of the Communist International simply did not understand...Chinese society, the Chinese nation, or the Chinese revolution. For a long time even we did not have a clear understanding of the objective world of China, still less the foreign comrades![85]

On another and crucial aspect of this matter, however, Mao Tse-tung did

---

[83] For articles illustrating a range of views on this issue, see the contributions to the authoritative inner-party journal *Tang-shih yen-chiu*, hereafter *TSYC* (Research on party history) by Lin Yun-hui, 'Lueh lun Mao Tse-tung t'ung-chih tui Li-san lu-hsien ti jen-shih ho ti-chih' (A brief account of Comrade Mao Tse-tung's understanding of and resistance to the Li-san line), *TSYC* 4 (1980) 51–9; T'ien Yuan, 'Tsai lun Mao Tse-tung t'ung-chih tui Li-san lu-hsien ti jen-shih ho ti-chih' (More on Comrade Mao Tse-tung's understanding of and resistance to the Li-san line), *TSYC* 1 (1981) 65–71; and Ling Yü, 'Mao Tse-tung t'ung-chih ho Li-san lu-hsien ti kuan-hsi t'ao-lun tsung-shu' (A summary of the discussion regarding Comrade Mao Tse-tung's relationship to the Li-san line), *TSYC* 3 (1982) 78–80. The resolution of 7 October 1930 is quoted in an article by Ch'ü Ch'iu-pai in *Shih-hua* (True words) (Shanghai) 2 (9 December 1930), 3–4. For Mao's letter of 19 October, see 'Kei Hsiang tung t'e-wei hsin' (Letter to the East Hunan Special Committee), *MTTC, pu-chüan*, 3.157–8.

[84] For a brief summary of some of Li's statements about China's role in the world revolution, see S. Schram, *Mao Tse-tung*, 148–9.

[85] Talk of 30 January 1962, in S. Schram, *Mao Tse-tung unrehearsed*, 172. (See also the official version, translated in *Peking Review* 27 (1978) 14.)

not take the same line as Li Li-san. Li set out quite explicitly to provoke Japanese and other imperialist intervention in North-east China, and thereby to unleash a 'world revolutionary war' into which the Soviet Union would be drawn whether she liked it or not.[86] With such a strategic vision Mao could not possibly agree, for it implied that the fate of the Chinese revolution would ultimately be decided outside China, and not by the Chinese themselves. He was, of course, acutely conscious of the weight of the imperialist presence in China, and of the importance of the international factor in the Chinese revolution. It was, however, a corollary of the shift in his sociological perspective, between 1923 and 1926, that since the main foundations of the old reactionary order were to be found in landlord domination in the countryside, and not in the influence of the imperialists and their urban allies, victory in the Chinese revolution could only be achieved by mobilizing the workers, peasants and other exploited classes throughout the length and breadth of the land to destroy this 'feudal power' of the landlords and their political agents.

Whatever Mao's position in the summer of 1930, the retreat from Changsha in September 1930 marked a crucial turning point in his thinking toward a long-term strategy of encircling the cities from the countryside. In such a context, the military tactics he had been developing since he had ascended the Ching-kang-shan in 1927, and joined forces there with Chu Te in 1928, became an explicit and integral part of Mao's political thought.

According to Mao's own statement, it was in 1931, by the time Chiang Kai-shek's third 'encirclement and annihilation' campaign had been defeated, that 'a complete set of operational principles for the Red Army' took shape.[87] The earliest known text in which these principles were expounded is a short book entitled *Guerrilla war*, dated 1934. This was not in fact by Mao, though his name and picture appeared on it, but by Chu Te, P'eng Te-huai and others.[88] It may well have been the first systematic formulation of the strategic ideas Mao was to put forward in debates at the Tsun-yi Conference, which marked a decisive stage both in the emergence of a new military line, and in opening the road to his rise to supreme power in the party eight years later.[89] In December 1936, Mao delivered a series of lectures entitled *Problems of strategy in China's revolutionary war*, reviewing in

---

[86] Li's 'plot' to involve the Soviet Union in a war for the sake of the Chinese revolution naturally excites great indignation on the part of the Soviet authors; see, for example, Grigoriev, 365–7.

[87] Mao, *SW* 1.213.

[88] For a summary of a portion of this work, see Ch'en Po-chün, 'Lun k'ang-Jih yu-chi chan-cheng ti chi-pen chan-shu: hsi-chi' (On the basic tactic of the anti-Japanese guerrilla war: the surprise attack), *Chieh-fang*, 28 (11 Jan. 1938) 14–19. The above information regarding authorship is from Pao Shih-hsiu of the PLA Academy of Military Science.

[89] On the Tsun-yi Conference see Benjamin Yang, 'The Zunyi Conference as one step in Mao's rise to power', *CQ* 106 (June 1986) 235–71, and Jerome Ch'en's reply in *CQ* 111 (September 1987).

detail the lessons of the five encirclement campaigns, and restating his case against his critics. Finally, in 1938, he wrote two works regarding guerrilla tactics in the special circumstances of the Anti-Japanese War: *Questions of strategy in the Anti-Japanese guerrilla war*, and *On protracted war*. A third book, *Basic tactics*, was ascribed to him in some editions.[90]

Military tactics is a specialized domain, in which I have little competence. Here I view the matter from the interface between war and politics. Mao himself summed up the whole question when he wrote: 'Our strategy is "pit one against ten", and our tactics are "pit ten against one"; these contrary and yet complementary propositions constitute one of our principles for gaining mastery over the enemy.'[91]

The meaning of this aphorism is, of course, as Mao explained at length in the remainder of the passage, that while the Red Army at that time was greatly inferior in numbers and equipment to the Kuomintang and other white forces in the country as a whole, and even in each separate theatre of operations, it should fight only when it enjoyed overwhelming superiority on the battlefield. Such a tactical advantage should be obtained by concentrating the greater part of one's own forces against isolated white units, and thus 'destroying the enemy one by one'. And this, in turn, while it depended partly on skill in using troops, was very largely the result of superior intelligence, obtained by the Red Army thanks to its intimate links with the population.

The methods of the Communists for mobilizing the peasantry and thereby obtaining not only information regarding the adversary's movements but other advantages, such as voluntary service by the masses as porters or auxiliary troops, were different from anything envisaged by China's ancient military strategist Sun Tzu, yet Mao's strictly tactical principles were strikingly similar to those of Sun Tzu, who wrote:

By discovering the enemy's dispositions and remaining invisible ourselves, we can keep our forces concentrated while...the enemy must be split up into fractions. Hence there will be a whole pitted against separate parts of the whole, which means that we shall be many in collected mass to the enemy's separate few [literally, 'ten against one']....And if we are thus able to attack an inferior force with a superior one, our opponents will be in dire straits.[92]

---

[90] Some of the editions of this book have Mao's name on the title page, others do not, and his authorship is doubtful. Although it appears in a bibliography of Mao's works published by the PLA (Chung-kuo jen-min chieh-fang chün cheng-chih hsueh-yuan hsun-lien pu t'u-shu tzu-liao kuan, *Mao Tse-tung chu-tso, yen-lun, wen-tien mu-lu* (Peking), Feb. 1961, 28), the weight of the evidence is against attributing it to Mao. In the introduction to my English translation (*Basic tactics*), I have sketched an interpretation of the stages in the elaboration of Mao's military tactics. [91] Mao, *SW* 1.237.

[92] Sun Tzu, *The art of war*, Giles' trans., Ch. VI, par. 13.

Mao himself, questioned in his later years about what he had learned from the Chinese classics, was generally whimsical and frequently contradictory in his replies. In one of his most balanced statements, he said in 1968 that he had read the *Romance of the three kingdoms* before he began to fight in 1927, and that he had taken a look at Sun Tzu before writing his own works on military tactics in 1936–8.[93] There is no doubt, in any case, that he very frequently quoted, in these writings, both from Sun Tzu and from historical works, as well as from novels such as the *Romance of the three kingdoms* and *Water margin*.

How did Mao Tse-tung contrive to justify in theoretical terms the view that a Communist Party of uncertain composition, operating primarily through the instrumentality of the army, in a highly ambiguous social context, could yet constitute the vanguard of the proletariat? A crucial issue here is the role of the subjective factors in defining man's class nature, and the possibility of modifying a person's objective essence by changing his thinking. We have seen that Mao's emphasis on the importance of subjective attitudes goes back to 1917. One of the most striking formulations of the period under consideration here is to be found in his report of 28 November 1928 on the struggle on the Ching-kang-shan. Discussing the problem raised by the fact that the greater part of his small Red Army was made up not of workers, or even of proper peasants, but of rural vagabonds or *éléments déclassés*, Mao said:

The contingent of *éléments déclassés* should be replaced by peasants and workers, but these are not available now. On the one hand, when fighting is going on every day, the *éléments déclassés* are after all especially good fighters. Moreover, casualties are mounting high. Consequently, not only can we not diminish the *éléments déclassés* now in our ranks, but it is even difficult to find more for reinforcements. In these circumstances, the only method is to intensify political training, so as to effect a qualitative change in these elements.[94]

In his letter of January 1930 to Lin Piao, Mao criticized Lin for 'overestimating the importance of objective forces and underestimating the importance of subjective forces'.[95] By 'objective forces' Mao meant in particular the white armies, which were outside the Communists' direct control, whereas 'subjective forces' referred to the Red Army, which they perceived from inside, and whose motivation and strategy they therefore understood. But it is plain that he was also talking about objective factors in the broader sense of objective historical circumstances, and subjective factors in the sense of the human capacity to influence those circumstances by 'conscious action'.

[93] Dialogue with Red Guards, 28 July 1968, in *Miscellany of Mao Tse-tung thought*, 476 (JPRS no. 61269). Chinese in *Mao Tse-tung ssu-hsiang wan-sui* (1969), 694.
[94] *MTTC* 2.36–7; *PTMT* 268–9.   [95] *MTTC* 2.130.

This element in Mao's thinking had been, as I suggested earlier, reinforced by the context of military struggle in which he developed his ideas and undertook to make revolution from 1927 onwards. Mao saw war as the highest manifestation of 'conscious action' and the supreme test of the human spirit. He put the point in a passage which he liked so much that he repeated it in almost identical words in 1936 and in 1938:

Conscious activity is a distinctive characteristic of man, especially of man at war. This characteristic is manifested in all of man's acts, but nowhere more strongly than in war. Victory or defeat in a war is decided on the one hand by the military, political, economic, and geographical conditions, by the character of the war, and by international support on both sides. But it is not decided by these alone; these alone constitute only the possibility of victory or defeat; they do not in themselves decide the issue. To decide the issue, subjective efforts must be added, efforts in directing and waging the war, i.e. conscious activity in war.

People who direct a war cannot strive for victories beyond the limit allowed by the objective conditions, but within that limit they can and must strive actively for victory. The stage of action for these directors of war must be built upon objective conditions, but on this stage, they can direct the performance of many living dramas, full of sound and colour, of power and grandeur...[96]

This passage eloquently expresses what I have called Mao Tse-tung's 'military romanticism', born out of the experience of many years of bitter struggle for survival. It would, however, be a gross over-simplification to interpret Mao's faith in the limitless capacities of man, and especially of the Chinese people, solely in terms of his romantic temperament, or of his life of combat. His emphasis on subjective factors corresponded also, as I have already suggested, to the necessities of revolution in a transitional society made up of many disparate elements.

It is this aspect of Chinese reality which provides the link between the military and political dimensions of Mao's thought and experience. Just as the outcome of a battle can rarely be predicted with certainty, but depends in part, as Mao stressed in the passage just quoted, on subjective factors such as the courage of the soldiers and the tactical skill of the commanders, so the terms of the political combat appeared less clearly defined in China than in Western Europe or even in the former Russian empire. Although the Chinese Communist Party and the Kuomintang might be regarded loosely as the representatives respectively of the workers and of the capitalists, the socio-economic weight of the peasants in the former, and of the landlords in the latter, was in fact greater. Moreover, the picture was significantly modified by the impact of the foreign presence. Marx and Engels, with reference to the Polish question, and Lenin, with reference to the colonies in the twentieth century, had

[96] *MTTC* 6.98–9; *PTMT* 284–5.

already established the principle that the behaviour of classes within a given society might be modified by a reaction of solidarity against the foreign oppressor. Mao Tse-tung, for his part, did not merely accept this as a theoretical possibility; he was persuaded, from the early 1930s onward, that an alliance for the pursuit of national goals could be effectively realized, and that its establishment depended in large part on the success of the Communists in modifying the subjective attitudes of other strata of Chinese society, apart from the workers and their immediate allies the peasantry.

This concern with national unity as the condition of national salvation, though it marked Mao's thought and policies to a greater or lesser degree from beginning to end, by no means signified that he had become a mere nationalist. Even in the late 1930s, as he concluded and implemented a new alliance with Chiang Kai-shek, Mao made crystal clear that the Chinese Communist Party had no intention of abandoning its maximum programme. And in the late 1920s and early 1930s, social revolution was the main focus of his thought and action. Nor did he approach it solely in terms of moral values and psychological transformation. Though he believed that objective social realities could be modified by changes in consciousness, he also saw participation in revolutionary action as one of the most effective means for changing men's thinking. Indeed, an acute awareness of the interaction between the subjective and the objective, and the deliberate manipulation of this dialectic was one of the hallmarks of Mao Tse-tung's thought, and one of the secrets of his political success.

The concept of revolutionary struggle as an instrument for promoting cultural revolution was formulated by Mao as early as 1927, in his Hunan peasant report, where he wrote: 'The abolition of the clan system, of superstitions, and of one-sided notions of chastity will follow as a natural consequence of victory in the political and economic struggles. ... The idols should be removed by the peasants themselves...'[97]

Throughout the ensuing two decades, the countryside remained the main theatre of Mao's experiments both in social and in cultural revolution. The heart of his activity in this domain was, of course, land reform. Details of the changing line toward various social categories, especially the rich peasants, cannot be presented here. (For a brief summary, see *The Cambridge History of China*, 13.191–3.)

An episode which offers particularly striking illustration of Mao's faith in the technique of changing attitudes through revolutionary struggle was the 'land verification movement' of 1933–4. Mao may not have launched this, but he did place his stamp on it in 1933. The ostensible economic goal of this

97 *MTTC* 1.237–8; *PTMT* 259.

campaign, which was to determine whether or not land reform had been properly carried out, in fact merely provided the framework within which to pursue essentially political aims. Given the inherited prestige of the landlords and rich peasants, and the fact that they had the advantage of literacy and facility in speech, Mao was convinced that whatever changes were made in the formal property structure, these formerly privileged elements would succeed in one way or another in worming their way back into positions of authority in the peasant associations. The only way to prevent such a disguised return to the old order of things was constantly to stir up the peasantry at the grass roots and encourage poor peasants to engage in struggle against their former exploiters, in order to develop their self-confidence and allow the conviction to take root that henceforth they were the masters of society.

This movement offers many parallels with the way land reform was carried out subsequently, in 1946–8 and after 1950. The mass meetings, at which the peasants were encouraged to 'speak their bitterness' against the landlords for their previous oppression, followed in some cases by the execution of the worst offenders, were designed not only to break the spirit of the gentry, but above all to allow the peasants to rid themselves of their inferiority complex and stand up as men at last. Thus Mao undertook to carry out a cultural revolution in the sense of a change in attitudes toward authority, and used revolutionary struggle as an instrument toward this end. But while this concern was prominent in his line from beginning to end, the political context within which he applied these techniques changed significantly over the years.

A crucial aspect of the tactical situation during the period of the Kiangsi Soviet Republic was the contradiction between military and political imperatives. In order to obtain maximum support from the population, Mao Tse-tung and Chu Te had practised in earlier years the principle of 'luring the enemy deep' into the heart of the base area, where land reform had been carried out and the sympathy for the Red Army was therefore warmest. These tactics meant, however, that the faithful supporters of the Communist forces were frequently exposed to the perils and losses of war, and this undermined the credibility of the Chinese Soviet Republic to constitute a veritable state within a state, since it could not protect its own citizens. In a sense, the 'forward and offensive strategy' constituted a response to this dilemma – a response which consisted in putting the political imperative of defending the prestige and integrity of the soviet republic ahead of realistic evaluation of the military possibilities. It ended in disaster, but that does not necessarily mean that Mao's earlier tactics would have worked in 1934. In any case, it was only the rapidly accelerating Japanese advance into China, and the consequent threat to China's very survival as an independent nation, which effectively allowed the Communists to break out of the dilemma in which they found themselves. Moreover, it was only in the new circumstances which took shape in 1935–7 that Mao, who had had little of any theoretical interest to say for several years, once more began to speak out in confident tones. No doubt the fact that he was again in a strong position in the party, whereas in 1933–4 he had been reduced to little more than a figurehead, had something to do with his new eloquence. But the phenomenon also resulted, unquestionably, from the fact that a war for national liberation was something about which he had a great deal to say. Even in the early 1930s, Mao's statements about the relation between the internal and external enemies of the revolution were suggestive of what was to come.

The evolution which brought Communists and Kuomintang, and the old enemies Mao Tse-tung and Chiang Kai-shek, once more into an alliance was very much against the grain of both parties. What was the theoretical justification which Mao put forward for the second united front?

In September 1931, when the Japanese action in Manchuria first brought to the fore the issue of resistance to foreign aggression, the position of the Chinese Communist Party regarding collaboration with the bourgeoisie was basically similar to that of the Comintern, summed up in the slogan of 'class against class'. Nevertheless, although this was understood to mean in principle the struggle for hegemony between the proletariat and the bourgeoisie, Mao's sociological vision of the concrete struggle remained that which he had entertained in 1926. A letter of 25 September 1931, signed by Mao and others, to 'our brothers the soldiers of the White Army', after calling on them to kill their reactionary superior officers and unite with the workers, peasants, and toiling masses to overthrow the 'fucking Kuomintang government', continued:

confiscate the land of the landlord class and distribute it among the poor peasants; confiscate the food and the houses of the wealthy and distribute them among the poor; let the workers do only eight hours of work a day; then, organize yourselves to run your own affairs. In this way, you will have created a government of workers, peasants, and soldiers, that is, a soviet government.[98]

Clearly, for Mao the countryside was where the Chinese revolution principally was at. In this text, the 'Kuomintang militarists' were treated as the 'running dogs of imperialism', as well as the creatures of the landlord class, just as in Mao's writings of the 1920s, but the domestic reactionary role of the Kuomintang in 'exploiting and butchering the

98 *MTTC* 3.14; *PTMT* 219.

masses' was still given the greatest prominence. To the extent that Mao's attack focused on the problem of resistance to Japanese aggression, his position was the mirror image of Chiang Kai-shek's 'unify before resisting'. Since 'only the Red Army' could 'overthrow imperialism and really defend the people', it was necessary first to deal with the domestic enemy, in order to make possible effective action against the foreign invader.

In April 1932, in the wake of the Japanese aggression against Shanghai in January of that year, the Chinese Soviet government declared war on Japan, thus bringing questions of foreign affairs closer to the centre of its political strategy. A change in Mao's outlook regarding collaboration with other political forces was signalled by a declaration of 17 January 1933, which offered, on certain conditions (cessation of attacks on the soviet regions, granting of democratic rights, and arming of the masses against Japan), to conclude an agreement with 'any armed force', that is, with any dissident commander prepared to deal with the Communists.[99] Although this position still remained within the framework of the 'united front from below' laid down in the line of the Comintern, that is to say, an alliance with the supporters of other political movements rather than with their leaders, the willingness to deal with high-ranking officers of the Kuomintang (though not with Chiang Kai-shek himself) marked a significant step toward the 'united front from above' which was to be set up in 1937.

In the proclamation on the northward march of the Red Army to fight Japan, which he signed on 15 July 1934 together with Chu Te, Mao called once again for a 'national revolutionary war', and an alliance with those willing to wage such a war, while striving to overthrow the 'band of traitors of the Kuomintang'.[100] Nevertheless, while Mao Tse-tung gave high place to nationalism as an idea and a political force, he was markedly more reticent than the Soviet leaders about going all the way to a second united front, and the declaration of 1 August 1935 calling for such a front was in fact issued from Moscow on behalf of the Chinese Communist Party by Wang Ming, in the context of the Seventh Comintern Congress.

For their part, Mao and his comrades found it far more distasteful than did Stalin to embrace once again Chiang Kai-shek, whom they knew as the butcher of their friends and perceived as a traitor to the revolution. By the end of 1935, as his forces regrouped in December in Wayaobao, Mao was prepared to cooperate not only with the 'national bourgeoisie' but with those sectors of the capitalist class who were linked to European

[99] *Su-wei-ai Chung-kuo*, 91–4; MTTC 3.183–5.   [100] MTTC 4.363–7; PTMT 220–2.

and American imperialism, and were therefore inclined to oppose 'Japanese imperialism and its running dogs'. But Chiang Kai-shek, as the 'chieftain' of the 'camp of traitors to the nation', and the representative of the evil gentry, warlords and compradors, was specifically excluded from the proposed united front.[101]

In fact, indirect contacts with this 'traitor' had already been established during 1935. In April 1936, Chang Hsueh-liang met with Chou En-lai, and urged the Communists to stop fighting Chiang and concentrate on the Japanese, promising to use his influence with Chiang to persuade him to accept such a truce. On 5 May 1936, a telegram was accordingly addressed directly to the Military Affairs Council in Nanking, and this was subsequently characterized by Mao as marking the 'abandonment of the anti-Chiang Kai-shek slogan'.[102] Henceforth, Mao was in regular contact with Chang Hsueh-liang, Yang Hu-ch'eng and other political and military leaders about the possibility of cooperation against Japan,[103] writing in particular to Chang on 5 October 1936 expressing his desire for an 'agreement between the Kuomintang and the Communist Party to resist Japan and save the country'. On 1 December 1936, Mao signed, together with eighteen other senior Communist political and military leaders, a letter to Chiang himself, expressing the hope that he would change his ways, so posterity would remember him not as the man responsible for China's ruin, but as 'the hero who saved the country and the people'.[104]

All of these gestures, which were based on political realism, did not mean that the feelings of the Communists toward Chiang had changed fundamentally. When he was taken prisoner by Chang Hsueh-liang and Yang Hu-ch'eng in Sian on 12 December, there was an instinctive reaction on the part of Communist cadres, high and low, that it would be very agreeable to put him on trial for his crimes against the revolution, but there is no evidence that such a policy was seriously considered by Mao and others at the top level. On the contrary, Mao Tse-tung wrote to Yen Hsi-shan on 22 December 1936 assuring him that 'we do not in the least wish to take revenge on Nanking'.[105] Mao's frequently reported rage on receipt of a peremptory telegram from Moscow ordering him not to kill Chiang was therefore provoked not by frustration at being deprived

---

[101] Report of 27 December 1935, Mao, *SW* 1.153–78.

[102] Mao, *SW* 1.264, 279–80. On the secret negotiations between the CCP and the KMT in 1935–6, and Mao's continuing reluctance to compromise with Chiang, see the article by John Garver, 'The origins of the Second United Front: the Comintern and the Chinese Communist Party', *CQ* 113 (March 1988).

[103] See the numerous letters from the second half of 1936 in *Selected letters*, 30–97.

[104] *Ibid.* 78–9, 87–90.   [105] *Ibid.* 95–7.

of his victim, but by Stalin's doubts about his loyalty, or his common sense.[106]

In any case, once embarked on a policy of cooperation with the Kuomintang, the Chinese Communists, and Mao in particular, showed themselves inclined to throw themselves into it with a will. The reason was, manifestly, that for them the salvation of the Chinese nation was not merely, as for Lenin, the basis for tactical manoeuvres; it was a value in itself.

Mao could not, of course, call for a change of such importance without justifying it, both for himself and for his followers, in terms of the stage currently reached by the Chinese revolution, and the tasks which could accordingly be pursued at that time. He began to sketch out his ideas on this theme in his speech of 27 December 1935 just mentioned; they were fully elaborated and given their definitive formulation only in 1939–40. But before continuing this discussion of Mao's political thought, which reached a notably higher level of maturity and complexity during the Yenan period, it is necessary to give some account of the emergence, in 1937, of philosophical ideas which were to occupy an increasingly central place in his thinking as a whole.

NATIONAL CONTRADICTIONS AND SOCIAL CONTRADICTIONS 1937–1940

While Mao Tse-tung had occasionally touched on philosophical questions in his writings of the 1920s and 1930s, it was in the winter of 1936–7 that he first undertook the serious study of Marxist philosophy. Edgar Snow has recorded how Mao interrupted the interviews, which were to form the basis for his autobiography, in order to devour a pile of Soviet works on philosophy in Chinese translation which had just reached the Communist capital of Pao-an. Having read these, Mao proceeded almost immediately to deliver a series of lectures on dialectical materialism, of which the works now known as 'On practice' and 'On contradiction' were originally the concluding sections.[107]

Only 'On practice' and 'On contradiction' have, of course, been

---

[106] For details regarding the sequence of events, and further references, see *The Cambridge History of China* (hereafter *CHOC*), 13, ch. 12 by Lyman Van Slyke. The above interpretation is based on interviews with Hu Hua and Li Hsin, respectively on 10 and 23 September 1982 in Peking.

[107] 'Pien-cheng-fa wei-wu-lun (chiang-shou t'i-kang)' (Dialectical materialism – lecture notes) in *K'ang-chan ta-hsueh*, 6 to 8 (April to June 1938). This portion of the text includes chapter 1, and the first six sections of chapter 2. It is not known whether or not the remainder of the work was serialized in *K'ang-chan ta-hsueh*. Sections 7 to 10 of chapter 2 were included in a version circulated during the Cultural Revolution (*Mao Chu-hsi wen-hsuan*), and the whole of the first two chapters, less section 11 of chapter 2 (corresponding to 'On practice'), was reproduced in *MTTC* 6.265–305. Subsequently, two editions of the work containing the original version of

officially published in China since 1949, respectively in 1950 and 1952. The evidence that Mao did in fact deliver a course of lectures on dialectical materialism in 1937 is, however, conclusive and irrefutable.[108] It is therefore of some moment that, when asked about the matter by Edgar Snow in 1965, Mao denied authorship of *Dialectical materialism*.[109] It is true that he generally preferred people to read his works only in editions revised and approved by himself, but he did not always go to the trouble of explicitly repudiating items no longer thought suitable.

The reasons for Mao's sensitivity in this case are not far to seek. A reputation as a Marxist theoretician and philosopher has been regarded, since Lenin's day, as one of the indispensable qualifications for leadership within the Communist movement. It was no doubt with the aim of establishing his credentials in this respect (as Stalin had sought to do before him) that Mao had originally delivered these lectures. His rivals in the party, with whom he was to have an ongoing trial of strength during the next five or six years, were all schooled in Moscow, and he thus felt himself vulnerable to the charge that he was nothing but a leader of peasant guerrillas, with no grasp of Marxist theory and no capacity for dealing with abstract categories. It soon became apparent, however, that Mao's lectures on dialectical materialism did not effectively serve their purpose. In very large part, they amounted (especially in the early sections) to unashamed plagiarism of his Soviet sources, and where Mao had expressed himself in his own words, the result was often very crude.[110]

'On practice' have come to light, and one of these also contains chapter 3, corresponding to 'On contradiction'. The complete text appears in *MTTC, pu-chüan*, 5.187–280. For a translation of selected passages and a detailed analysis both of the form and of the content of the original version of 'On contradiction', see Nick Knight, 'Mao Zedong's *On contradiction* and *On practice*: pre-liberation texts', *CQ* 84 (December 1980), 641–68. Mr Knight has also published a complete translation: *Mao Zedong's 'On contradiction'. An annotated translation of the pre-liberation text.*

[108] It suffices to mention three points, any of which would be sufficient in itself. The first is that, as already indicated, a considerable portion of the text was published at the time in *K'ang-chan ta-hsueh*. The second is the reference to this work by Chang Ju-hsin, then (with Ch'en Po-ta) one of those most actively engaged in building up Mao as a theoretician, in an article published in *Chieh-fang jih-pao* (18 and 19 February 1942), where he characterized it as the most important source on Mao's methodology and dialectics. Finally, almost the whole text of the work, broken up into fragments by theme, is reproduced in an authorized compilation on Mao's philosophical thought: *Mao Tse-tung che-hsueh ssu-hsiang (chai-lu)*, 11–14, 19–21, 49–51, 53–5, 64–9, 97–9 and *passim*.

[109] As originally published in *The New Republic*, this disclaimer was strong, but Mao carefully edged away from a flat statement that he had never given any such lectures; when the interview was re-published as an appendix to *The long revolution*, it was 'improved' to make of it a categorical denial of authorship. A comment by Snow (*The long revolution*, 194–5) suggests that this may have been done at the request of the Chinese authorities, or of Mao himself.

[110] On Mao's plagiarism, see the note in my article 'Mao Tse-tung and the theory of the permanent revolution, 1958–1969', *CQ* 46 (April–June 1971), 223–4; also K. A. Wittfogel, 'Some remarks

I shall not analyse here Mao's lectures as a whole, but will focus on the two essays that did become an integral part of 'Mao Tse-tung Thought'. While epistemology was often dealt with at some length in writings and translations from Soviet works to which Mao was exposed in 1936–7, and often came (like 'On practice') relatively near the end of one-volume surveys of Marxist philosophy, the prominence given by Mao to the subject of contradictions was without parallel in any of his potential sources. Most of these had a section on the unity and struggle of opposites and related topics, but it was generally short, and in no case was it placed, as in Mao's lectures, at the end, thus making it the culmination and synthesis of the whole course.

Many reasons could no doubt be given for the prominence Mao attached to contradictions. Two of them flow naturally from the interpretation of his thought already sketched in this work. On the one hand, his understanding of dialectics was strongly marked by Taoism and other currents in traditional Chinese thought. On the other, he was, as I have stressed throughout, acutely aware of the complex and ambiguous character of Chinese society (in other words, of the contradictions within it), and sought to incorporate these insights into his revolutionary tactics. The first of these characteristics might be seen by some as a flaw in his understanding of dialectics; the second might well be construed as an advantage.

Some idea of the importance attached by Mao to contradictions can be gained from the fact that the portion of his lecture notes devoted to this topic constitutes nearly half of the whole work, and runs to approximately

on Mao's handling of concepts and problems of dialectics', *Studies in Soviet thought*, 3.4 (Dec. 1963), 251–77. In the context of the view (explicitly stated in 1981, but implicit since 1978 or 1979) that Mao Tse-tung was a man subject to human error, both the fact that Mao did indeed lecture on dialectical materialism in 1937, and his debt to other authors, especially to Ai Ssu-ch'i, have now been officially placed on record in China.

See the materials in *Chung-kuo che-hsueh*, 1.1–44, including Mao's extensive reading notes on Ai's *Che-hsueh yü sheng-huo* (Philosophy and life) dated September 1937, a letter of early 1938 from Mao to Ai about a point in this work, and an article (Kuo Hua-jo, 'Mao chu-hsi k'ang-chan ch'u-ch'i kuang-hui ti che-hsueh huo-tung' (Chairman Mao's brilliant philosophical activity during the early period of the anti-Japanese war)) discussing the variants between the original versions of 'On practice' and 'On contradiction' and those in Mao, *SW*. Other writings by Ai which Mao certainly read included his translation of an article by Mitin from the Great Soviet Encyclopedia, *Hsin che-hsueh ta-kang* (Outline of the new philosophy) (Tu-shu sheng-huo ch'u-pan-she, 1936), from which he cribbed many passages, and *Ta-chung che-hsueh* (Philosophy for the masses), which a reader of *K'ang-chan ta-hsueh* (8, 187) showed an embarrassing tendency to confuse with Mao's lectures. Much fuller information on Mao's study of philosophy during the Yenan period is contained in a 550-page volume of the Chinese and Soviet texts he read, with his marginal annotations, recently published in China. See *Mao Tse-tung che-hsüeh p'i-chu-chi* (Mao Tse-tung's collected annotations on philosophy). Hereafter *Philosophical annotations*. For a summary of the contents, see the review by Shih Chung-ch'üan, *Che-hsüeh yen-chiu* (Philosophical Research), 10 (1987) 3–9, 40.

25,000 characters, as compared to about 22,000 for the *Selected works* version. While there are significant differences between the two texts, the correspondence is sufficiently close to dispose once and for all of the theory, put forward by Arthur Cohen and others, according to which Mao could not possibly have written such a work at all in 1937. Mao Tse-tung did, however, find it no easy task in the early 1950s to put this article into satisfactory shape. On 8 March 1951, he wrote to Ch'en Po-ta and T'ien Chia-ying, indicating that he had revised 'On contradiction' yet again, but that the last section especially still required further work, so this item should not be included in the forthcoming first volume of the Chinese edition of his *Selected works*.[111] Why was this portion of the lectures so much superior to the earlier sections? In essence, the answer lies, I think, in the fact that Mao was dealing not only with notions which appealed to him, but with their concrete application to the circumstances of the Chinese revolution. The first chapter of *Dialectical materialism* was, on the other hand, in large part simply a summary of the history of philosophy in Greece and the West, as perceived by Soviet authors. Here Mao could only copy his sources, and was in no position to add anything of himself.[112]

It is commonly held that Soviet journals (which had praised 'On practice' in 1950) took no notice of 'On contradiction' two years later because they objected to the implied challenge to Stalin's theoretical primacy. There is no doubt whatever that this was indeed a factor, but it is altogether possible that the Soviets also found Mao's understanding of dialectics strange and heretical. On many occasions in the 1950s Mao complained that the *Concise philosophical dictionary* made a speciality of criticizing his view of contradictions, and on one occasion he noted that he was speaking of the fourth

[111] It is true that the earliest text of this work available outside China was published nearly a decade later. (For details see the Bibliography under Mao.) On the other hand, editions of Mao's writings which appeared in 1946–7 do not commonly show extensive rewriting. Moreover, this version has been cited by Soviet scholars who were certainly not bent on enhancing Mao Tse-tung's reputation for theoretical maturity during the Yenan period. If it had been rewritten, as Cohen argues, to take account of Stalin's works of the late 1930s, Soviet specialists would certainly have pointed this out. For Cohen's argument (now invalidated), see A. Cohen, *The communism of Mao Tse-tung*, 14–28. Mao's letter of 8 March 1951 was read out to me by Kung Yü-chih, Deputy Director of the Research Centre on Party Literature, in a conversation of 4 January 1988. Professor Kung has also confirmed in print both Mao's authorship of the lecture notes on dialectical materialism, and the fact that the 1946 Dairen edition was simply a reprint of what had been reproduced in mimeographed form in Yenan in 1937, without editorial changes. See his article '"Shih-chieh lun" san t'i' (Three points regarding 'On practice'), in *Lun Mao Tse-tung che-hsüeh ssu-hsiang* (On Mao Tse-tung's philosophical thought), 66–86, especially 66–72.

[112] This point is underscored by the fact that, following these sources, Mao included in the original version of 'On contradiction' a whole section repudiating formal logic as incompatible with dialectics. (See Knight, trans., 15–17.) According to Kung Yü-chih, he removed this in 1951 because he had changed his views after reading Stalin's *Marxism and questions of linguistics*, and taking note of the ensuing discussion in Soviet philosophical circles.

edition of this work (published in Moscow in 1953) which reflected, he said, Stalin's views. The Soviet complaint was that the transformation of birth into death was 'metaphysical', and that the transformation of war into peace was wrong.[113]

A case can be made regarding the para-traditional character of Mao's dialectics in his old age, when (in 1964) he abandoned two of the three basic axioms of Marxist and Hegelian dialectics, including the negation of the negation.[114] And while his outlook in 1937 was more derivative, and therefore on the whole more orthodox in Marxist terms, it could be argued that he was already leaning in the direction he was to follow a quarter of a century later. Perhaps the clearest pointer is to be found in the statement that 'the law of the unit of opposites' is 'the fundamental law of thought',[115] which seems to place this axiom in a higher category than the other two principles (the negation of the negation, and the transformation of quantity into quality) Mao subsequently rejected.[116]

The original version of Mao's lecture notes contains an allusion to the fact that Lenin regarded the unity of opposites as the 'kernel of dialectics',[117] and in 1957 Mao cited the relevant fragment explicitly: 'In brief, dialectics can be defined as the doctrine of the unity of opposites. This grasps the kernel of dialectics, but it requires explanations and development.'[118] This remark of Lenin's occurs, however, in rough reading notes on Hegel's *Logic*, and the passage summarizing Hegel's ideas to which it refers mentions both the negation of the negation, and the transformation of quantity into quality.[119]

To pursue this problem further would take us too far from the mainly political concerns of this work toward the consideration of strictly philosophical issues. Mao's analysis of Chinese society, and the theoretical considerations he drew from it, lie on the other hand at the centre of our concerns, and can serve as a convenient transition from philosophy to other

---

[113] Mao, *SW* 5.368; Schram, *Mao unrehearsed*, 109 (speech of 20 March 1958).
[114] I have discussed this problem in Part 2 below, pp. 138–41. See also F. Wakeman, *History and will*, 297–9, 310, 323–6, etc.
[115] Mao, *SW* 1.345.
[116] This point was noted by Wang Jo-shui in a conversation of 7 May 1982 in Peking, though Mr Wang did not agree that Mao's emphasis on the unity and struggle of opposites reflected traditional influences. Steve Chin has interpreted Mao's stress on the unity of opposites as a new theoretical development going well beyond Marx and Engels. (Steve S. K. Chin, *The thought of Mao Tse-tung*, 60–4.) The preface to a 1946 edition of the lectures points out that the sections on the other two laws are 'missing'. *MTTC, pu-chüan*, 5.279. Note also Mao's disagreement with Ai Ssu-ch'i's view that mere differences (such as between pen, ink and table) do not necessarily constitute contradictions: *Chung-kuo che-hsueh*, 1.29.
[117] Knight, trans., 39.   [118] Mao, *SW* 5.366.
[119] V. I. Lenin, 'Conspectus of Hegel's *Science of logic*', *Collected works* 38, 222–3.

aspects of Mao's thought. It has often been argued, and up to a point the claim is accepted even by Cohen, that Mao's most notable contribution to the science of dialectics lay in his elaboration of the concepts 'principal contradiction' and 'principal aspect of the principal contradiction'. I should like to suggest, to begin with, that Mao's use of these categories can be linked directly to his subtle understanding of Chinese reality. A Marxist revolutionary in a society of the type observed by Marx himself, which was perceived as increasingly polarized into capitalists and proletarians, should have been in no doubt as to which were the basic contradictions between classes, or between the productive forces and the mode of production. In broad terms, this pattern was expected to remain more or less the same until the conflict was resolved by revolution. In China, on the other hand, where neither the internal situation nor relations with foreign powers were stable or predictable, it was not merely an intriguing intellectual problem, but a pressing tactical necessity, to determine which factor, or contradiction, was crucial or dominant at a given time.

One of the earliest Soviet writings translated in China, a volume published in 1933, devoted a section to the 'leading' (*chu-tao*) aspect of contradictions, but stated that this was in general always *the same*: for example, in the contradictions between base and superstructure, the base was always dominant.[120] This is one of the points in Mao's essay which Cohen finds most significant; he draws attention to the passage which reads:

> Some people think that...in the contradiction between the productive forces and the relations of production, the productive forces are the leading aspect; in the contradiction between theory and practice, practice is the leading aspect; in the contradiction between the economic foundation and its superstructure, the economic foundation is the leading aspect, and that there is no change in their respective positions.... True, the productive forces, practice, and the economic foundation generally manifest themselves as the leading and decisive factors...But there are times (*yu shih*) when such aspects as the relations of production, theory and the superstructure in turn manifest themselves as the leading or decisive factors; this must also be admitted. When the productive forces cannot be developed unless the relations of production are changed, the change in the relations of production plays the leading and decisive role.... When the superstructure – politics, culture, and so on – hinders the development of the economic foundation, political and cultural reforms become the leading and decisive factors...[121]

Cohen makes much of this passage in his argument that Mao did not write 'On contradiction' in 1937; Mao could not, he says, have gone against

---

[120] Hsi-lo-k'e-fu [Shirokov] *et al.*, trans. by Li Ta *et al. Pien-cheng-fa wei-wu-lun chiao-ch'eng* (Course of instruction in dialectical materialism), 295.

[121] *Pien-cheng wei-wu-lun*, 93; *MTTC, pu-chüan*, 5.264. There are some variants in this passage, but with

Marxist 'determinism' in this fashion until Stalin had shown him the way. The facts speak otherwise. It would seem that Mao derived his 'voluntarism' directly from the study of Lenin (to whom the term was, after all, first applied), and also from his own personality, and the experience of the Chinese revolution. Indeed, the original text of 'On contradiction' puts even more emphasis on subjective factors.

The most important variant here is the replacement of the expression 'there are times' by 'in certain circumstances'. The implication of this formulation, inserted in the *Selected works*, would appear to be that such circumstances, or the totality of the necessary preconditions, will be present only for limited periods, at times of crisis or revolution. The looser 'at times' might be taken, on the other hand, to suggest that this reversal of roles between basis and superstructure might last for a significant period. This conclusion is reinforced by the sentence which follows immediately the passage just quoted (in both versions, original and rewritten): 'The creation and advocacy of revolutionary theory plays the principal and decisive role in those times of which Lenin said, "Without revolutionary theory there can be no revolutionary movement".'[122] Since Lenin saw this axiom as applicable to the whole historical period in which the proletarian revolution was to be planned, organized and carried out, Mao's use of it here can well be interpreted to mean that, while generally speaking the superstructure does not play the leading and decisive role in historical change, one of those 'times' when it does will occur, in fact, in China during a large part of the twentieth century.

One final point about Mao as a philosopher concerns his debt to Stalin. The current version of 'On contradiction' has a long and fulsome passage about Stalin's analysis of the peculiarities of the Russian Revolution as a 'model in understanding the particularity and universality of contradiction'.[123] This turns out to have been completely absent from the original version, where Mao illustrates his point rather by the exegesis of a quotation from Su Tung-p'o, who is said to have thoroughly understood the relation between the universal and the relative.[124]

the exception of the replacement of *chu-tao* (leading) by *chu-yao* (principal), Mao made no systematic changes in 1952 in those portions which I have actually quoted here. (The translation is from *PTMT* 199; see also Nick Knight, trans., 28 and notes.) The materials in *Philosophical annotations* show that Mao had read the book cited in the previous note between November 1936 and April 1937, and written a 1200-character comment on the passage devoted to the principal aspect of the contradiction. Despite his criticism of it, Mao recommended Shirokov's book for study by cadres (*Selected letters*, 189).

122 Knight, trans., 28.
123 Mao, *SW* 1.229–30.
124 *Pien-cheng wei-wu-lun*, 86; *MTTC*, *pu-chüan*, 5.258; Knight, trans., 24, and 146. The passage in

Chapter 2 of *Dialectical materialism* contains the statement that, because the 'dialectical materialist currents developing in China today do not result from taking over and reforming our own philosophical heritage, but from the study of Marxism-Leninism', we must 'liquidate the philosophical heritage of ancient China', which reflected the 'backwardness of China's social development'.[125] Plainly, this statement was the product of a momentary feeling of intimidation on Mao's first exposure to Marxist dialectics. It was entirely superseded by his call, in October 1938, for the 'sinification of Marxism', and did not represent a consistent position even in 1937.

If we look now concretely at Mao Tse-tung's analysis of strategic and tactical problems in the late 1930s, a fundamental issue is that of the relation between the Chinese Communist Party and the 'general staff of the world proletariat' in Moscow. Mao's view of this matter was absolutely clear. He summed it up in 1936 when, replying to a question from Edgar Snow as to whether, in the event of a Communist victory, there would be 'some kind of actual merger of governments' between Soviet China and Soviet Russia, he declared: 'We are certainly not fighting for an emancipated China in order to turn the country over to Moscow!' And he continued, spelling out the basis for this rejoinder:

The Chinese Communist Party is only one party in China, and in its victory it will have to speak for the whole nation. It cannot speak for the Russian people, or rule for the Third International, but only in the interests of the Chinese masses. Only where the interests of the Chinese masses coincide with the interests of the Russian masses can it be said to be 'obeying the will' of Moscow. But of course this basis of common benefit will be tremendously broadened once the masses of China are in democratic power and socially and economically emancipated, like their brothers in Russia.[126]

This passage shows that Mao, in 1936, felt the bond of solidarity uniting all the world's Communist Parties. But it also makes plain that for him solidarity did not mean subservience. Other things being equal, an 'emancipated China' – that is, a China ruled by the Communist Party – would have more intimate ties with the Soviet Union than with other countries. But if things were *not* equal – if Moscow did not show the respect for China's interests which Mao regarded as normal and

---

question is from Su's famous poem 'The red cliff', and reads as follows: 'If we regard this question as one of impermanence, then the universe cannot last for the twinkling of an eye. If, on the other hand, we consider it from the aspect of permanence, then you and I, together with all matter, are imperishable' (Cyril Drummond Le Gros Clark, *The prose-poetry of Su Tung-p'o*, 128).

[125] *MTTC* 6.275; *PTMT* 186.

[126] Reproduced from Edgar Snow's manuscript in *PTMT* 419.

appropriate – China's policy, under his guidance, might take a different direction.

There were those in the Chinese Communist Party in the 1930s who did not adopt the same independent attitude, just as there were those in later years who were prepared to be more flexible than Mao in dealings with Moscow. The history of the struggle between Mao Tse-tung and the so-called 'internationalist' (i.e. pro-Soviet) faction in the Chinese Communist Party from 1935 to 1945 is a long and complicated story, which has been told elsewhere (*CHOC* 13, ch. 12). Here our concern is not with power relations between Moscow and the Chinese Communist Party, or its various factions, but rather with the nature and significance of the theories by which Mao asserted his independence from Soviet tutelage. And among the concepts Mao put forward in the late 1930s, the boldest and most unequivocal symbol of his belief in the uniqueness of the Chinese revolution, and the need for the Chinese to solve their own problems in their own way, was that of the 'sinification of Marxism'.

This slogan was in fact used by the Chinese Communists only for a relatively short period, which began in 1938, when Mao first made the term his own, and reached its culmination in 1945 when, at the Seventh Congress of the Chinese Communist Party, Liu Shao-ch'i hailed Mao's gigantic achievements in creating theories which were 'thoroughly Marxist, and at the same time thoroughly Chinese'. But if the term itself was relatively ephemeral, the concerns it expresses were present before 1938, and have not only survived but grown in importance since the establishment of the Chinese People's Republic.

Mao Tse-tung's reasons for putting forward this idea are not difficult to understand. The concept of sinification symbolized the affirmation of China's national dignity in the face of the patronizing and domineering attitude of the Comintern; it was therefore valuable not only as a weapon in the inner-party struggle, but as a slogan for appealing to non-Communist opinion at a time of national crisis. But it also reflected a genuine conviction on Mao's part that in the last analysis an ideology of Western origin would not work in the Chinese context, unless it were adapted to the mentality and conditions of the Chinese people.

Exactly what sinification meant to Mao in 1938 is a more complex question. To call for the 'nationalization' of Marxism (as Liu Shao-ch'i put it in 1945),[127] not only in China but in other non-European countries, implies the adaptation of Marxist theories to national reality at many different levels, from language and culture to the economic and social structure of largely pre-capitalist agrarian societies. Moreover, the

[127] Carrère d'Encausse and Schram, 260.

question also arises as to which 'Marxism', or what elements of Marxism, are to be sinified.

The intermingling of the various dimensions of the problem is evoked in Mao Tse-tung's classic statement regarding sinification, in October 1938, when he said in part:

'Today's China is an outgrowth of historic China. We are Marxist historicists; we must not mutilate history. From Confucius to Sun Yat-sen we must sum it up critically, and we must constitute ourselves the heirs to this precious legacy. Conversely, the assimilation of this legacy itself becomes a method that aids considerably in guiding the present great movement. A Communist is a Marxist internationalist, but Marxism must take on a national form before it can be of any practical effect. There is no such thing as abstract Marxism, but only concrete Marxism. What we call concrete Marxism is Marxism that has taken on a national form, that is, Marxism applied to the concrete struggle in the concrete conditions prevailing in China, and not Marxism abstractly used. If a Chinese Communist, who is a part of the great Chinese people, bound to his people by his very flesh and blood, talks of Marxism apart from Chinese peculiarities, this Marxism is merely an empty abstraction. Consequently, the sinification of Marxism – that is to say, making certain that in all of its manifestations it is imbued with Chinese characteristics, using it according to Chinese peculiarities – becomes a problem that must be understood and solved by the whole party without delay. We must put an end to writing eight-legged essays on foreign models; there must be less repeating of empty and abstract refrains; we must discard our dogmatism and replace it by a new and vital Chinese style and manner, pleasing to the eye and to the ear of the Chinese common people.[128]

The simplest and least controversial aspect of Mao's conception of sinification is that dealt with in the last sentence of this quotation. Obviously, if Marxism is to have any impact in a non-European country, it must be presented to the people of that country in language which is not only intelligible to them but vivid and meaningful in the light of their mentality and traditions, rather than in jargon literally translated from another language and another culture. But such sinification of the form of Marxism, though indispensable in Mao's view, was only the outward manifestation of a more fundamental enterprise, aiming to transform the very substance of Marxism in order to adapt it to Chinese conditions.

In seeking to clarify the issues involved here, let us look first of all at the meaning of Mao Tse-tung's statement: 'There is no such thing as abstract Marxism, but only concrete Marxism.' In the light of his other writings in Yenan days, the ideas underlying this assertion could perhaps be spelled out as follows. The theory of scientific socialism was first expounded by Marx. Certain aspects of his writings – for example, his analysis of capitalism, and of the transition from capitalism to socialism, the

[128] MTTC 6.260–1; PTMT 172–3.

centrality of class struggle, and the basic axioms of dialectics – are of universal validity, but the theory as a whole reflects both its origins in the nineteenth century, and Marx's specifically European mentality and experience. When we talk, therefore (like Stalin and everyone else from Lenin on down), about applying the universally valid principles of Marxism to Chinese conditions, it is the timeless kernel of these theories which we should seek to grasp and adapt to our needs.

And what is that timeless kernel? Mao himself, in the report of October 1938 already quoted, declared: 'We must not study the letter of Marxism and Leninism, but the standpoint and methodology of its creators, with which they observed and solved problems.'[129] In February 1942 he called upon his comrades of the Chinese Communist Party to 'take the standpoint, viewpoint and methods of Marxism-Leninism, apply them to China, and create a theory from the conscientious study of the realities of the Chinese revolution and Chinese history'.[130]

These formulations raise two problems. What did Mao mean by 'standpoint', 'viewpoint', and 'methods'? And what was the relation between such attitudes or principles derived from Marxism, and the 'method' which, he said, could emerge from the assimilation of the precious legacy of China's past?

As for the first point, the current Chinese interpretation is that Mao was talking about adopting the standpoint of the proletariat, the viewpoint of historical materialism, and the method of dialectics. But if Mao was indeed referring to aspects of Marxism as broadly defined as these, does it not follow that, in his view, the theories of Marx himself constituted in fact 'German Marxism', just as the ideas of Lenin were characterized by his critics in the early twentieth century as 'Russian Marxism'? In other words, by 'abstract Marxism' Mao meant 'absolute Marxism', or Marxist theory unconditionally valid in all countries and at all times. And when he said that such Marxism 'did not exist', he meant that Marx's own writings were merely one concrete incarnation of the standpoint, viewpoint and methods which he had devised, not necessarily superior to the application of the same principles by Stalin, or by Mao himself. In any case, theory had real existence and meaning only in its concrete expression.

For Mao it was not, however, merely a question of applying Marxism to China; he also proposed, as we have seen, to enrich it with elements drawn from China's experience. Nor were the 'Chinese peculiarities' with which Mao proposed to imbue his Marxism merely the economic traits China shared with other Asian countries. They were also the 'precious qualities' which, as he put it in 1938, had been exhibited 'in the history

[129] *PTMT* 171.   [130] *MTTC* 8.75; *PTMT* 179–80.

of our great people over several millennia', and had been shaped both by historical experience and by the genius of the Chinese people.

The view that China today bears the imprint of the past is in no way remarkable. Marxists, at least those of the Leninist persuasion, have long agreed that social customs and forms of political organization, though they change in the wake of modifications in the economic infrastructure of society and as a result of the class struggles these engender, are themselves a variable in the historical equation. But in Mao's view, were cultural realities basically determined by levels of technology and 'modes of production', or did the 'national peculiarities' he stressed constitute for him an independent, or partially independent, variable? In my opinion, there is very little doubt that for Mao Tse-tung culture, both in the narrow and in the broad sense, constituted a partially autonomous dimension of human experience.

Precisely how central this theme was to Mao Tse-tung's whole vision of revolution in China is indicated by the extraordinary statement, in the passage quoted earlier from his report of October 1938, that the assimilation of the Chinese heritage 'itself becomes a method that aids considerably in guiding the present great movement'. The preceding injunction to 'sum up critically' the experience of the past does not carry the same implications, for in it the active and guiding role appears to rest with the 'viewpoint and methodology' of Marx and Lenin, which is to be used to sort out the wheat from the chaff in the record of Chinese history. The suggestion that a deeper knowledge of the past will not merely widen the revolutionaries' understanding of their own society, but will actually provide an instrument for leading the revolution is something else again, and opens vistas without precedent in the history of Marxism down to 1938. Mao himself was plainly dubious about the sweeping implications of the formulation 'this legacy . . . becomes a method', for he removed these words with his own hand during the revision of this text for the *Selected works*.[131]

What was the nature of this method, which Mao said could be distilled from the experience of 'historic China', and what elements in the past were to be drawn upon in producing it? He did not spell this out explicitly, but there are hints in his writings of the Yenan period that he was thinking about a domain which could be loosely defined as that of the art of

---

131 Information from P'ang Hsien-chih of the Research Centre on Party Literature under the Central Committee, January 1988. Ray Wylie has discussed the problem of the 'sinification of Marxism' and its significance from a parallel but somewhat different perspective, placing greater emphasis on the philosophical issue of the relation between the universal and the particular and its implications for the originality of 'Mao Tse-tung thought': Ray Wylie, *The emergence of Maoism: Mao Tse-tung, Ch'en Po-ta, and the search for Chinese theory, 1935–1945*, 55–8, 88–95 and *passim*.

statecraft.[132] Thus, in another section of the report of October 1938 in which he first put forward the idea of sinification, Mao dealt with the problem of making proper use of cadres – which, he said, had been referred to in the past as 'employing people in the administration' (*yung-jen hsing-cheng*). He went on to discuss the continuity between the present and the past in the following terms:

Throughout our national history there have been two sharply contrasting lines on the subject of the use of cadres, reflecting the opposition between the depraved and the upright, one being to 'appoint people on their merit', and the other being 'to appoint people by favouritism'. The former was the policy of sagacious rulers and worthy ministers in making appointments; the latter was that of despots and traitors. Today, when we talk about making use of cadres, it is from a revolutionary standpoint, fundamentally different from that of ancient times, and yet there is no getting away from this standard of 'appointing people on their merit'. It was utterly wrong in the past, and is still utterly wrong today, to be guided by personal likes and dislikes, to reward fawning flatterers and to punish the honest and forthright.[133]

Here Mao was clearly indicating that in his view there were standards of political conduct which remained valid for Communist revolutionaries in the present, even though they were originally evolved in the context of a pre-capitalist and bureaucratic society.

Rather more surprisingly, Mao Tse-tung also found positive elements in Confucian philosophy. Commenting in 1939 on an article by Ch'en Po-ta on this theme, Mao indicated that he was basically in agreement, but that, in criticizing Confucius' doctrine of the rectification of names as 'idealist', Ch'en had failed to note that, from the epistemological standpoint, it contained important elements of truth, because of its emphasis on the link between theory and practice. He also saw Chu Hsi's interpretation of Confucius' theory of the mean as parallel to the Communists' principle of struggle on two fronts, against left and right deviations. Not going far enough (*pu chi*), he said, stood for rightism; going too far (*kuo*) stood for leftism.[134]

Appeals of this kind to the national past were, of course, singularly appropriate at a time when Mao Tse-tung was concerned to address himself to the widest possible spectrum of opinion, in order to promote the establishment of a new united front. They must also be taken seriously, however, as an expression of the substance of his thinking. Before turning to the analysis of Mao's ideas specifically about the alliance with bourgeois nationalists against Japanese aggression, let us explore further his

---

[132] On this tradition, see *CHOC* 11, 145–7.
[133] Mao, *SW* 2.202, supplemented by *MTCC* 6.250–1.
[134] 'Chih Chang Wen-t'ien' (To Chang Wen-t'ien), 20 Feb. 1939, *Selected letters*, 144–8.

interpretation of Chinese history, especially in the nineteenth and twentieth centuries, for it is this context which served to define the current stage of the Chinese revolution as he saw it, and accordingly the tactics appropriate at such a time.

The most systematic statement of Mao's views regarding Chinese history in general dating from the Yenan period is to be found in the first chapter of *The Chinese Revolution and the Chinese Communist Party*. (Strictly speaking, this text was not drafted by Mao himself, who wrote only the second chapter of the work, but Mao did choose to include it in his *Selected works*, and thereby took responsibility for the contents.) The details of this wide-ranging discussion fall for the most part outside the scope of this volume, but certain points should be noted.

To begin with, Mao here places the transition from slave-holding society to feudalism at the beginning of the Chou dynasty, or roughly in the eleventh century BC. The relevant passage reads as follows:

[China's] feudal society, beginning with the Chou and Ch'in dynasties, lasted about 3,000 years...
It was the feudal landlord state which protected this system of feudal exploitation. While the feudal state was torn apart into rival principalities under the Chou, it became an autocratic and centralized feudal state after Ch'in Shih-huang unified China, though a degree of feudal separatism remained...[135]

Thus the Ch'in dynasty was seen as marked simply by a change in the form of the state, and not by a transition from one mode of production to another.[136]

The notion of an 'autocratic and centralized feudal state', which may appear to Western readers to be a contradiction in terms, was the formula arrived at by Mao and his comrades, after the debates of the 1920s and 1930s about the nature of traditional society, in order to assert simultaneously the 'feudal' (and hence universal) character of Chinese society and its uniqueness. At the same time, there remained in the original version of this text of 1939 traces of the notion of China as an 'Asiatic' society, which had in principle been repudiated. Thus, Mao asserted that Chinese society prior to the Opium War had been completely stagnant for centuries, and was only prodded into motion by the impact of the West.[137]

---

[135] Mao, *SW* 2.307–8; *MTTC* 7.100–1.
[136] Although there was ongoing scholarly controversy on this point, it did not become a burning political issue until the *p'i-Lin p'i-K'ung* campaign of 1973–4. The views put forward at that time were in flat contradiction with those Mao had espoused in 1939.
[137] In 1952, he would insert into *SW* the thesis, more agreeable to national pride, that changes were already at work which would have led to the birth of capitalism in China even without foreign intervention (Mao, *SW* 2.307–9; *MTTC* 7.100–3).

Two other points in Mao's survey of Chinese history are worthy of special emphasis. We have seen that, in 1919, Mao Tse-tung had boldly made what he called a 'singular assertion': 'one day, the reform of the Chinese people will be more profound than that of any other people, and the society of the Chinese people will be more radiant than that of any other people'. Twenty years later, the same faith in the exceptional capacities of his compatriots found expression in passages such as this:

In the many-thousand-year history of the Chinese people, many national heroes and revolutionary leaders have emerged. China has also given birth to many revolutionary strategists, statesmen, men of letters and thinkers. So the Chinese people [min-tsu] is also a people with a glorious revolutionary tradition and a splendid historical heritage.[138]

Secondly, Mao continued, as he had done since 1926, to give particular emphasis to the role of the peasantry. Not only were the 'hundreds of peasant revolts' throughout Chinese history characterized as the decisive cause of each and every dynastic change, but these 'peasant revolts and peasant wars', on a 'gigantic scale...without parallel in world history' were said to form the only 'real motive force of China's historical evolution'. At the same time, however, Mao stressed the limitations on such actions by the peasants alone, in a 'feudal' society, as far as their capacity to promote the development of the productive forces or change the mode of production was concerned. On this point, he wrote:

each peasant revolt and peasant war dealt a blow to the existing feudal regime; thus to some extent it changed the productive relations of society and to some extent furthered the development of the productive forces of society. However, since neither new productive forces nor new modes of production nor a new class force nor an advanced political party existed in those days, and the peasant wars and revolts consequently lacked the leadership of an advanced class and an advanced political party, such as the correct leadership given by the proletariat and the Communist Party today, the peasant revolutions invariably failed, and the peasants were utilized...by the landlords and the nobility as a tool for bringing about dynastic changes. Thus, although some social progress was made after each peasant revolutionary struggle, the feudal economic relations and feudal political system remained basically unchanged.[139]

When and how, in Mao's view, did a situation arise in which the proletariat and the Communist Party could exercise 'correct leadership' over the Chinese revolution? As he saw it, this process took place in two stages. First, the 'feudal' relations of production which had existed until the

[138] Mao, SW 2.306; MTTC 7.99.
[139] Mao, SW 2.308–9; MTTC 7.102. Here, and elsewhere in SW, Mao replaced the term he had originally used for peasant uprisings, pao-tung (revolt, armed rebellion), with ch'i-i (righteous uprising). The nuance lies, of course, in the fact that pao-tung suggests something more sporadic and less directly linked as a precursor to the rural revolution led by the Communists.

nineteenth century were partly broken down, and the position of the old ruling class undermined by the impact of the West and the ensuing development of capitalism, and of an embryonic bourgeoisie. At this stage, the landlord class, backed by the imperialists, still constituted the ruling class of Chinese society, but the bourgeois elements were the natural leaders of the revolutionary challenge to the existing order. Then, in a second stage, conditions became ripe for the proletariat to assert its hegemony over the revolution.

In Mao's interpretation, this transition took place roughly at the time of the May Fourth movement; the periods of bourgeois and proletarian hegemony he referred to respectively as the 'democratic' or 'old democratic' revolution and the 'New Democratic' revolution. Before discussing his periodization of modern Chinese history, let us consider what precisely he meant by 'New Democracy', for this concept was not only important in its day, but has continuing relevance to China's later problems.

Since 'New Democracy' was intended to be a category of Marxist-Leninist analysis, it is necessary to remind ourselves briefly of the doctrinal background. Marx had considered that, as a matter of course, the capitalist stage in the development of society would be characterized by the domination of the bourgeoisie, just as the feudal stage had been marked by the domination of the nobility. The bourgeois-democratic revolution which constituted the decisive phase in the transition from feudalism to capitalism would likewise be the task of the bourgeoisie. As for the proletariat, it would support the bourgeoisie in the democratic revolution, meanwhile prodding it forward to satisfy in so far as possible the immediate demands of the workers, until the time came to put an end to the capitalist system by a socialist revolution led by the proletariat.

The writings of Marx and Engels regarding revolution in pre-capitalist societies, especially those which had felt the impact of Western colonialism, are fascinating and suggestive, but at the same time fragmentary and contradictory. In any case, it is impossible (whatever attempts may have been made) to extract from them a clear tactical line for the guidance of Asian revolutionaries. At the time of the 1905 Revolution, first Trotsky and then Lenin put forward the view that, in such backward lands, the 'bourgeois-democratic revolution' could take place under the hegemony of the proletariat, that is, in a political context dominated by the Communist Party. This idea, subsequently elaborated by Stalin, Mao and many others, has been an axiom of Marxism, as interpreted by the Soviets and their disciples, ever since.

Thus, the class nature of a given historical stage was effectively dissociated from the class character of the actors in such a stage. The proletarian dictatorship, or some precursor or variant of it, can, it has been postulated for three-quarters of a century, preside over a 'bourgeois' revolution which will constitute the functional equivalent of the capitalist stage in the development of Western societies.

To return now to the nature and significance of Mao Tse-tung's ideas regarding this stage, which he baptized 'New Democratic', it is of interest to note not only how he defined its content, but when he postulated that it had begun. For it was in this context that Mao undertook to justify the new alliance with the Nationalists, in terms of the evolving balance of forces, and the aims of the revolution at that time.

In some passages Mao dated the transition from 'old' to 'new' democracy in 1919 precisely, and for purposes of convenience the dividing-line between 'modern' and 'contemporary' Chinese history was fixed beginning in Yenan days at the time of the May Fourth movement. Mao was, however, naturally aware that decisive changes such as this do not occur overnight, and for the most part he situated the emergence of 'New Democracy' more loosely in the period from the outbreak of the First World War to the foundation of the Chinese Communist Party (that is, in the 'May Fourth period' as commonly and broadly defined). In *On new democracy*, Mao wrote in January 1940: 'A change...occurred in China's bourgeois-democratic revolution after the outbreak of the first imperialist world war in 1914 and the founding of a socialist state on one-sixth of the globe as a result of the Russian October Revolution of 1917.'[140]

The reasons here given or suggested for the change in the nature of China's revolution include the weakening and discrediting of Western 'bourgeois democracy, the emergence of an alternative model in the new Soviet republic, and also the possibility of material and moral assistance from the Soviets. It was partly for this last reason that Mao, following Stalin (who himself was following Lenin), declared China's New-Democratic revolution to be an integral part of the proletarian-socialist world revolution. On this theme, he wrote:

In an era in which the world capitalist front has collapsed in one corner of the globe... and has fully revealed its decadence everywhere else, in an era in which the remaining capitalist portions cannot survive without relying more than ever on the colonies and semi-colonies... in such an era, a revolution in any colony or semi-colony that is directed against imperialism... no longer comes within the old category of the bourgeois-democratic world revolution, but within the new category...

[140] Mao, *SW* 2.343; *MTTC* 7.153.

Although during its first stage or first step, such a revolution in a colonial and
semi-colonial country is still fundamentally bourgeois-democratic in its social
character, and although its objective demand is still fundamentally to clear the
path for the development of capitalism, it is no longer a revolution of the old
type, led *entirely* by the bourgeoisie, with the aim of establishing a capitalist
society and a state under bourgeois dictatorship. It is rather a revolution of the
new type, *with the participation of the proletariat in the leadership*, or led by the
proletariat, and having as its aim, in the first stage, the establishment of a
new-democratic society and a state under the joint dictatorship of all the
revolutionary classes...[141]

This passage speaks of a 'joint dictatorship', and the words in italics (which
Mao removed in 1952) imply that the proletariat might not even enjoy
primacy among the various dictators. Indeed, in the original version of
On new democracy Mao went so far as to state explicitly that, if the Chinese
bourgeoisie should prove itself capable of leading the people in 'driving
out Japanese imperialism and introducing democratic government', they
(i.e., the Kuomintang) would continue to enjoy the people's confidence.[142]
It was plain, however, that this was merely a rhetorical gesture to Chiang
Kai-shek, and that Mao fully intended his own party to exercise hegemony
on behalf of the proletariat within the 'joint dictatorship of all the
revolutionary classes'. In *The Chinese Revolution and the Chinese Communist
Party*, addressed directly to party members rather than to a non-party
audience of intellectuals (as was *On new democracy*), Mao said bluntly,
'Unless the proletariat participates in it and leads it, the Chinese revolution
cannot... succeed.'[143] And on the eve of victory in June 1949, he put the
same view more categorically still: 'Why did forty years of revolution
under Sun Yat-sen end in failure? Because in the epoch of imperialism
the bourgeoisie cannot lead any genuine revolution to victory.'[144]

In sum, though he expressed it with varying degrees of frankness, Mao's
view from the time he first began to use the term 'New Democracy' in
1939 was that in China, after 1919 or thereabouts, leadership of the
revolution rightfully belonged to the proletariat. How could he claim such
a role for a class which, in the second decade of the twentieth century,
was only beginning to develop, and for a party which counted, until the
alliance with the Nationalists in 1923–7, only a handful of members? Apart
from the fact that the Communists, as already noted, enjoyed external
support and sympathy from the Soviet Union, Mao argued as follows:

As distinct social classes, the Chinese bourgeoisie and proletariat are new-born
and never existed before in Chinese history.... They are twins born of China's

---

[141] Carrère d'Encausse and Schram, 252; *MTTC* 7.153–4. (The words in italics have been removed
in Mao, *SW*.)   [142] Carrère d'Encausse and Schram, 254; *MTTC* 7.162.
[143] Mao, *SW* 2.325; *MTTC* 7.126.   [144] Mao, *SW* 4.422; *MTTC* 10.305.

old (feudal) society, at once linked to each other and antagonistic to each other. However, the Chinese proletariat emerged and grew simultaneously not only with the Chinese national bourgeoisie but also with the enterprises directly operated by the imperialists in China. Hence, a very large section of the Chinese proletariat is older and more experienced than the Chinese bourgeoisie, and is therefore a greater and more broadly-based social force.[145]

This is an ingenious argument, and not without substance. Nevertheless, Mao's assertion of proletarian hegemony from 1917–21 onwards must be read not as a statement of fact about the strength of the opposing political forces, but as an assertion that, from this time forward, it was appropriate, and not wholly unrealistic, for the Communists to *strive* for leadership over the national revolution.

If such was indeed Mao's intimate conviction, even though he did not always state this openly, was it not meaningless or hypocritical to talk about a 'united front' at all? Or, to put it differently, would not such an alliance necessarily assume the character of a 'united front from below', that is, of an attempt to mobilize the rank and file of the Kuomintang against its leadership? Not necessarily, especially if we interpret Mao's periodization, as I have done above, in the sense that, in the late 1930s, it had long been legitimate for the Communists to seek to assert their hegemony. For what was legitimate might not, at any given time, be expedient, or politically 'correct'. If the external threat from Japan to China's very existence as an independent state, and therefore to the possibility of political change within the country, became so grave that the struggle against Japan replaced the struggle against Chiang Kai-shek as the Communists' number one policy goal, and if the Kuomintang was not only militarily and politically stronger than the Communists but willing to fight Japan, then it might be appropriate to accept, for a time, Kuomintang predominance in such a struggle.

As noted above, Mao had accepted by December 1935 the need for a new united front, and he had agreed, by late 1936, that Chiang Kai-shek must be the titular leader of such an alliance. It was in October 1938, in his report to the sixth plenum of the Central Committee, that Mao went farthest in recognizing the leading role of the Kuomintang, not only during the Anti-Japanese War, but in the phase of national reconstruction which would follow it. In a paragraph entitled 'The Kuomintang has a brilliant future' he declared:

The Kuomintang and the Communist Party are the foundation of the Anti-Japanese United Front, but of these two it is the Kuomintang that occupies first place....In the course of its glorious history, the Kuomintang has been responsible for the

[145] Mao, *SW* 2.310; *MTTC* 7.104–5.

overthrow of the Ch'ing, the establishment of the Republic, opposition to Yuan Shih-k'ai...and the great revolution of 1926–7. Today it is once more leading the great anti-Japanese war. It enjoys the historic heritage of the Three People's Principles; it has had two great leaders in succession – Mr Sun Yat-sen and Mr Chiang Kai-shek....All this should not be underestimated by our compatriots and constitutes the result of China's historical development.

In carrying out the anti-Japanese war, and in organizing the Anti-Japanese United Front, the Kuomintang occupies the position of leader and backbone [*chi-kan*]...Under the single great condition that it support to the end the war of resistance and the United Front, one can foresee a brilliant future for the Kuomintang...[146]

Although this report expressed the softest line ever taken by Mao Tse-tung toward Chiang Kai-shek and the Kuomintang, it was by no means the blank cheque it might at first glance appear. The 'single great condition' alone, stated in the last sentence of the preceding quotation, limited severely the scope of Mao's concessions to Chiang. To the extent that he regarded Chiang and the Kuomintang as, in the long run, congenitally incapable of supporting unflinchingly the united front and the war against Japan, Mao looked forward to the time when his acceptance of Chiang's leadership would necessarily lapse. Moreover, though the original 1938 text of this report did not speak, as do the rewritten extracts in the *Selected works*, of leadership by the Communists, it did refer to 'the way in which the Communists should become conscious of their own role and strengthen themselves, in order to be in a position to assume their great responsibilities in the national war'. And these responsibilities he defined succinctly by saying that the Communists 'should exercise the role of vanguard and model in every domain'.[147] Quite obviously, if the Kuomintang should falter in its leadership, its place would be taken by those who had already established themselves as 'vanguard and model'.

Finally, Mao's proposal, in his report of October 1938, that the 'bloc within' should be resuscitated, and that Communists should once more join the Kuomintang as individuals, was a two-edged and ambiguous one. For though he offered in advance to give Chiang Kai-shek a complete list of all such Communists with dual party membership, thus satisfying one of the conditions which Chiang had laid down following the 'reorganization' of May 1926, he also sought to persuade Chiang to turn the Kuomintang into a 'national league'. The aim of this second proposal was all too obviously to weaken the Leninist stranglehold which had made it impossible, in 1926–7, for the Communists to manipulate the

146 *MTTC* 6.198; *PTMT* 228–9.
147 *MTTC* 6.243–4; *PTMT* 229.

Kuomintang from within. It is therefore not surprising that Chiang saw this as a 'Trojan horse' manoeuvre, and rejected it.[148]

In a little over a year, Mao's position evolved, as we have already seen, from recognition that the Kuomintang must take 'first place' in the united front to the assertion of Communist leadership as an accomplished fact. In *On new democracy* (January 1940) this bald claim was covered with a rhetorical fig leaf; in *The Chinese Revolution and the Chinese Communist Party* (December 1939) it was quite unambiguous.[149] *The Chinese Revolution and the Chinese Communist Party*, though written chiefly for a Communist audience, was openly sold. In his Introduction to the inner-party periodical *The Communist* (October 1939), Mao did not even raise the question of who should exercise hegemony; he simply assumed that leadership belonged to the Communists, and proceeded to discuss how they should go about exercising it.

Apart from the question of leadership, two directly related points merit discussion here: Mao's views regarding the role of various classes in the revolution, and about the nature of the political movement or regime which should represent the revolutionary forces.

In essence, Mao's view regarding the class forces supporting the revolution at the time of the Anti-Japanese War was simple and consistent. He saw them as composed of Stalin's four-class bloc of the 1920s, with the addition of a certain portion of the 'comprador bourgeoisie' tied to powers whose interests were in conflict with those of Japan. Understandably, the line enclosing possible allies was drawn most tightly in the Introduction to *The Communist*, and most loosely in *On new democracy*. In the former, the peasantry is characterized as a 'firm' ally of the proletariat, and the urban petty bourgeoisie as a 'reliable' ally. As for the national bourgeoisie, it will take part in the struggle 'against imperialism and the feudal warlords' at 'certain times and to a certain extent', because it suffers from foreign oppression, but it will also 'vacillate and defect' on occasion 'because of its economic and political flabbiness'. The bourgeoisie or big bourgeoisie, even when it joins the united front against the enemy, 'continues to be most reactionary', opposes the development of the proletarian party, and ultimately plans to capitulate to the enemy and split the united front.[150]

The original version of *On new democracy* exhibits one curious anomaly:

[148] Schram, *Mao Tse-tung*, 202–3. For the text of Mao's proposal, see *MTTC* 6.228–9.

[149] *MTTC* 7.129; *PTMT* 230–1.

[150] Mao, *SW* 2.228–89; *MTTC* 7.228–9. The passage (paragraph 3) putting a slightly more optimistic view of the (comprador) bourgeoisie was added in *SW* and does not appear at all in the 1939 text. On Stalin and the four-class bloc, see Carrère d'Encausse and Schram, 55, 227–29.

it refers throughout to a three-class, rather than a four-class bloc. The difference is one of form rather than substance, but it is not without interest. It results from lumping together the peasantry (which has always been regarded by Marxists as petty-bourgeois in nature) with the urban petty bourgeoisie, and calling the resulting category '*the*' petty bourgeoisie, instead of counting the peasants as a separate class. Thus we read, for example, that in 1927–36, as a result of the 'going over of the Chinese bourgeoisie to the counter-revolutionary camp...only two of the three classes originally composing the revolutionary camp remained...': the proletariat and the petty bourgeoisie (including the peasantry, the revolutionary intellectuals, and other sections of the petty bourgeoisie).[151]

With the coming of the Anti-Japanese War, continued Mao, the Chinese revolution, 'pursuing its zig-zag course', had again arrived at a united front of three classes. But this time, he added,

the scope is much broader. Among the upper classes, it includes all the rulers; among the middle classes, it includes the petty bourgeoisie in its totality; among the lower classes, it includes the totality of the proletarians. All classes and strata of the country have become allies, and are resolutely resisting Japanese imperialism.[152]

It is quite clear that the swallowing-up of the peasantry in the catch-all category of the 'petty bourgeoisie' served to attenuate the emphasis on the unique character of China's revolution, and especially on one of its original traits: guerrilla warfare in the countryside. In his Introduction to *The Communist*, Mao made of these aspects of China's experience one of the main themes of his analysis:

since China is a semi-colonial and semi-feudal country, since her political, economic and cultural development is uneven, since her economy is predominantly semi-feudal and since her territory is vast, it follows that the character of the Chinese revolution in its present stage is bourgeois-democratic, that its principal targets are imperialism and the feudal forces, and that its basic motive forces are the proletariat, the peasantry, and the urban petty bourgeoisie, with the national bourgeoisie etc. taking part at certain times and to a certain extent; it also follows [*sic*] that the principal form of struggle in the Chinese revolution is armed struggle.

It is not quite clear why the last conclusion should follow from the facts enumerated by Mao Tse-tung in this sentence, but it is obviously a valid

---

[151] *MTTC* 7.196; Carrère d'Encausse and Schram, 256–7. There is an intriguing prefiguration of this three-class analysis in Mao's reply of November 1925 to a survey by the Young China Association (*MTTC*, *pu-chüan*, 2.127), in which he declared that though he was a Communist and a partisan of a 'proletarian social revolution', a single class was not in a position, in China, to overthrow the internal and external forces of reaction, so the 'national revolution' must be carried out by the proletariat, the petty-bourgeoisie, and the left wing of the middle class (*chung-ch'an chieh-chi*).   [152] *MTTC* 7.197–8; Carrère d'Encausse and Schram, 257.

one. 'Indeed,' Mao goes on, 'the history of our party may be called a history of armed struggle. Comrade Stalin has said, "In China the armed people are fighting armed counter-revolution. That is one of the specific features of the Chinese revolution." This is perfectly true.' The quotation from Stalin represents a particularly cynical instance of citing out of context; when Stalin made this statement in December 1926 the 'armed people' he was talking about were represented by Chiang Kai-shek, in whose fidelity to the cause he still had full confidence, and Mao knew this very well. Still, once again, the point was well taken: 'armed struggle in China', added Mao, 'is, in essence, peasant war and the party's relations with the peasantry and its close relation with the peasant war are one and the same thing'.[153]

In this text, Mao Tse-tung characterizes the united front, armed struggle, and party-building as the Chinese Communist Party's three 'magic weapons'. I have spoken previously at some length of the place of armed struggle in Mao's strategy. As for the united front, his essential message in the Introduction to *The Communist* is that it should be marked by both unity and struggle. The precise form such unity should take is not discussed, but as we have already seen Mao laid down in the other two basic texts of this same period that the vehicle for cooperation should be the 'joint dictatorship of all the revolutionary classes'. In *The Chinese Revolution and the Chinese Communist Party* he also referred to it as the 'joint revolutionary-democratic dictatorship of several revolutionary classes over the imperialists and reactionary traitors'.[154] The term 'revolutionary-democratic dictatorship' was obviously modelled on Lenin's 'revolutionary-democratic dictatorship of the workers and peasants', a slogan first coined at the time of the 1905 Revolution and often reiterated thereafter. Mao's dictators were, of course, more numerous than Lenin's; the difference he explained, as we have already seen, by the special conditions of a country under foreign domination.

The third of Mao's 'magic weapons', party-building, meant in fact something far more sweeping and significant than would at first glance appear. It implied defining a correct doctrine, and unifying and rectifying the party on the basis of that doctrine. A passage somewhat modified in the *Selected works* noted that, if in the past the Chinese Communist Party had been unsuccessful in its pursuit of consolidation and 'bolshevization', this was because its members had not adequately linked Marxism to the concrete practice of the Chinese revolution, and did not have an adequate knowledge of Chinese history and of Chinese society.[155]

[153] Mao, *SW* 2.286–7; *MTTC* 7.72.   [154] *MTTC* 7.129; *PTMT* 230.
[155] Mao, *SW* 2.292–3; *MTTC* 7.79–80.

This meant, quite plainly, that they did not yet have the benefit of the 'sinified Marxism' which Mao Tse-tung was then engaged in elaborating, precisely in the works we have been discussing. In other words, the 'party-building' for which Mao called in October 1939 was destined to take the form of the great rectification or *cheng-feng* campaign which, in 1942–3, definitively established his ideological predominance in the party.

THE TRIUMPH OF MAO TSE-TUNG'S THOUGHT 1941–1949

When Mao had first put forward the slogan of adapting Marxism to Chinese conditions, his main concern, as I have already suggested, was to shape the approach of the Chinese Communist Party to fit the political and cultural circumstances of the time. The next main phase in the development of his ideas on this theme, in 1941–3, was much more directly linked to Mao's struggle with his rivals in the party, and the views he propagated were explicitly designed to serve his interests in that struggle.

The same was true of other aspects of Mao's thought. If the philosophical core of his thinking had taken shape as early as 1937 with the theory of contradictions, in a wide range of other domains, from economic work to literature and from administrative principles to the interpretation of the Marxist heritage, the definitive formulation of Mao's ideas prior to 1949 dates from the early 1940s. And in all of these areas the links between ideology and political in-fighting are palpable and direct.

This book focuses, of course, primarily on ideas rather than on historical fact. The following succinct chronology brings out clearly, however, the concrete significance of certain theoretical statements:

5 May 1941. Mao makes a speech to a cadre meeting in Yenan criticizing 'scholars of Marxism-Leninism' who 'can only repeat quotes from Marx, Engels, Lenin and Stalin from memory, but about their own ancestors...have to apologize and say they've forgotten'.

1 July 1941. Adoption of Central Committee resolution on 'strengthening the party spirit', stressing the importance of discipline and of absolute subordination of cadres at all levels to higher authority.

13 July 1941. Sun Yeh-fang writes a letter to Liu Shao-ch'i (using the pen name Sung Liang), referring to the two opposing deviations of slighting theoretical study and scholasticism, and asking for some 'Chinese examples' of the correct relation between theory and practice. Liu replies the same day stressing the difficulties of sinifying Marxism, and blaming the lack of progress thus far partly on the fact that few Chinese Communist Party members can read Marx in the original.

23 January 1942. Mao orders army cadres to study his Ku-t'ien Resolution of December 1929 until they are thoroughly familiar with it.

1 February and 8 February 1942. Mao delivers his two keynote speeches on rectification. In the second of these, he complains that his 1938 call for 'sinification' has not been heeded.

May 1942. Mao delivers two talks to the Yenan Forum on Literature and Art, but these are not published for nearly a year and a half.

December 1942. Mao delivers a report *On economic and financial problems.*

20 March 1943. Mao elected chairman of the Politburo of the Chinese Communist Party, and chairman of the three-man Secretariat, with the right to outvote the two other members.

April 1943. Movement to investigate cadres pressed forward vigorously in Yenan – in fact, a harsh purge of dissident or anti-Maoist elements in the party, under the control of K'ang Sheng.

26 May 1943. Mao, commenting on the dissolution of the Comintern, declares that, although Moscow has not intervened in the affairs of the Chinese Communist Party since the Seventh Comintern Congress of August 1935, the Chinese Communists have done their work very well.

1 June 1943. Resolution, drafted by Mao, on methods of leadership puts forward the classic formulation of the 'mass line'.

6 July 1943. Liu Shao-ch'i publishes the article 'Liquidate Menshevik thought in the party', hailing Mao as a true Bolshevik and denouncing the 'International faction' as Mensheviks in disguise.

19 October 1943. Mao's 'Yenan Talks' finally published in *Chieh-fang jih-pao.*

April 1945. Apotheosis – Mao's thought written into the party constitution as the guide to all the party's work, and Mao hailed by Liu Shao-ch'i for his earth-shaking contributions in 'sinifying' or 'nationalizing' Marxism.[156]

These facts have, of course, been selected and arranged to suggest that the establishment of Mao Tse-tung's absolute predominance in the party was, from the outset, a primary goal of the rectification campaign of 1942–3. Though they may sharpen and oversimplify the picture to some extent, I do not believe that they distort the broad outline.

---

[156] Most of these events are well known, and since the main stuff of this work is ideas rather than facts, I shall not footnote them all in detail. Liu Shao-ch'i's article 'Liquidate Menshevik thought', and the Central Committee resolution of 1 July 1941 are translated by Boyd Compton, *Mao's China: party reform documents, 1942–44.* The 1 June 1943 resolution and Mao's speeches (except *On economic and financial problems*) are to be found in Mao, *SW* and many other sources, including the Compton volume. Liu's letter to 'Comrade Sung Liang' has long been known to exist. See my discussion of it in 'The party in Chinese Communist ideology', in J. W. Lewis, ed. *Party leadership and revolutionary power in China,* 177.

It has now been reprinted, and Sung Liang identified as Sun Yeh-fang (*Hung-ch'i* 7 (1980) 2–4), but Sun's original letter is not included in this version. For the latter, see Liu Shao-ch'i, *Lun tang* (On the party), 345–6. For key passages from Liu's report of April 1945 (which has recently been reprinted in China), see Carrère d'Encausse and Schram, 259–61. Regarding Mao's formal position in the party from March 1943, see *TSYC* 2 (1980) 77–8.

To be sure, Mao wrote, with real or feigned modesty, in April 1943, when the rectification campaign had basically achieved its objectives, that his thought, which was a form of Marxism-Leninism, was not in his own opinion fully mature and thought out, and did not constitute a system. It was, he said, still not in the stage where it should be preached or advocated (*ku-ch'ui*), except perhaps for a few pieces contained in the documents studied during the campaign.[157] The fact remains, however, that it was quite clearly regarded, from 1943 onwards, and especially from 1945, as the definitive exemplar of the adaptation of Marxism-Leninism to Chinese conditions, and the summing-up and culmination both of Marxism and of Chinese culture.[158]

If we accept that Mao, after his humiliation at the hands of the '28 Bolsheviks' in 1932–4, and a long hard struggle, from 1935 to 1943, to establish his own political and ideological authority, at length achieved this goal in the course of the rectification campaign, what sort of political and economic system did he establish at that time in the Yenan base area, and what were the principles underlying it? It has been repeatedly argued that the essence of the Yenan heritage lies in an intimate relationship between the party and the masses. There is much truth in this, but the matter should not be looked at too one-sidedly.

In the second section above, I evoked the classic directive of 1 June 1943 on the 'mass line', and argued that this was an ambiguous concept, which pointed in two directions: toward Leninist elitism, and toward the genuine involvement of people in their own affairs.

To suggest that ordinary people may be a source of ideas from which correct policies are elaborated, and that they can in turn understand these policies, rather than blindly applying them, marked a very great rupture with one of the central themes of traditional Chinese thought. According to the *Analects*: 'The people may be made to follow a path of action, but they may not be made to understand it.'[159] This is one of the Confucian prejudices that Mao strove for half a century to break down. As already emphasized, he did not, however, cast doubt in so doing on the Leninist axiom that class consciousness can only be imported into the working class from outside, and more broadly that the Communist Party must provide ideological guidance to society as a whole.

---

[157] 'Chih Ho K'ai-feng' (To Ho K'ai-feng), 22 April 1943, *Selected letters*, 212–13.

[158] On this point, Ray Wylie (273–4) is, in my opinion, right, and Franz Schurmann wrong, about the interpretation of Liu Shao-ch'i's report to the Seventh Congress, and of the party statutes adopted on that occasion. Whether or not, in the early 1950s, the Chinese adopted a distinction between 'pure' and 'practical' ideology is quite another question, which I shall not take up here.

[159] *Confucian analects*, 8, ch. 9, in James Legge, *The Chinese classics*, 1.211.

Within the broad limits defined by Mao's insistence both on a measure of initiative and involvement from below, and on firm centralized guidance from above, there is room for an infinite variety of formulations and shades of emphasis. From Yenan days onwards, Mao Tse-tung rang the changes on these themes. Consistently, however, at least until the Cultural Revolution, he regarded centralized leadership as in the last analysis even more important than democracy.

Mao's ideas about methods of work and patterns of organization had taken shape progressively during a decade and a half of military and political struggle in the countryside, from the Autumn Harvest uprising to the rectification campaign. Now, in the early 1940s, the lessons of this experience were summed up, systematized, and applied to economic work as well as to guerrilla tactics.

A key slogan of this time was 'centralized leadership and dispersed operation' (*chi-chung ling-tao, fen-san ching-ying*). Such an approach was particularly appropriate in circumstances where only a relatively small proportion of the total area controlled by the Communists was located in the main Yenan base area, and the technical level of the economy was so low that rigorously centralized planning of inputs and outputs was neither possible nor desirable. Even in these circumstances, however, the accent was by no means on continued and unmitigated dispersion of responsibility and effort. Mao Tse-tung made this point quite unequivocally in his report of December 1942, *On economic and financial problems*.[160] Asking the rhetorical question why the self-sufficient industry of the Border Region should be run in such a dispersed fashion, Mao replied:

The main reason is that the labour force is divided among the various branches of the party, government and army. If it were centralized, we would destroy their activism. For example, we encouraged 359 Brigade to set up the Ta-kuang Textile Mill and did not order it to combine with a government mill because most of the several hundred employees at the mill were selected from the officers and men of 359 Brigade. They work to produce the bedding and clothing requirements of the Brigade and their enthusiasm is high. If we centralized, we would destroy this enthusiasm.... Adopting the policy of 'dispersed operation' is correct and ideas aimed at centralizing everything are wrong. However, enterprises of the same kind carried out within the same area should be centralized as much as possible. Unlimited dispersal is not profitable. At present we are already carrying out...centralization of this kind....Perhaps this process of dispersal at first and centralization later cannot be avoided...[161]

[160] Only the first part of this very long work appears in the current canon of Mao, *SW*. The passages quoted below are from part 7, 'On developing a self-sufficient industry', *MTTC* 8.263–4.
[161] The translation is that of Andrew Watson, *Mao Zedong and the political economy of the border region*, 149–50.

Later in the same section, listing the economic measures which should be pursued in 1943, Mao placed second (immediately after increased capital investment) that of 'establishing a unified leadership for the whole of self-supporting industry, overcoming the serious anarchy which exists now'.[162] In order to achieve this result, he called for the establishment of a 'unified plan', drawn up under the 'unified leadership' of the Finance and Economy Office (*Ts'ai-ching pan-shih-ch'u*), but at the same time he specified that agriculture, industry and commerce should not be 'put entirely in the hands of one single official organization for the whole Border Region'. Instead, the unified plan should be 'handed over to the party, government and army systems for separate implementation'. Nevertheless, Mao's final conclusion was that the problem of unified leadership was 'the central problem in advancing self-supporting industry during 1943'.[163]

The sentence just quoted poses explicitly the problem of the relation between party, state and army, which remained a central and often controversial issue after 1949. A key concept, introduced in Yenan, conveys the essence of the party's unifying and guiding role as conceived at that time. The term is *i-yuan-hua* – literally 'to make one', 'to make monolithic'. It has sometimes been translated 'to coordinate', but that is probably too weak a rendering; 'to unify', which has also been used, is unsatisfactory because it seems best to reserve this English term as the equivalent for *t'ung-i*, just as 'centralized' is best kept for translating *chi-chung*. The English equivalent which I propose to use is 'integrate', but this question of translation is less important than the concerns which underlay the adoption of the Chinese expression in the early 1940s. Because this concept has hitherto received far less attention than democratic centralism or the mass line, I shall give a number of illustrations of its use, before summing up my understanding of its significance.

The *locus classicus* of this term seems to be found in the resolution of the Politburo dated 1 September 1942, 'On the unification of party leadership in the anti-Japanese bases, and adjusting the relations between various organizations'.[164]

This resolution asserts explicitly and forcefully the link between party-government and party-army relations on the one hand, and the

---

[162] Watson, *Mao Zedong*, 160.

[163] *MTTC* 8.265, 273; Watson, *Mao Zedong*, 151, 160–1.

[164] This is one of the documents studied in the course of the rectification campaign, and an English translation can be found in Boyd Compton, *Mao's China*, 161–75. Authorship of the resolution has not been officially attributed to Mao, but the Chinese text is included in the Tokyo *MTTC*, 8.155–63.

hierarchical structure of each individual organization on the other. Paragraph 8 of the resolution begins as follows:

The integration [*i-yuan-hua*] of party leadership is [to be] expressed on the one hand in the mutual relations between party, governmental, and mass organizations at the same level; on the other hand, it is [to be] expressed in the relations between upper and lower levels. In this [latter respect], strict adherence to the principle of obedience of lower to higher echelons and obedience of the entire party to the central committee is of decisive significance in unifying party leadership...[165]

A somewhat clearer definition and explanation of the meaning of the elusive term *i-yuan-hua* is to be found in the decision of 1 June 1943, drafted by Mao Tse-tung, from which I quoted earlier the well-known paragraph on the 'mass line'. In an immediately following passage (paragraph 7) of this directive, Mao declares:

In relaying to subordinate units any task... a higher organization should in all cases go through the leader of the lower organization concerned, so that he may assume responsibility, thus achieving the goal of combining division of labour with unified leadership [*i-yuan-hua*]. A department at a higher level should not go solely to its counterpart at the lower level (for instance, a higher department concerned with organization, propaganda or counter-espionage should not go solely to the corresponding department at the lower level), leaving the person in overall charge of the lower organization (such as the secretary, the chairman, the director or the school principal) in ignorance or without responsibility. Both the person in overall charge and the person with specific responsibility should be informed and given responsibility. This *i-yuan-hua* method, combining division of labour with unified leadership, makes it possible, through the person with overall responsibility, to mobilize a large number of cadres...to carry out a particular task, and thus to overcome shortages of cadres in individual departments and turn a good number of people into cadres for one's own work. This, too, is a way of combining the leadership with the masses...[166]

It will have been seen (as well as such things can be seen in translation) that *i-yuan-hua* is twice used as an appositive for 'combining division of labour with unified leadership'. The sense, plainly, is that the necessary division of labour between various organs can exist without posing a threat to the unity of the movement only on condition that the whole system be penetrated and controlled by a unifying force in the shape of the party. To convey this function, the English equivalent 'to integrate' seems most appropriate.

The use of the term *i-yuan-hua*, with its strong verbal force, reflects the perception, on the part of the Chinese Communist leadership, of the situation that prevailed in the early 1940s in the base areas, which were

[165] Compton, 171–2; translation modified on the basis of the Chinese text in *MTTC* 8.161.
[166] *SW* 3.120–1; revised on the basis of *MTTC* 9.29, to take account of changes (which are not particularly extensive) in the official Chinese text as compared to the 1943 version.

fragmented, often isolated, and exposed to enemy attack. In such circumstances, the various agencies of political, economic, and administrative control could scarcely be effectively integrated. They stressed, therefore, the necessity of *making* things monolithic (*i-yuan-hua*), because excessive dispersal in fact prevailed.

One might assume that, once the Chinese Communists had established their authority throughout the whole of the country and set up the People's Republic of China, dispersionism would no longer be a threat. In fact, for many complex historical and practical reasons, the problems of fragmentation and of divided authority by no means evaporated in 1949, and the concept of 'integrated leadership' therefore did not become irrelevant, even though the whole context did, of course, change radically with the conquest of power.

CONCLUSION: TOWARD A PEOPLE'S DEMOCRATIC MODERNIZING AUTOCRACY?

As indicated in the third section above, Mao had already in 1939–40 characterized the regime to be established after the war as a 'joint dictatorship of several revolutionary classes', and had made it fairly clear that this dictatorship was to be under the effective control of the proletariat, or of its 'vanguard', the Chinese Communist Party. When the prospect of a 'coalition government' with the Kuomintang, which Mao had envisaged as a useful tactical expedient in 1944–5, finally evaporated in 1946, and was replaced by open civil war, there was no longer any reason for maintaining the slightest ambiguity about the party's immediate political goals. Mao therefore spelled out, on 30 June 1949, in an article written to commemorate the 28th anniversary of the foundation of the Chinese Communist Party, the precise nature of the 'people's democratic dictatorship' which he proposed to establish three months later.

As for the class nature of the new state, Mao defined the locus of authority in terms of what has often been called a concentric-circle metaphor. The 'people' who were to exercise the dictatorship would be composed of the working class, the peasantry, the urban petty bourgeoisie and the 'national bourgeoisie'. Of these four classes, the workers would enjoy hegemony, and the peasants constituted their most reliable allies. The petty bourgeoisie were to be largely followers, while the national bourgeoisie had a dual nature: they were part of the people, but at the same time exploiters. Consequently, those elements among them who behaved badly could be re-classified as not of 'the people', and find themselves on the receiving end of the dictatorship, the objects rather than the subjects of revolutionary change.

Mao made no mystery at all of the form of the state which was to represent these four classes. Replying to imaginary critics who complained that the Communists were 'autocrats', he declared:

My dear sirs, you are right, that is just what we are. All the experience the Chinese people have accumulated through several decades teaches us to enforce the people's democratic dictatorship – which one could also call people's democratic autocracy (*tu-ts'ai*), the two terms mean the same thing – that is, to deprive the reactionaries of the right to speak and let the people alone have that right...

Don't you want to abolish state power? Yes, we do, but not right now; we cannot do it yet. Why? Because imperialism still exists, because domestic reaction still exists, because classes still exist in our country. Our present task is to strengthen the people's state apparatus – mainly the people's army, the people's police, and the people's courts – in order to consolidate the national defence and protect the people's interests. Given this condition, China can develop steadily, under the leadership of the working class and the Communist Party, from an agricultural into an industrial country, and from a new-democratic into a socialist and communist society, abolish classes and realize the Great Harmony [*ta-t'ung*].

In this task of guiding the development of China 'from an agricultural into an industrial country', Mao said that 'the education of the peasantry' was 'the serious problem'. For, he added: 'The peasant economy is scattered, and the socialization of agriculture, judging by the Soviet Union's experience, will require a long time and painstaking work.'[167]

These brief quotations evoke several crucial dimensions of the problem of carrying out a Marxist revolution in China after 1949. On the one hand, Mao's theory of the 'people's democratic dictatorship' was the lineal descendant of Lenin's 'revolutionary-democratic dictatorship of the workers and peasants', and of Stalin's 'four-class bloc', and Mao himself freely acknowledged this ideological debt, and went out of his way to stress the relevance of Soviet experience. Indeed, however unorthodox his road to power, as soon as victory was plainly within his grasp Mao had announced his intention of doing things henceforth in the orthodox way. 'From 1927 to the present,' he declared in March 1949, 'the centre of gravity of our work has been in the villages – gathering strength in the village in order to surround the cities, and then taking the cities. The period for this method of work has now ended. The period of "from the city to the villages" and of the city leading the village has now begun. The centre of gravity of the party's work has shifted from the village to the city.'[168] Hence Mao's statement: 'the serious problem is the education of the peasantry', in other words, the bringing of modern knowledge, and the resources of the modern industrial sector, from the cities to the countryside. Hence the stress, in 1949, on working-class leadership of the

---

[167] Mao, *SW* 4.418–19.   [168] Mao, *SW* 4.363.

'people's dictatorship'. Hence the attempt, which was to be made in the early 1950s, to draw large numbers of real flesh-and-blood workers into the Chinese Communist Party, in order to 'improve' its class composition.

And yet, despite all this, and despite Mao's explicit statement, in 1962, that during these early years there had been no alternative to 'copying from the Soviets',[169] his article of 30 June 1949 itself contained, in the passage quoted above, elements that point in a significantly different direction. Thus the traditional term 'autocracy' (*tu-ts'ai*) was used as a synonym for dictatorship (*chuan-cheng*), *ta-t'ung* or 'Great Harmony' was used as an equivalent for communism, and the unique character of China's revolutionary experience was repeatedly underscored.

The question of whether or not the Chinese revolution after 1949 followed a course which could be characterized as 'orthodox' in Marxist terms, and of when, how, and why it diverged from the Soviet model is not a proper topic for discussion here, since it will be taken up in Part 2 of this volume. What does seem appropriate, in summing up the record of Mao's development as a theorist of revolution during the period ending in 1949, is to consider which of the trends that were to emerge during the first three decades of the People's Republic were already implicit in his thinking prior to the conquest of power, if people had only had the wit to read the signs of the times.

One domain where, in my opinion, this is not the case is that of the political economy of development. There are, of course, those who argue that 'Maoist economics' was born in Yenan, if not before. While it is certainly true that there are significant hints of Mao's future economic thinking to be found in the experience of the Yenan base areas (as summed up in *On economic and financial problems*), these beginnings were too one-sided to justify the conclusion that the ideas of the Great Leap Forward of 1958 were in any sense implicit in them. They involved only peasant self-help and not the complex multi-faceted organization which characterized the communes; only a stress on indigenous methods, and not large-scale inputs or modern technology. In a word, there was no 'walking on two legs' combining the large and the small, the modern and the traditional in Yenan, and no idea of 'walking on two legs' in Mao's writings of the period. As already noted, Mao proposed in 1949 to transform China 'from an agricultural into an industrial country' through a process of modernization and economic development. And the rural population, though it would participate actively in this process, was to have no say as to the ultimate destination: it would have to accept 're-education', and the resulting change in its mentality and way of life.

[169] Schram, *Mao unrehearsed*, 178 (speech of 30 January 1962).

Thus, if one can distinguish a certain existential continuity between the self-sufficient economy of Yenan and the new policies adopted under the slogan of self-reliance (*tzu-li keng-sheng*) a decade and a half later, there was no intellectual continuity in terms of detailed policy formulations, and certainly no unbroken chain of development in Mao's own thinking, since he explicitly repudiated in 1949 many of the rudimentary ideas he had put forward in the early 1940s. There was, to be sure, as already noted, substantial continuity in the philosophical core of Mao Tse-tung's thought, from 1937 to the early 1960s at least. But if Mao's theory of contradictions was ultimately incompatible with the logic of the Soviet model of economic development, Mao himself did not discover this until the period of the Great Leap.

The one domain in which there was almost total continuity in Mao's approach from the 1930s to the 1970s was that of patterns and methods for the exercise of political authority. Moreover, in this case it should have been possible, I would argue, to discern in Mao's speeches and writings prior to 1949 the signs of many things to come.

Mao declared that the new regime he was about to set up could be called a 'people's democratic autocracy' just as well as a 'people's democratic dictatorship'. Too much should not be made of this terminological difference, for *tu-ts'ai* was sometimes used in years past, when Marxist expressions did not yet all have standard equivalents in Chinese, as a translation for 'dictatorship'. None the less, to the extent that it carries an aura of old-fashioned Chinese-style autocracy, this term in fact sums up rather well the essence of Mao's approach to political leadership.

On the one hand, he promoted grass-roots participatory democracy on a larger scale than any other revolutionary leader of modern times. In this respect he served the Chinese people well, and helped to prepare them for the next stage in their political development. But at the same time he regarded the promotion of democracy as feasible only within the framework of a 'strong state'. In this he was, in my opinion, correct. Unfortunately, his idea of a strong state was something very like an autocracy, in which he, as the historic leader of the Chinese revolution, remained in the last analysis the arbiter as to what political tendencies were legitimate, and which were not.

As stressed above in the third section, Mao sought to promote, in the period from 1939 onwards, a 'new democratic' revolution in China which would be a kind of functional equivalent of the capitalist stage in the development of European society. On the one hand, this meant, of course, modernization and industrialization, in order to create the economic foundation on which socialism could ultimately be established. But he was also bent on completing the work of China's abortive capitalist stage in another sense, by continuing the attack on the old Confucian values launched at the time of the May Fourth movement. Indeed, he actually wrote, in August 1944, in a letter calling for emancipation from the old family system: 'There are those who say we neglect or repress individuality [*ko-hsing*]; this is wrong. If the individuality which has been fettered is not liberated, there will be no democracy, and no socialism'.[170] One must none the less ask whether this goal was compatible with Mao's outlook as a whole.

Behind this, and the other questions I have just posed, lurk the fundamental issues raised by the process of cross-cultural borrowing which has been under way in China since the beginning of this century, and has still not led to any clear-cut result. The violent rejection of traditional Chinese values in favour of ideas of Western origin which had characterized, on the whole, the May Fourth period, had been succeeded in the 1930s, in the context of the Anti-Japanese War, by a reaffirmation of the dignity of Chinese culture. In the case of Chiang Kai-shek and the Kuomintang, this swing of the pendulum had led virtually to the negation of the whole May Fourth spirit, and the assertion that Confucianism provided the answer to all the world's problems. Mao Tse-tung, as an adherent of that most radical of Westernizing philosophies, Marxism-Leninism, could not go to such an extreme, but there is none the less a certain parallelism between the trends in Kuomintang ideology which led to the writing of *China's destiny*, and Mao's call for 'sinification'.

In the late 1940s, as nationwide victory approached, Mao Tse-tung began to emphasize more strongly, as noted above, explicitly Marxist concerns such as the need for leadership by the cities and by the working class, and the central role of industrialization in transforming both Chinese society and Chinese culture. But could 'feudal' culture truly be abolished, and could a party truly undergo reform and acquire a more democratic work style, under the guidance of an 'autocrat', albeit a benevolent one? Could a 'people's democratic autocracy', such as Mao Tse-tung set up in 1949, truly carry out modernization, if this included by implication profound changes in the traditional political culture? Or would the form of such a regime ultimately vitiate or distort the content? That is the question which can be clearly seen to hang over Mao's political creed, at his moment of triumph in 1949.

---

[170] 'Chih Ch'in Pang-hsien' (To Ch'in Pang-hsien), 31 August 1944, *Selected letters*, 239.

PART 2

MAO TSE-TUNG'S THOUGHT
FROM 1949 TO 1976

Like Lenin, Mao Tse-tung, on coming to power, continued to develop his ideas in a context different from that within which he had operated while in opposition. In so doing, he modified, adapted and elaborated positions which he had adopted earlier. In many respects there was substantial continuity, but there were also startling ruptures and reversals and, in addition, Mao struck out in new directions which he had never previously had the occasion to explore.

One important constant in the development of Mao Tse-tung's thought was his concern to adapt Marxism, or Marxism-Leninism, to the economic and social reality of a backward agrarian country, and to the heritage of the Chinese past, which for Mao was no less real. Prior to the conquest of power, the first aspect of this project involved devising theoretical justifications for attributing to the peasantry a political role greater than that implied by the model of the October Revolution, and more specifically for the strategy of surrounding the cities from the countryside. In this respect, it might have been assumed, and probably was assumed by Mao himself in 1949, that Chinese practice, and Chinese theory, would move closer to that of the Soviet Union. Having taken power in the cities as well as in the countryside, the Chinese Communist Party was effectively in a position to develop modern industry, and thus to create its own supposed class basis as the 'vanguard of the proletariat', and to open a road to convergence with more advanced countries under Communist rule.

During the first few years of the People's Republic, such a trend appeared to be emerging, but it was rapidly reversed, and a decade after 1949 China and the Soviet Union were moving farther apart than they had ever been before. These events have been chronicled in Volume 14 of *The Cambridge History of China*, and in many other works. What interests us here is, of course, the role played by Mao Tse-tung and his ideas in these changes of direction. I shall argue that the explanation lies partly in the continuing weight of the peasantry in Chinese society, and the influence of ideas current among the peasantry on Mao himself. But that is by no means the whole answer. The influence of the Yenan matrix, both in terms of an ethos of struggle and sacrifice, and in terms of decentralized and self-reliant methods of economic work, must also be taken into account. Yet another factor manifestly important, but difficult to assess, is Mao's goal, already mentioned, of adapting Marxism to China. Although the term he had put forward in 1938 to evoke this process, 'the sinification of Marxism', had gone out of use by the early 1950s, largely because Stalin resented the suggestion that there might be other theoretical authorities in the world Communist movement apart from himself, the impulse it expressed remained very much part of Mao's thinking.

Mao's conviction that Chinese culture was a great, perhaps a unique, historical achievement strengthened his sentiments of national pride. On the other hand, his explicit aim was to enrich Marxism with ideas and values drawn from the national past, and thereby render it more potent as an agent of revolutionary transformation, and ultimately of Westernization, not to replace it with some kind of neo-traditionalism in Marxist dress. None the less, it became increasingly hard, especially in his later years, to determine whether the basic structure of 'Mao Tse-tung Thought' was Chinese or Western.[1]

This is particularly the case of his theory of contradictions, though it can legitimately be asked whether Mao, during his last decade and a half, was as interested in such intellectual issues as he had been in the past, or whether he was above all preoccupied with achieving his own goals, which he regarded as by definition revolutionary. Another ambiguous element in Mao's thought is the stress on the role of subjective forces, 'conscious activity', and the superstructure which runs through the whole of his career from beginning to end. To the extent that this reflects a Promethean impulse, which was not prominent in pre-modern Chinese culture, or in other non-European civilizations, it cannot be seen as a traditionalistic element in Mao's thought. On the other hand, to the extent that the display of virtue by the ruler came to be seen as the chief guarantee of happiness, and the emulation of virtue became a key instrument of social control, the parallels with imperial China are obvious.

In Mao's final years, he was, of course, explicitly likened to the first Ch'in emperor, presented as a great revolutionary precursor, and a master in the use of revolutionary violence. And yet, at the very same time, the idea of mass participation, and of relying on the masses, which was a real (though often misunderstood) element in the Yenan heritage, was also trumpeted more loudly than ever.

---

[1] For a discussion of the complex and ambiguous relation between 'traditional' and 'modern' elements in Mao's thought and behaviour, see my article, 'Party leader or true ruler?' in Schram, ed. *Foundations of state power.*

Proletarian party and peasant constituency, the logic of modernization and the ethos of revolutionary war, Marxism and the Chinese tradition, determinism and voluntarism, salvation through virtue and salvation through technology, autocracy and mass democracy – these are some of the contradictions with which Mao wrestled during the years from 1949 to 1976.

In discussing the complex record of his efforts to deal with these and other issues, I shall adopt an approach partly thematic and partly chronological. In many important respects, the second half of 1957 constituted a great climacteric in Mao's life, marked by changes in outlook and personality which were to cast their shadow over the whole of his last nineteen years. The account of many aspects of Mao Tse-tung's thought will therefore be divided into two halves, before and after 1957. This pattern will not, however, be applied rigidly, especially as some key ideas of Mao's later years did not even emerge until well after 1957.

FROM PEOPLE'S DEMOCRACY TO CONTRADICTIONS AMONG THE PEOPLE

Patterns of rule

This first theme is one for which, precisely, 1957 does not appear to have seen a decisive change in Mao's thinking, but where there was a very great element of continuity from the Ching-kang-shan and Yenan to the early 1960s. Throughout this period, his thought was strongly marked by an insistence on the need for firm leadership by a political elite.

This trait is, in fact, an integral part of the 'mass line' itself, so often romanticized, or sentimentalized, during the Cultural Revolution to signify a project for allowing the people to liberate themselves and to run things in their own spontaneous way. In fact, while Mao Tse-tung saw the process of government as in part an educative process, he had no Spockian notions to the effect that the 'students' should be entirely free to decide what they should learn. On the contrary, the 'mass line', correctly understood, must be seen not as the negation or polar opposite of Lenin's conception of 'democratic centralism', but as a complementary idea, emphasizing a particular dimension of the relation between leaders and led.

At the same time, it must be recognized that the concept of the 'mass line' does evoke a real and significant aspect of the theory and leadership methods of the Chinese Communist Party, rooted in that party's experience. The emphasis on close links with the masses emerged during the Kiangsi period, for the obvious reason that without such links the fragile bases could not possibly have survived.[2] The term 'mass line' was not first used by Mao Tse-tung, and has been credited to other leaders such as Chou En-lai.[3] These ideas were, however, at the centre of Mao's own thinking, as expressed in particular in the Ku-t'ien Resolution of December 1929, and it was Mao who gave the concept its definitive formulation.

His classic definition, put forward in Yenan in 1943 at a time when so many aspects of the experience of the Chinese Communist Party were being drawn together and systematically formulated for the first time, reads in part as follows:

all correct leadership is necessarily from the masses, to the masses. This means: take the ideas of the masses (scattered and unsystematic ideas) and concentrate them (through study turn them into concentrated and systematic ideas), then go to the masses and propagate and explain these ideas *until the masses embrace them as their own*, hold fast to them and translate them into action.[4]

As the italicized words make plain, the people, though taken into the confidence of the leaders of the revolutionary movement, were in the end to be made to embrace, and to interiorize, ideas which, if left to themselves, they were quite incapable of elaborating in systematic form. As I argued in Part 1, there is an obvious parallel here with Lenin's thinking, and it is therefore not surprising that, at about the same as he put forward this formulation of the 'mass line', Mao should have reaffirmed in its full Leninist rigour the principle of centralized guidance by a revolutionary elite. 'Some comrades', he complained in his speech of 1 February 1942,

do not understand the party's system of democratic centralism; they do not know that the Communist Party not only needs democracy, but needs centralization even more. They forget the system of democratic centralism, in which the minority is subordinate to the majority, the lower level to the higher level, the part to the whole and the entire membership to the Central Committee . . .[5]

The polarity between firm leadership from above, and willing (if not entirely spontaneous) participation from below, is a crucial problem in the theory and practice of Leninism. The contradictions inherent in any such conception of democracy under guidance are acute, and in his efforts to resolve them, Mao Tse-tung shifted the balance now one way, now the other, from the 1940s to the 1960s. Consistently, however, at least until the Cultural Revolution, he underscored the primacy of centralism over democracy.

---

[2] See above, pp.44-8 and 86-7.
[3] See, for example, Ting Wei-chih and Shih Chung-ch'üan, 'Ch'ün-chung lu-hsien shih wo-men tang ti li-shih ching-yen ti tsung-chieh' (The mass line is the summation of the historical experience of our party), *Wen-hsien ho yen-chiu*. 1983 hui-pien pen (*Documents and research.* Collected volume for 1983), 420-8, esp. 421-2.   [4] Mao, *SW* 3.119. (Italics added.)   [5] Mao, *SW* 3.43-4.

And yet, while Mao was in no sense a partisan of what Lenin stigmatized as 'tailism' (more accurately translated 'backsideism'), that is, of following the rank and file rather than leading them, he was prepared, to a greater degree than Lenin, not to mention Stalin, to listen to the people and take account of their views. Such was the case, at least, until the 1960s. Another dimension of the problem of the 'mass line' must also be noted, however. At issue was not merely the relation between the leaders and the led, but the nature, and in particular the social composition, of the party's members and supporters.

A Communist Party was, for Lenin as for Marx, the party of the proletariat, even though Lenin expanded the social basis of the movement to make a somewhat larger place for the peasants. Mao, however, while continuing to talk about proletarian hegemony, had recruited, from 1927 onwards, among a much wider range of social categories: rural vagabonds or *éléments déclassés* (*yu-min*), shopkeepers, office workers, minor civil servants, and intellectuals of all descriptions, as well as 'national capitalists', 'patriotic gentry' and others. Most of these categories were relatively low on the scale of social privilege, and in this sense belonged to the 'people' rather than the 'elite'. All the same, whereas 'masses' (or 'toiling masses') was in the Soviet context essentially a synonym for the workers plus reliable elements among the peasantry, used instead of more precise class labels to stress the inchoate character of the followers, and therefore their need for leadership, for Mao it signified rather the overwhelming majority of the Chinese people who could, in the end, be made to rally to the revolution.[6]

The precise role of the various classes in Mao's pattern of socialist development will be considered in subsequent sections. The simple fact of the heterogeneity of the 'masses' with which he had to deal carries, however, certain implications about the nature and function of leadership in the political order he sought to create.

As noted in Part 1, Mao Tse-tung had envisaged, in 1944–5, the possibility of a 'coalition government' with the Kuomintang as a tactical expedient appropriate to the circumstances at that time. In 1949, on the other hand, speaking with the uninhibited frankness which the imminent possession of total power allowed him to exercise, Mao spelled out, in an article of 30 June, the quite different relations between political and social forces which would prevail under the 'people's democratic dictatorship' that he proposed to establish.

The term 'people's democracy' had, in fact, been introduced by Mao as

---

[6] For a discussion of these issues from a somewhat different methodological perspective, see Tang Tsou, 'Marxism, the Leninist party, the masses, and the citizens in the rebuilding of the Chinese state', in Schram, *Foundations of state power*, 257–89.

early as May 1939, in his speech on the 20th anniversary of the May Fourth movement. 'The present stage', he said then, 'is not socialism, but destroying imperialism and the feudal forces, transforming this [present] semi-colonial and semi-feudal position, and establishing a people's democratic system (*jen-min min-chu chu-i ti chih-tu*).'[7] Now, in 1949, characterizing the new people's democratic regime, Mao alluded to a distinction he had employed in *On new democracy* between the 'state system' (*kuo-t'i*) and the 'system of government' (*cheng-t'i*).[8] Not surprisingly, since they viewed the matter in a Marxist framework, Mao and other writers in the early years of the Chinese People's Republic defined the 'state system' primarily in class terms. Thus, one reference work for political study by basic-level cadres, first published in 1952, said in part:

The state system is the class essence of the state. The question of the state system is the question of the place of the various social classes in the state, i.e., it is the question of which class controls the political power of the state. For the most part, the state system of the various countries of the world at the present time can be divided into three types: (1) the capitalist state system, marked by the dictatorship of the reactionary bourgeoisie; (2) the socialist state system, marked by the dictatorship of the working class; and (3) the new-democratic state system, marked by the joint dictatorship of the various revolutionary classes, led by the working class and with the worker-peasant alliance as the foundation.[9]

This had been the classification laid down by Mao in 1939–40. The state established in 1949 was called a people's dictatorship, rather than a proletarian dictatorship, because it was seen as a hybrid form adapted to the circumstances prevailing during the 'period of transition' from postwar reconstruction to the building of socialism. While it was an axiom of Marxism that power, in a society where capitalism had begun to develop, could be exercised only by the proletariat or by the bourgeoisie, and not by any intermediate class or combination of classes, Lenin had put forward, in 1905, the formula of the 'revolutionary-democratic dictatorship of the workers and the peasants' to characterize the political system under which certain reforms could be carried out in Russia prior to the establishment of a full-blooded proletarian dictatorship. Mao's 'People's Democratic Dictatorship' was a lineal descendant of this Leninist concept, which had been applied to China and other Asian countries by the Comintern in the 1920s and 1930s.[10]

In 1949, Mao defined the locus of sovereignty in such a state in terms of

---

[7] *MTTC* 6.328. Apart from variations resulting from changes in the Chinese text, the translation in Mao, *SW* 2, 243 is so imprecise that 'people's democratic system' becomes simply 'people's democracy'.   [8] Mao, *SW* 2.351–2.

[9] Ch'en Pei-ou, *Jen-min hsüeh-hsi tzu-tien* (People's study dictionary), 288–9.

[10] Mao, *SW* 4.417–22. On Mao's evolving ideas regarding the role of various classes in the Chinese revolution and the hegemony of the proletariat, see above, pp. 38–42, 48–52 and 75–82.

concentric circles, or of an atom or onion metaphor. The hard or heavy centre was made up of the working class, which was to exercise hegemony through the party presumed to represent it. Next closest to the centre were the peasants, said to constitute the most reliable allies of the proletariat. Then came the petty bourgeoisie, who were to be largely followers. As for the national bourgeoisie, they had a dual nature; they were patriotic, but they were also exploiters. They therefore dwelt on the outer fringes of the 'people', perpetually in danger of flying off into the camp of the 'non-people' hostile to the revolution.

These four classes (corresponding, of course, to Stalin's 'four-class bloc' of the 1920s) were to exercise the 'people's democratic dictatorship'. Since the 'state system' was thus made to include not only the class nature of the state but also the mode of rule (dictatorship), what realm of meaning was left to be covered by 'system of government'? Most definitions of the *cheng-t'i* of the Chinese People's Republic in its earliest years[11] refer back to Mao's formulation in *On new democracy*, where he wrote in part:

As for the question of the 'system of government',[12] this is a matter of how political power is organized, the form in which one social class or another chooses to arrange its apparatus of political power to oppose its enemies and protect itself. . . . China may now adopt a system of people's congresses, from the national people's congress down to the provincial, county, district and township people's congresses, with all levels electing thir respective governmental bodies. But if there is to be a proper representation for each revolutionary class according to its status in the state, a proper expression of the people's will . . . then a system of really universal and equal suffrage, irrespective of sex, creed, property or education, must be introduced. Such is the system of democratic centralism. . . .

The state system, a joint dictatorship of all the revolutionary classes and the system of government, democratic centralism – these constitute the politics of New Democracy. . . .[13]

This passage was, of course, written in 1940, when Mao was still operating within the context of the United Front with the Kuomintang and the position of the Chinese Communist Party was relatively weak. By 1949, his idea of a 'Republic of New Democracy' stressed rather the need for dictatorship over the 'reactionary' classes than direct elections based on universal suffrage as the key to genuine democracy. The affirmation of 'democratic centralism' as the basic organizational principle of the new state remained, on the other hand, intact.

But while he showed his debt to the Soviet example by maintaining key

---

[11] See, for example, *Jen-min ta hsien-chang hsueh-hsi shou-ts'e* (Handbook for the study of the people's Constitution), 135; *Jen-min ta hsien-chang hsueh-hsi tzu-liao* (Materials for the study of the people's Constitution), 31.

[12] In the original version, this reads 'political power' (*cheng-ch'üan*), rather than 'system of government' (*cheng-t'i*), but the latter term is used in the first sentence of the ensuing paragraph, so the overall sense of the passage is not substantially affected. (See *MTTC* 7.165–6.)   [13] Mao, *SW* 2.352.

Leninist slogans such as democratic centralism, Mao also used, in his article of 30 June 1949, terms and concepts of Chinese origin. Thus he deliberately asserted, in a passage quoted in Part 1, that the old-fashioned word '*tu-ts'ai*' or autocracy meant the same thing as dictatorship (*chuan-cheng*). To be sure, this compound had occasionally been employed as a translation for 'dictatorship' in the early period, when Marxist expressions did not all have standard equivalents in Chinese. Mao cannot, however, have been unaware of the traditional overtones *tu-ts'ai* would have for his readers, any more than he was unaware of the connotations of the ancient term of *ta-t'ung*, or 'Great Harmony', which had been refurbished half a century earlier by K'ang Yu-wei, and which he employed as a synonym for 'communism'.

In 1953, when a committee headed by Mao was engaged in drafting a Constitution for the People's Republic of China, an eight-line rhyme was coined to sum up the criteria for the proper functioning of the political system:

> Great power is monopolized,
> Small power is dispersed.
> The party committee takes decisions,
> All quarters carry them out.
> Implementation also involves decisions,
> But they must not depart from principles.
> Checking on the work
> Is the responsibility of the Party Committee.[14]

In other words, there should be participation, by the citizens and by lower-level cadres, but it must be kept firmly under centralized control.

Mao's speech of 25 April 1956 to the Politburo, entitled 'On the ten great relationships', is unquestionably one of his half-dozen most important utterances after 1949, and one of the two or three most authoritative statements of his administrative philosophy. This remains the case, in my view, even if the economic ideas Mao expounded on this occasion were in large part derived, as noted below, from reports by the planners.

Section v, on the relationship between the Centre and the localities, must be interpreted in the context of the speech as a whole, which tended above all to argue that the one-sided and doctrinaire pursuit of any policy goal was self-defeating. Thus, if you really wanted to develop heavy industry, you must not neglect light industry and agriculture, and in order to build up new industrial centres in the hinterland it was necessary to make proper use of the existing industry in the coastal areas. Reasoning in similarly dialectic fashion, Mao said, on the question which concerns us here:

---

[14] 'Sixty articles on work methods', *Wan-sui* (supplement), 34. (My translation; see also the version in Jerome Ch'en, *Mao papers*, 68.)

The relationship between the Centre and the localities is also . . . a contradiction. In order to resolve this contradiction, what we now need to consider is how to arouse the enthusiasm of the localities by allowing them to run more projects under the unified plan of the Centre.

As things look now, I think that we need a further extension of local power. At present it is too limited, and this is not favourable to building socialism.[15]

In the last analysis, Mao continued to attach supreme importance to the cohesion and efficiency of the state as a whole, and he valued decentralization and grass-roots initiative within the limits thus set. Summing up his discussion in Section v of 'On the ten great relationships', he declared:

There must be proper enthusiasm and proper independence. . . . Naturally we must at the same time tell the comrades at the lower levels that they should not act wildly, that they must exercise caution. Where they can conform, they ought to conform . . . Where they cannot conform . . . then conformity should not be sought at all costs. Two enthusiasms are much better than just one . . . In short, the localities should have an appropriate degree of power. This would be beneficial to the building of a strong socialist state.[16]

The emphasis on centralism is even stronger in the official version than in the unofficial text from which I have been quoting. The new text adds, at this point: 'In order to build a powerful socialist state, we must have strong and united leadership by the Centre, we must have unified planning and discipline throughout the whole country; disruption of this necessary unity is impermissible.'[17]

Although these differences of emphasis were clearly evident at the time when the official version of 'On the ten great relationships' was published three months after Mao's death, it was impossible at that time to assess their significance for lack of information about the sources, and the course of editorial work on this key text. Indeed, some observers regarded the new passages added at that time as forgeries. Information subsequently published enables us to clarify these issues.

This talk, while it dealt at length with the problems of patterns of rule which concern us here, was in the first instance an attempt to define an overall strategy for economic development. For a month and a half, in February and March 1956, Mao Tse-tung had listened, in the company of some leading members of the party and of the government, to reports from a large number of economic departments. On 25 April 1956, he summed up his own understanding of the conclusions which flowed from these discussions at an enlarged session of the Politburo; on 2 May, he repeated

---

[15] This quotation is taken from the version of Mao's speech reproduced by the Red Guards in 1967–9, as translated in Schram, *Mao unrehearsed*, 71–2.   [16] *Mao unrehearsed*, 73.   [17] Mao, *SW* 5.294.

substantial portions of this talk, in revised form, before the Supreme State Conference. The official version is a marriage of the two.[18]

Despite his abiding emphasis on a strong centralized state, Mao's immediate concern in 1956 was with widening the scope of local authority, since he regarded the existing degree of centralization as self-defeating. In another talk at the same April 1956 Politburo meeting, he said: 'The relationship between the lower echelons and the higher echelons is like that of a mouse when it sees a cat. It is as if their souls have been eaten away, and there are many things they dare not say.'[19]

But how was effective centralization to be combined with an 'appropriate degree' of local power? This problem, in Mao's view, was inextricably linked to the issue of dual versus vertical control, which is explicitly raised in Section v of 'On the ten great relationships':

At present dozens of hands are meddling in local affairs, making them difficult to manage ... Since the ministries don't think it proper to issue orders to the party committees and people's councils at the provincial level, they establish direct contact with the relevant departments and bureaux in the provinces and municipalities and give them orders every day. These orders are all supposed to come from the central authorities, even though neither the Central Committee of the party nor the State Council knows anything about them, and they put a great strain on the local authorities. . . . This state of affairs must be changed.

. . . We hope that the ministries and departments under the central authorities will . . . first confer with the localities on all matters concerning them and issue no order without full consultation.

18 The 25 April version was disseminated only to upper-level party cadres at the time; in December 1965, 'On the ten great relationships' was circulated down to the *hsien* and equivalent levels, but this text, while dated 25 April, was in fact an edited version of the 2 May 1956 talk. The latter, since it was delivered before a non-party audience, was understandably less explicit and forceful in dealing with various issues such as relations with the Soviets. (On one point, the proclamation of the 'Hundred Flowers' slogan, Mao had in fact gone well beyond his April position on 2 May, but that passage, to which I shall return below, was not included in the December 1965 text.) It was such a truncated version of Mao's 2 May talk which the Red Guards reproduced under the title 'On the ten great relationships' and which was translated in the West in the 1970s. Only in July 1975 were the two speeches combined, at the suggestion of Teng Hsiao-p'ing, into what was to become the official version. The editorial work was done by Hu Ch'iao-mu, under Teng's authority. Approved by Mao at the time for inner-party distribution, it was published only in December 1976. In the light of these facts, the title of the article I wrote immediately after its appearance (S. Schram, 'Chairman Hua edits Mao's literary heritage: "On the ten great relationships"', *CQ* 69, March 1977) now appears slightly ironic.

All the information in the above note is taken from *Kuan-yü chien-kuo i-lai tang ti jo-kan li-shih wen-t'i chüeh-i chu-shih pen (hsiu-ting)* (Annotated edition of the Resolution [of 27 June 1981] on some questions of party history since 1949. Revised); hereafter, 1981 Resolution, annotated edn). This volume, compiled by the 'Research Centre on Party Literature under the Central Committee' (Chung-kung chung-yang wen-hsien yen-chiu-shih), the organ responsible for the publication of all writings by Mao Tse-tung (as well as other leaders including Liu Shao-ch'i, Chou En-lai and Teng Hsiao-p'ing) is unquestionably authoritative. The openly published, revised edition of this work is slightly fuller than the original *nei-pu* version which appeared in 1983, and is therefore to be preferred. In the case of the 'Ten great relationships', the relevant passage is virtually identical.

19 *Wan-sui* (1969) 35; *Miscellany of Mao Tse-tung thought*, 30. Hereafter *Miscellany*.

The central departments fall into two categories. Those in the first category exercise leadership right down to the enterprises, but their administrative offices and enterprises in the localities are also subject to supervision by the local authorities. Those in the second have the task of laying down guiding principles and mapping out work plans, while the local authorities assume the responsibility for putting them into operation.[20]

The last paragraph of the quotation refers to the policy, adopted in 1956–7, of keeping only large-scale or important enterprises, especially in the field of heavy industry, under the direct control of the central ministries, and handing other industrial and commercial enterprises over to the lower levels. (See *CHOC* 14, 125–9, 181–4.) The complex pattern which resulted has been the subject of many studies. Two decades ago, Franz Schurmann drew a distinction which remains useful between what he called 'decentralization I', involving the transfer of decision-making power to the production units themselves, and 'decentralization II', signifying the transfer of power to some lower level of regional administration. He viewed Ch'en Yun as an advocate of the former view, which would have led China in the direction of a Yugoslav-type economy, and Mao Tse-tung and Liu Shao-ch'i as partisans of the second. He found, however, that Ch'en Yun's approach constituted a 'contradictory' combination of centralization, decentralization I, and decentralization II.[21]

Harry Harding, who uses a six-fold set of criteria for approaching the problem, likewise concludes that the policy (in fact drafted by Ch'en Yun) adopted by the third plenum in the autumn of 1957 was an 'eclectic' one, combining centralization and decentralization.[22] Such a contradictory or 'eclectic' approach was, in reality, characteristic of everyone in the leadership at the time; the differences were matters of emphasis. During the Great Leap Forward, Schurmann added, this policy of combining centralism and democracy in a 'unity of true opposites' consisted in 'centralization of general policy impulses and decentralization of specific policy impulses'.[23] Plainly, what he calls here 'general policy impulses' are in essence what Mao's 1953 jingle referred to as *ta-ch'üan* or 'great power'; 'specific policy impulses' (or the right to generate them) can be equated with *hsiao-ch'üan*, 'small power'.

On 31 January 1958, Mao revised the 'Sixty articles on work methods',

---

[20] This version is based primarily on the official Chinese text, as translated in *Selected works*, 5.293, but the translation has been modified in places, sometimes making use of the phrasing employed in *Mao unrehearsed*, 72.

[21] Franz Schurmann, *Ideology and organization in Communist China*, 175–6, 196–8.

[22] Harry Harding, *Organizing China. The problem of bureaucracy 1949–1976*, 107–15, 175–82. Both Schurmann and Harding rely to a great extent on secondary sources for Ch'en's views; Ch'en Yun's own words can now be read in N. Lardy and K. Lieberthal, eds., *Chen Yun's strategy for China's development.*   [23] Schurmann, *Ideology*, 86–7.

the directive constituting in effect the blueprint for the Great Leap Forward. In Article 28 of this directive, the 1953 jingle is first quoted, and then explained in the following terms:

'Great power is monopolized' [ta-ch'üan tu-lan] is a cliché which is customarily used to refer to the arbitrary decisions of an individual [ko-jen tu-tuan]. We borrow this phrase to indicate that the main powers should be concentrated in collective bodies such as the Central Committee and local party committees, we use it to oppose dispersionism. Can it possibly be argued that great power should be scattered? . . . When we say, 'All quarters carry them out', this does not mean that party members do so directly. It is rather that there must first be a phase in which party members enter into contact with those who are not party members in government organs, enterprises, cooperatives, people's organizations, and cultural and educational organs, discuss and study things with them, and revise those parts [of higher-level directives] which are inappropriate [to the particular conditions]; only then, after they have been approved by everybody, are they applied.[24]

This text, it will be seen, deals both with relations between levels, and with the coordinating role of the party. Mao's deliberate emphasis on the parallel between the current maxim ta-ch'üan tu-lan and the term tu-tuan, which normally refers, as he says, to the arbitrary or dictatorial decisions of an individual, shows once again that he did not shrink back from asserting the need for strong, centralized rule − or from implementing such ideas in practice.

How could such centralization be combined with the exercise of real and significant, though subordinate, 'small power' at lower levels? Primarily through the coordinating role of the party, to which the greater part of Mao's commentaries on the 1953 jingle are devoted. Although he did not here employ the term i-yuan-hua, meaning 'to integrate', 'to make monolithic', or 'to make monistic', which had figured so largely in his administrative philosophy during the Yenan period,[25] it is clear that the impulse expressed in this concept was at the centre of his thinking. In remarks of April 1956, he recalled that, in response to the emergence of excessive decentralization and local independence in the base areas of the Yenan period, the Central Committee had adopted a resolution on strengthening the 'party spirit' [tang-hsing, a translation of the Russian 'partiinost']. 'Integration [i-yuan-hua] was carried out', he continued, 'but a great deal of autonomy was preserved.'[26]

24 Wan-sui (supplement) 34–5. (My translation.)
25 For a more detailed discussion of the emergence and significance of this concept, see my article 'Decentralization in a unitary state: theory and practice 1940–1984', in S. Schram, ed. The scope of state power in China, 81–125, especially 87–9; also pp. 80–96 above.
26 Wan-sui (1969) 36; Miscellany, 31. The 'Resolution on strengthening the party spirit' adopted by the Politburo on 1 July 1941 (Compton, Mao's China, 156–60) did not in fact use the term i-yuan-hua, but referred to the importance of centralization, and of 'unified will, action and discipline'. Manifestly, Mao regarded this decision as the first step in a process of establishing integrated party control which found further expression in 1942 and 1943.

In comments of January 1958 on the 1953 jingle, Mao referred to the fact that the system of one-man management had been discredited. He included among the most basic organizational principles to be observed 'the unity of collective leadership and individual role', which he equated with 'the unity of the party committee and the first secretary'.[27] This can be taken as a reaffirmation of Mao's Yenan-style understanding of *i-yuan-hua* or integrated leadership, as opposed to Kao Kang's ideas on the subject. For Kao, *i-yuan-hua* had a sense very close to its literal meaning of 'to make monolithic'. A monolithic pattern of organization implied, in his view, that each entity such as a factory could be responsible to only one outside authority, which in practice meant the relevant ministry in Peking. The factory manager, as the agent or point of contact of this authority, must therefore have unchallenged authority within the factory. According to Mao's view, which was the prevailing view in the late 1950s, integration had to be carried out not merely at the national level, but in the localities. Otherwise, even 'small power' could not be dispersed without leading to confusion. And the agent of integration could only be the party committee at each level. Party control, whether at the Centre or in the localities, involved, as Mao made clear, first taking decisions on matters of principle, and then subsequently checking on their implementation.

Further discussion of the leading role of the party can best be deferred until we consider Mao's political and economic strategy at the time of the Great Leap Forward as a whole. Meanwhile, to round off this discussion of patterns of rule, it suffices to recall that in his speech of January 1962, after asserting that centralism and democracy must be combined 'both within the party and outside', and stressing once again, as he had in Yenan, that centralism was even more important than democracy, Mao went on to say that genuine centralization was possible only on a basis of democracy, for two main reasons. On the one hand, if people were not allowed to express themselves they would be 'angry' and frustrated, and therefore would not participate willingly and effectively in political and economic work. And, on the other hand:

If there is no democracy, if ideas are not coming from the masses, it is impossible to establish a good line . . . Our leading organs merely play the role of a processing plant in the establishment of a good line and good . . . policies and methods. Everyone knows that if a factory has no raw material, it cannot do any processing . . . Without democracy, you have no understanding of what is happening down below; the general situation will be unclear; . . . and thus you will find it difficult to avoid being subjectivist; it will be impossible to achieve unity of understanding and unity of action, and impossible to achieve true centralism.[28]

---

[27] Talk of 11 January 1958 at the Nanning Conference, *Wan-sui* (1969) 148; *Miscellany*, 79–80. *Wan-sui* (supplement) 34–5.   [28] *Mao unrehearsed*, 163–4.

Here the term 'democratic centralism' is made to cover both the fundamental dilemma of combining effective 'centralized unification' with active support and initiative from below, and the problem of the upward and downward flow of ideas evoked by the slogan of the 'mass line'. Mao's overall view of this cluster of issues is clearly reflected in the metaphor of the 'processing plant'. To be sure, this plant is incapable of producing anything meaningful if it is not constantly fed with information and suggestions, but in the last analysis the correct line can only be elaborated by the brain at the centre. The deprecatory adverb 'merely' before 'processing plant' does not change the fact that this is where the decisive action takes place.

Such was, broadly speaking, Mao's view of democracy and centralism, from Yenan days to the early 1960s. At the same time, although an overarching consistency marked, as I said at the beginning of this section, his line on these matters, there was undeniably a certain change of emphasis in 1957–8. This shift was closely linked to Mao's increasing radicalism, both in economic matters and in the domain of class struggle, which will be discussed in the following sections. It had, however, a direct impact on the questions of the structure of power we are considering here.

I noted earlier that, although Mao did seek, within the limitations imposed by his ultimate attachment to the ideal of a 'strong socialist state', to foster the participation of the people in the country's affairs, the scope for political choice involved in such practices was slight. Above all, Mao gave little thought to the establishment of a political system democratic in its structure and mechanisms, and not merely in the sense that it was held to represent the 'people'.

That is, of course, one of the criticisms which has been made of him in China since 1978, to which I shall return in the Conclusion to this book. It is important to note, however, that from the time of the Great Leap, Mao Tse-tung attached even less importance to institutions than he had previously done. In a word, down to 1956 or 1957, while defining democracy in terms of the class character of the state rather than in terms of political mechanisms, he none the less treated the state structure as something which had to be taken into account.

For example, in his April 1956 discussion of centralization and decentralization, Mao declared:

According to our Constitution, the legislative powers are all vested in the central authorities. But, provided that the policies of the central authorities are not violated, the local authorities may work out rules, regulations and measures in the light of their specific conditions and the needs of their work, and this is in no way prohibited by the Constitution.[29]

---

[29] Mao, *SW* 5.294. This version is substantially identical in substance with the unofficial text (*Mao unrehearsed*, 72), except that the latter contains an explicit reference to the National People's Congress as the sole legislative body.

In his speech of 27 February 1957, 'On the correct handling of contradictions among the people', Mao emphasized that democracy was a means and not an end, and he poured scorn on Western ideas and practices such as parliamentary democracy and the two-party system.[30] China's own political system he treated whimsically and cavalierly, but he did at least take note of its existence. Discussing the problem of whether the not very numerous counter-revolutionaries still present in the country should be liberated in a big way (ta fang), even though under the Constitution they were supposed to be objects of the dictatorship, Mao quoted an imaginary critic as saying: 'This is laid down in the Constitution. You are the Chairman; aren't you supposed to observe the Constitution?' His very characteristic response to this dilemma was to suggest that most, thought not all, of these people should be released, but that one should certainly not announce such a policy publicly.[31]

By the time of the Great Leap Forward, Mao had come to set very little store indeed by such institutional niceties. But since this evolution in Mao Tse-tung's thought was a direct consequence of the radical climate engendered by the ongoing revolution in the economy and in society, let us turn to those dimensions of the matter, before examining Mao's approach to political power in his later years.

Patterns of development

In approaching Mao's ideas regarding patterns of socialist development, it is perhaps worth emphasizing by way of introduction that his attitude toward modernization and industrialization was consistently positive. There has been a tendency in recent years to treat Mao as a believer in some kind of pastoral utopia, a partisan of a 'steady-state' economy as an alternative to our so-called advanced industrial society. In reality, throughout the twenty-seven years during which he presided over the destinies of the People's Republic of China, Mao never ceased to call for rapid economic progress, and for progress defined in quantitative terms: tons of steel, tons of grain, and all the rest.

The very use of the term 'modernization' was often taken, in the recent past, as a manifestation of Western cultural arrogance, because it seemed to imply that, in joining the 'modern' world, the peoples of Asia and Africa would necessarily become like the Americans or the Europeans. In fact, Mao himself had no such scruples, and consistently defined China's economic aims in these terms, from the 1940s to the 1960s. Thus, for example,

[30] Mao, SW 5.398.
[31] This passage has been removed from the June 1957 edited text of Mao's speech (Mao, SW 5.398–9). See the text as delivered in Hsüeh-hsi wen-hsüan (Selected documents for study), 201–2. The content of Mao's February 1957 speech will be discussed in detail below.

in his report of April 1945 to the Seventh Party Congress, he said China's agriculture must be made to progress from its 'old-style, backward level' to a 'modernized (*chin-tai-hua ti*) level', in order to provide markets for industry, and 'make possible the transformation of an agricultural country into an industrial country'.[32]

Industry was, in Mao's view, of primary importance because of the role it played, or could play, in assuring the wealth and power of the Chinese state. Noting, in his article 'On the people's democratic dictatorship', that 'Imperialism, a most ferocious enemy, is still standing alongside us,' Mao added (in a comment removed from the *Selected works* text): 'A very long time must elapse before China can achieve genuine economic independence. Only when China's industry has been developed, so that economically China is no longer dependent on foreign countries, will she enjoy genuine independence.'[33]

I spoke in the introduction to Part 2 of the continuing weight of the peasantry in Chinese society, and of the influence of this fact, and of peasant ideology, on Mao Tse-tung himself. This factor undeniably existed, and was of crucial importance, but it manifested itself very much more strongly from 1955, and especially from 1958 onwards. On the eve of the conquest of power, in contrast, Mao repudiated, or in any case played down, the significance of the party's rural experience. 'From 1927 to the present,' he declared in March 1949,

the centre of gravity of our work has been in the villages – gathering strength in the villages, using the villages in order to surround the cities, and then taking the cities. The period for this method of work has now ended. The period of 'from the city to the village' and of the city leading the village has now begun. The centre of gravity of the party's work has shifted from the village to the city.[34]

In other words, hitherto we have been doing it the unorthodox way, because that is the only way in which we could win victory, but henceforth we will do it in the orthodox Marxist, or Leninist way, with guidance and enlightenment radiating outward from the urban industrial environment to the backward peasants in the countryside. Such a perspective was clearly in evidence in Mao's article of June 1949, 'On the people's democratic dictatorship', in which, after declaring that state power could not be abolished yet because imperialism and domestic reaction still existed, and that the present task, on the contrary, was to strengthen the people's state apparatus, he went on to say:

---

[32] *MTTC* 9.244. (The clause referring to agricultural modernization has been excised from the current official version of this speech in Mao, *SW* 3.297.)

[33] *MTTC* 10.304; see also Mao, *SW* 4.421, where the last two sentences quoted are missing.

[34] Mao, *SW* 4.363.

Given this condition, China can develop steadily, under the leadership of the working class and the Communist Party, from an agricultural into an industrial country, and from a new-democratic into a socialist and communist society, abolish classes and realize the Great Harmony [*ta-t'ung*].

In this task of guiding the development of China 'from an agricultural into an industrial country', it would be relatively easy, in Mao's view, to re-educate and re-mould the national bourgeoisie. 'The serious problem,' he declared, 'is the education of the peasantry.' For, he added, 'The peasant economy is scattered, and the socialization of agriculture, judging by the Soviet Union's experience, will require a long time and painstaking work.'[35]

Mao's stress on educating the peasants, and on working-class leadership of the 'people's dictatorship' which was to do the educating, appears to offer clear confirmation of the reversal of priorities between cities and countryside he had announced in March 1949.

Another intriguing indication to this effect may be found in Mao's decision of December 1951 to abandon a formulation, put forward the previous spring by Liu Shao-ch'i and used thereafter by the Central Committee, according to which the 'semi-working class" (*pan kung-jen chieh-chi*) in the countryside was, like the urban working class, one of the classes leading the revolution. Although Mao himself had earlier characterized the 'semi-proletariat (the poor peasants)' as a leading class in the new-democratic revolution, he now found it 'erroneous' to attribute leadership to any class save the urban workers. This plainly marked a shift toward greater orthodoxy.[36]

Moreover, in the early 1950s, these ideological trends were translated into action by an energetic attempt to draw large numbers of real flesh-and-blood workers into the Chinese Communist Party, in order to 'improve' its class composition.

And yet, despite Mao's statement, in 1962, that during these early years there had been no alternative to 'copying from the Soviets',[37] he did not, like the Soviets, confuse the industrial revolution with the socialist revolution. And though scientific and technical modernization was a central and crucial strand in Mao's conception of socialist development, one may legitimately ask whether his broader vision of the Chinese revolution, even as he entertained it in 1949, would ultimately prove compatible with such technical modernization.

At the outset, the economic policies explicitly formulated by Mao were prudent and gradualist ones. Thus, in June 1950, he called for 'maintaining

[35] Mao, *SW* 4.418–19.
[36] 'Chih Liu Shao-ch'i' (To Liu Shao-ch'i), 15 December 1951, *Selected letters*, 427–8.
[37] *Mao unrehearsed*, 178

the rich peasant economy in order to facilitate the early rehabilitation of rural production', and summed up the overall goals as follows:

existing industry and commerce should be properly readjusted, and relations between labour and capital should be effectively and suitably improved; thus under the leadership of the socialist state sector all sectors of the economy will function satisfactorily with a due division of labour to promote the rehabilitation and development of the whole economy. The view held by certain people that it is possible to eliminate capitalism and realize socialism at an early date is wrong, it does not tally with our national conditions.[38]

Even after the beginning of the first five-year plan, Mao's perspective on these matters remained essentially similar. In August 1953, he defined the 'general line' for the period of transition as 'basically to accomplish the country's industrialization and the socialist transformation of agriculture, handicrafts and capitalist industry and commerce over a fairly long period of time'.[39]

In September 1954, he declared:

The people of our country should work hard, do their best to draw on advanced experience in the Soviet Union and other fraternal countries, be honest and industrious, encourage and help each other, guard against boastfulness and arrogance, and gird themselves to build our country, which is at present economically and culturally backward, into a great industrialized country with a high standard of modern culture in the course of several five-year plans.[40]

In November 1954, Mao Tse-tung called the attention of Liu Shao-ch'i and Chou En-lai to what he described as an 'erroneous formulation' in the extracts from the Soviet textbook of political economy just published in *People's daily*: 'Until socialism has been edified completely or to a very large extent, it is impossible that there should be socialist economic laws.'[41] In repudiating this view, Mao was quite plainly concerned with the theoretical foundations for China's claim to be already in some degree socialist in nature.

Nevertheless, as late as March 1955, Mao recognized that the road to socialism would be a long one:

It is no easy job to build a socialist society in a large country such as ours with its complicated conditions and its formerly very backward economy. We may be able to build a socialist society over three five-year plans, but to build a strong, highly industrialized socialist country will require several decades of hard work, say fifty years, or the entire second half of the present century.[42]

Then, suddenly, in the middle of 1955 Mao's attitude changed, and he

---

[38] Mao, *SW* 5.29–30.   [39] *Ibid.* 102.   [40] *Ibid.* 148–9.
[41] 'Chih Liu Shao-ch'i, Chou En-lai teng' (To Liu Shao-ch'i, Chou En-lai and others), 18 November 1954, *Selected letters*, 484–5.   [42] Mao, *SW* 5.155.

launched a movement for more rapid cooperativization in the countryside which, almost overnight, transformed the whole atmosphere of Chinese society. Mao's new mood, as well as his new framework of analysis, are vividly evoked by his annotations to the volume *Socialist upsurge in China's countryside*, written at the end of 1955, when the acceleration of cooperativization for which he had called on 31 July was proceeding still faster than he himself had predicted.[43]

In these texts, we can see clearly foreshadowed certain basic themes of the Great Leap Forward, and even of the Cultural Revolution, such as Mao's belief in the omnipotence of the subjective efforts of the mobilized masses to transform themselves and their environment. For example, in a passage praising the Wang Kuo-fan cooperative, nicknamed 'The Paupers' Co-op', which had accumulated 'a large quantity of the means of production' in three years by their own efforts, Mao commented: 'In a few decades, why can't 600 million paupers, by their own efforts, create a socialist country, rich and strong?' Noting, in another passage, that tens of millions of peasant households had swung into action during the second half of 1955, thus completely transforming the atmosphere in China, Mao commented: 'It is as if a raging tidal wave has swept away all the demons and ghosts.'[44]

In this context of enthusiasm for the zeal and fighting spirit of the peasants, Mao wrote in December 1955:

If you compare our country with the Soviet Union: (1) we had twenty years' experience in the base areas, and were trained in three revolutionary wars; our experience [on coming to power] was exceedingly rich ... Therefore, we were able to set up a state very quickly, and complete the tasks of the revolution. (The Soviet Union was a newly established state; at the time of the October Revolution, they had neither army nor government apparatus, and there were very few party members.) (2) We enjoy the assistance of the Soviet Union and other democratic countries. (3) Our population is very numerous, and our position is excellent. [Our people] work industriously and bear much hardship, and there is no way out for the peasants without cooperativization. Chinese peasants are even better than English and American workers. Consequently, we can reach socialism more, better, and faster . . .[45]

Thus, Mao suggested as early as 1955 that because they came to power after twenty years' struggle in the countryside, instead of by suddenly seizing the reins of government in the capital city, the Chinese Communists knew more in 1949 than Lenin and his comrades had known in 1917 about exercising authority over the population at the grass roots, and securing their support. Moreover, the Chinese peasantry, in his view, provided splendid human material for building a socialist society.

---

[43] *Socialist upsurge in China's countryside, passim*; Mao's commentaries are also reproduced in *Selected works*, 5.235–76.   [44] *Socialist upsurge*, 5–6, 159–60.   [45] *Wan-sui* (1969) 27; *Miscellany*, 29.

And yet, it was by no means a one-sided 'rustic' revolution which Mao sought to promote at this time. Though a distinctive feature of his 31 July 1955 speech on cooperativization had been the demand that in China, collectivization should come before mechanization, it was not to come very *far* before it, and the provision of the necessary tractors, pumps, and other industrial products was therefore urgent. More broadly, Mao continued to subscribe to the view he had put forward in 1949, according to which 'the serious problem' was 'the education of the peasantry'. The implication plainly was that these rural dwellers would have to be brought into the modern world by causing them to assimilate knowledge, and especially technical knowledge, originating in the cities. And, in this process, scientists, technicians, and other intellectuals would have a key role to play. Indeed, Mao recognized this in January 1956 when he declared, in the context of his Twelve-Year Programme for Agricultural Development, that the Chinese people 'must have a far-reaching comprehensive plan of work in accordance with which they could strive to wipe out China's economic, scientific and cultural backwardness within a few decades and rapidly get abreast of the most advanced nations in the world'. And he added that 'to achieve this great goal, the decisive factor was to have cadres, to have an adequate number of excellent scientists and technicians'.[46]

Mao therefore called, in January 1956, for a conciliatory and understanding approach to the intellectuals inherited from the old society. At a conference on the problem of the intellectuals called by the Central Committee, Mao underscored the various respects in which China was industrially and technologically backward, and in a dependent position because she could not make key products for herself, and commented:

There are some comrades who say not very intelligent things, such as 'We can get along without them [i.e., the intellectuals]!' 'I'm a revolutionary (*lao-tzu shih ko-ming ti*)!' Such statements are wrong. Now we are calling for a technical revolution, a cultural revolution, a revolution to do away with stupidity and ignorance (*ko yü-ch'un wu-chih ti ming*), and we can't get along without them. We can't do it by relying only on uneducated people (*lao-ts'u*) like ourselves.[47]

Mao's overall approach to building socialism in the mid-1950s is most cogently summed up in his speech of 25 April 1956 to the Politburo, 'On the ten great relationships'. In every domain, the lesson of this well-known utterance was the same: understand the interconnectedness of things, and do not seek to maximize one while neglecting the effects on others. Thus, as we have already seen, he called in the political domain for an increase in the power and initiative of the localities, in order to contribute to the building

---

[46] Speech of 25 January 1956, *Jen-min jih-pao*, 26 January 1956; extracts translated in Carrère d'Encausse and Schram, 293.   [47] *Wan-sui* (1969) 34.

of a strong socialist state. In the economic field, he called for reducing (but not reversing, as is sometimes suggested) the overwhelming priority to heavy industry, at the expense of agriculture and light industry, which he held to be self-defeating. But at the same time (thus illustrating his balance and even-handedness at the time) he urged that proper attention should be given to developing further the existing industrial base in Shanghai and other coastal cities, rather than putting all the available resources into spreading industry throughout the hinterland.[48]

In drafting this speech Mao Tse-tung had, as noted earlier, taken careful account of the views of Ch'en Yun and other experts in economic work, and 'On the ten great relationships' as a whole undoubtedly represented an attempt on his part to lay down a compromise position which would command wide agreement within the party. The fact that Mao thus adopted a moderate and conciliatory attitude on specific issues by no means implied, however, that he was prepared in all respects to bow to the will of the majority of his leading comrades.

Already, in his manner of launching an accelerated collectivization drive in 1955, Mao Tse-tung had shown his disposition to ride roughshod over all opposition on a matter close to his own heart.[49] In mid-1956, he revealed a similar intolerance once again, in a more veiled, but ominous manner. In early 1956, Mao had been persuaded that, as a result of the success of the 'high tide' of socialism in the countryside, all economic work could be accelerated. When, in the face of the resulting contradictions and disequilibrium, the important editorial of 20 June 1956 on 'Opposing adventurism' was drafted under the supervision of Chou En-lai, Mao saw the text in advance, but did not express himself one way or the other. His colleagues were left with the impression that he had endorsed this statement, but in fact he had reservations about it. While acknowledging that it was undesirable to go *too* fast in economic development, he was persuaded that China could go very fast. For a year and a half, he harboured his resentment at this editorial in general, and at Chou En-lai in particular, before giving vent to his feelings on the eve of the Great Leap Forward.[50]

Meanwhile, in the spring and summer of 1956, Mao not only launched

[48] *Mao unrehearsed*, 61–83; official text in Mao, *SW* 5.284–307.

[49] See the discussion in *CHOC* 14. 110–17, 167–9, and also my analysis in 'Party leader or true ruler?', 214–16.

[50] For Mao's continuing optimism and impatience, see his speech at the second plenum of 15 November 1956, Mao, *SW* 5.332–5. The importance of Mao's psychological reaction to the criticism of 'adventurism' is widely stressed in recent Chinese accounts of this period. In a conversation of 24 April 1986, Kung Yü-chih characterized it as perhaps the first step on the road to the Cultural Revolution. For a summary of evidence regarding Mao's anger at this editorial published during the Cultural Revolution, see Roderick MacFarquhar, *The origins of the Cultural Revolution. 1. Contradictions among the people 1956–1957*, 86–91. Regarding Chou En-Lai's contribution to the writing of the article of 20 June 1956, see Hu Hua, *Chung-kuo she-hui-chu-i ko-ming ho chien-she shih chiang-i* (Textbook on the history of China's socialist revolution and construction), 146.

the slogan of a 'Hundred Flowers', but adopted a very soft approach toward problems of classes and class struggle, the relation between the Communist Party and other forces in society, and the relation between right and wrong. These issues were dealt with in more detail in his speech of 27 February 1957, 'On the correct handling of contradictions among the people', but Mao had frequently referred to them in earlier texts. Because of the importance which 'class struggle' was to assume from 1957 to 1976, this theme merits detailed discussion in a separate section.

People, classes and contradictions

The theoretical framework in which Mao considered these matters prior to February 1957 was essentially that laid down in 1937 in 'On contradiction'. In this article, Mao had argued that although contradiction 'permeates each and every process from beginning to end', and although all contradictions involved struggle, they were not necessarily antagonistic, and contradictions different in nature should be resolved by different methods. In the text of this essay as Mao originally wrote it, the realm of 'non-antagonistic contradictions' was defined very broadly, and the scope of class struggle thereby restricted:

For instance, the contradictions between correct and incorrect ideas in the Communist Party, between the advanced and the backward in culture, between town and country in economics, between the forces and relations of production, between production and consumption, between exchange value and use value, between the various technical divisions of labour, between workers and peasants in class relations, between life and death in nature, between heredity and mutation, between cold and hot, between day and night – none of these exist in antagonistic form (*tou mei-yu tui-k'ang hsing-t'ai ti ts'un-tsai*).[51]

In the revised version of 1952, which constituted, of course, the standard of ideological orthodoxy during the period we are considering here, Mao drew the lines much more carefully, explaining that 'as long as classes exist, contradictions between correct and incorrect ideas in the Communist Party are reflections within the party of class contradictions', and that such contradictions *could* become antagonistic 'if the comrades who had committed mistakes did not correct them'. He also noted that, while the contradiction between town and country was non-antagonistic in the base areas, or in a socialist country, it was 'extremely antagonistic' in capitalist society, and under the rule of the Kuomintang.[52]

These are important differences as far as the tone of the work is con-

---

[51] Knight, trans., 38. (Translation slightly modified on the basis of the Chinese text.)
[52] Mao, *SW* 1.344–5.

cerned, and reflected an emphasis on the need to wage class struggle which Mao Tse-tung was to exhibit in greater or lesser degree throughout the 1950s, but as regarded the attitude adopted toward the only two classes which (as we have seen from our earlier consideration of 'On the people's democratic dictatorship') constituted a serious problem for the new regime, the line laid down was not significantly altered in 1951. The contradiction between the proletariat and the bourgeoisie was still to be resolved 'by the method of socialist revolution'; and that between the workers and peasants in socialist society, which in 1937 was supposed to be resolved by 'the socialization of agriculture', now called for the method of 'collectivization and mechanization in agriculture', which was really a more concrete way of saying the same thing.[53]

In June 1950, Mao Tse-tung confirmed the basic moderation of his approach at that time in a speech to the third plenum entitled, in the *Selected works*, 'Don't hit out in all directions' – in other words, don't struggle with too many classes at the same time. Summing up the party's current attitude toward that ambiguous class, the national bourgeoisie, he declared:

The whole party should try earnestly and painstakingly to make a success of its united front work. We should rally the petty bourgeoisie under the leadership of the working class and on the basis of the worker-peasant alliance. The national bourgeoisie will eventually cease to exist, but at this stage we should rally them around us and not push them away. We should struggle against them on the one hand, and unite with them on the other.[54]

By June 1952, things had progressed to the point where, in Mao's view, the contradiction between the working class and the national bourgeoisie had become the 'principal contradiction' in China; hence it was no longer appropriate to define the national bourgeoisie as an 'intermediate class'.[55]

And yet, in September 1952 he wrote to Huang Yen-p'ei that it would be unreasonable, throughout the whole period of the first five-year plan (that is, until 1957), to expect more than a small fraction of the bourgeoisie to accept socialist ideas. They must accept working-class leadership, but to ask them to accept working-class thought, and not to be concerned with making money, was 'impossible, and should not be done'.[56]

In the summer of 1955, Mao Tse-tung gave renewed impetus to class struggle in the countryside, in particular by adopting the distinction between 'upper' and 'lower' middle peasants, and treating the line between these two categories as the fundamental cleavage in Chinese rural society. Summing up the situation in his concluding speech at the sixth plenum of

---

[53] Knight, trans., 20; Mao, *SW* 1.321–2.   [54] Mao, *SW* 5.35.   [55] *Ibid.* 77.
[56] 'Chih Huang Yen-p'ei' (To Huang Yen-p'ei), 5 September 1952, *Selected letters*, 441–3.

October 1955, which formally endorsed his rural policies, Mao repeated that the Communists had two alliances, one with the peasants and the other with the national bourgeoisie. Both of them were 'indispensable', but of the two, the alliance with the peasants was 'principal, basic and primary', while that with the bourgeoisie was 'temporary and secondary'. Stressing the interrelationship between these two alliances, he said:

At the third plenary session in 1950, I spoke against hitting out in all directions. The agrarian reform had not yet been carried out in vast areas of the country, nor had the peasants come over entirely to our side. If we had opened fire on the bourgeoisie then, it would have been out of order. After the agrarian reform, when the peasants had entirely come over to our side, it was possible and necessary for us to start the movements against the 'three evils' and the 'five evils' [i.e., the three antis and the five antis]. Agricultural cooperation will enable us to consolidate our alliance with the peasants on the basis of proletarian socialism and not of bourgeois democracy. That will isolate the bourgeoisie once and for all and facilitate the final elimination of capitalism. On this matter we are quite heartless! On this matter Marxism is indeed cruel and has little mercy, for it is determined to exterminate imperialism, feudalism, capitalism, and small production to boot.

During the fifteen-year period of the first three five-year plans (of which three years had already elapsed), 'the class struggle at home and abroad will be very tense', he noted.[57] In fact, the socialist transformation of agriculture and of capitalist industry and commerce, which Mao said in the speech just quoted would take about three five-year plans, was carried through on all fronts by the end of 1956. Already, by early 1956, sensing the favourable prospects and feeling himself in a position of strength, Mao Tse-tung took, as we have seen, a far softer and more conciliatory line on class struggle, and especially on the role of bourgeois intellectuals, and stressed the importance of scientists and technicians.

Another reflection of the same trend was the ending of the discrimination previously exercised against non-proletarian elements in recruiting new party members. As already noted, strenuous efforts had been made in the early years of the Chinese People's Republic to recruit more workers into the party, in order to improve its class composition. Then, in 1956, the more rigorous selection procedures formerly applied to non-workers were abolished in the new party Constitution, on the grounds that, as Teng Hsiao-p'ing put it in his report to the Eighth Congress, 'the former classification of social status has lost or is losing its meaning'. It is perhaps worth recalling the details of Teng's argument, for they provide the background against which Mao's views on class developed during the last two decades of his life:

[57] Mao, *SW* 5.213–15.

The difference between workers and office employees is now only a matter of division of labour within the same class . . . Poor and middle peasants have all become members of agricultural producers' cooperatives, and before long the distinction between them will become merely a thing of historical interest. . . . The vast majority of our intellectuals have now come over politically to the side of the working class, and a rapid change is taking place in their family background. . . . Every year large numbers of peasants and students become workers, large numbers of workers, peasants, and their sons and daughters join the ranks of the intellectuals and office workers, large numbers of peasants, students, workers and office workers join the army and become revolutionary soldiers. . . . What is the point, then, of classifying these social strata into two different categories?[58]

To the extent that Teng here attached more importance to subjective attitudes, and willingness to work for the revolution, than to family origins, his views are consonant with a continuing (though not a consistent) trend in Mao's thinking. But to the extent that he indicated class struggle within Chinese society was rapidly dying away, his ideas obviously go completely against the tide which was later to emerge, and to swamp the party. That does not, of course, mean that Mao Tse-tung disagreed with him at the time. Even during the first upsurge of the Cultural Revolution, in 1966, when K'ang Sheng complained that the political report at the Eighth Congress had contained the theory of the disappearance of classes, Mao recognized that he had shared these views in 1956: 'I read the report, and it was passed by the congress; we cannot make these two – Liu and Teng – solely responsible.'[59]

How and why did Mao come to change his attitude toward classes and class struggle so dramatically that Liu became a decade later the 'number one capitalist roader'? The general context is well known. An aspect which merits emphasis is the crucial generational change in China's educated elite, which was inevitable in any case, but was accelerated by the events of 1957. During the early years after 1949, both technical and managerial cadres were, of necessity, to a very large extent people inherited from the old society, 'bourgeois' in their social origins, and/or in the sense that they had been trained in the West or in universities staffed by graduates of European, American or Japanese schools. Mao believed that the loyalty of these people could be gained, and that being already expert, they could be made red as well. The 'Hundred Flowers' policies Mao launched in the spring of 1956 were primarily designed to serve this aim of drawing the pre-1949 intellectuals into active participation in political and social life, improving their morale, and re-moulding them in the process.

In his speech 'On the ten great relationships' as originally delivered to the

[58] Eighth National Congress of the Communist Party of China, 2.213–14.   [59] Mao unrehearsed, 269.

party on 25 April 1956, Mao Tse-tung, while reiterating that 'inner-party controversies over principle' were 'a reflection inside the party of the class struggle in society', stressed the importance of exchanging ideas, especially in the scientific domain, with people in and outside China.[60] The 'Hundred Flowers' formula emerged in the course of the discussion of his report by the Politburo. In an intervention of 28 April, Mao declared that, if your views were true, more and more people could be expected to believe in them, adding that the party's orientation (*fang-chen*) in literature should be 'Let a hundred flowers bloom', and in scholarly matters, 'Let a hundred schools contend'.[61]

It was in the version of 'On the ten great relationships' presented on 2 May 1956 to the Supreme State Conference that Mao gave, for the first time, a systematic account of his ideas on this topic. According to the fullest available summary, he declared that spring had now come, and that a hundred flowers, and not just a few kinds, should be allowed to bloom. The formula of a hundred schools of thought contending dated, he recalled, from the Spring and Autumn and Warring States periods, when there were a hundred schools of leading philosophers, with many different doctrines, all freely engaging in controversy. The same thing, he said, was necessary at present. Within the limits set by the Constitution, the partisans of every sort of scholarly theory should be able to argue about the truth or falsity of their ideas without interference. We still haven't sorted out, he remarked, whether Lyssenko's ideas are right or wrong, so let each school put forward its ideas in the newspapers and journals.[62]

Not only were Lyssenko's ideas discussed in the newspapers, but in August 1956 at Tsingtao a large-scale scholarly conference debated for a fortnight the opposing views of genetics, under the slogan 'Let a hundred schools of thought contend!'[63] When one of the participants in this gathering subsequently expressed his enthusiasm in an article published in *Kuangming jih-pao*, Mao Tse-tung personally decided that it should be reprinted in *People's daily*, with a new title supplied by Mao: 'The way which the development of science must follow' (*fa-chan k'o-hsueh pi-yu chih lu*).[64]

The editorial of 5 April 1956 'On the historical experience of the dictatorship of the proletariat' had attracted widespread attention by

---

[60] Mao, *SW* 5.301–6.   [61] 1981 Resolution, annotated edn, 253–4.   [62] *Ibid.* 254.

[63] The full record of the formal discussions at this conference was published nearly thirty years later. See *Pai-chia cheng-ming – fa-chan k'o-hsueh ti pi-yu chih lu. 1956 nien 8 yueh Tsingtao i-ch'uan-hsueh tso-t'an hui chi-shih* (Let a hundred schools contend – the way which the development of science must follow. The record of the August 1956 Tsingtao Conference on genetics).

[64] *Ibid.* 10 (Introduction). For a fuller account, see Kung Yü-chih, 'Fa-chan k'o-hsueh pi-yu chih lu – chieh-shao Mao Tse-tung t'ung-chih wei chuan-tai "Ts'ung i-ch'uan-hsueh t'an pai-chia cheng-ming" i wen hsieh ti hsin ho an-yü' (The way which the development of science must follow – presenting Comrade Mao Tse-tung's letter and annotation relating to the re-publication of 'Let a hundred schools of thought contend viewed from the perspective of genetics'), *Kuang-ming jih-pao*, 28 December 1983.

reasserting the view, already stated by Mao in 1937, that contradictions continued to exist under socialism.[65] The related but distinctive idea of contradictions among the people first emerged in the autumn of 1956, in the aftermath of de-Stalinization in the Soviet Union, and of the Polish and Hungarian events. In his speech of 15 November 1956 to the second plenum, Mao indicated that class contradictions within Chinese society had already basically been resolved, though he spoke out firmly in support of class struggle and the dictatorship of the proletariat in dealing with counter-revolutionaries, and against Khrushchev's ideas of peaceful transition by the parliamentary road.[66]

So far as is known, Mao first used the actual phrase 'contradictions among the people' on 4 December 1956 in a letter to Huang Yen-p'ei, stating that while class struggles within China (as opposed to conflicts with imperialism and its agents) had 'already been *basically* resolved' (*i-ching chi-pen-shang chieh-chüeh le*), problems among the people would, in future, 'ceaselessly arise'.[67]

The *People's daily* editorial of 29 December 1956, entitled 'More on the historical experience of the dictatorship of the proletariat', constituted the first public exposition of Mao's ideas on this topic.[68] This text, which aimed to combat excessive discrediting of Stalin and of Soviet experience in the wake of the Polish and Hungarian affairs, took a slightly harder position, stating that no one adopting the standpoint of the people should 'place the contradictions among the people above the contradictions between the enemy and ourselves', adding: 'Those who deny the class struggle and do not distinguish between the enemy and ourselves are definitely not Communists or Marxist-Leninists.'[69]

At a conference of provincial and municipal party secretaries on 27 January 1957, Mao declared:

During the period of building [socialism], our experience of class struggle (which is partial), and contradictions among the people (which are primary) has been inadequate. This is a science, and we must study it very well.[70]

---

[65] For a translation, see *The historical experience of the dictatorship of the proletariat*, 10–11.

[66] Mao, *SW* 5.341–8 *passim*; 1981 Resolution, annotated edn, 531.

[67] 'Chih Huang Yen-p'ei' (To Huang Yen-p'ei), 4 December 1956, *Selected letters*, 514–15. (Mao himself underscored the adverb 'basically'.)

[68] See *The historical experience*, 21–64. The novelty of this formulation was widely noted at the time, and these ideas were commonly attributed to Mao. The fact that Mao had not previously expressed the same ideas in any unpublished text is confirmed by Liao Kai-lung, 'She-hui-chu-i she-hui chung ti chieh-chi tou-cheng ho jen-min nei-pu mao-tun wen-t'i' (The problem of class struggle and of contradictions among the people in socialist society), in Liao Kai-lung, *Ch'üan-mien chien-she she-hui chu-i ti tao-lu* (The road to building socialism in an all-round way), 245.

[69] *The historical experience*, 25.

[70] *Wan-sui* (1969) 89; *Miscellany*, 61. This source indicates simply that the meeting took place in January 1957; the date of 27 January is given in the version published in Mao, *SW* 5.359–83, which does not, however, include this passage.

A month later, Mao devoted the greater part of his celebrated speech 'On the correct handling of contradictions among the people' precisely to this science. In the original version of this talk, Mao expressed some reservations about the December editorial (even though he had personally revised it),[71] saying that it had not dealt explicitly with the problem of the national bourgeoisie, and had not made plain that the contradictions with this class were definitely contradictions among the people. To be sure, under certain circumstances they could become antagonistic, but one should not mistake well-intentioned criticisms for hostile attacks. Lenin had not had time to analyse this problem properly, and Stalin did not even try to make the distinction:

You could only speak favourably, and not unfavourably; you could only sing praises to his successes and virtues, but were not allowed to criticize; if you expressed any criticisms he suspected you of being an enemy, and you were in danger of being sent to a camp or executed . . .

Leftists are left opportunists. The so-called 'leftists' raise the banner of the 'left', but they are not really left, for they exaggerate the contradictions between ourselves and the enemy. Stalin, for example, was such a person . . .

China, too, said Mao, had suffered from such errors, especially during the campaign against counter-revolutionaries.[72]

The original text of Mao's 27 February speech contained extremely long and important passages both on the differences between China and the Soviet Union, and on the related problem of war and peace, which I shall discuss below in the section on the Sino-Soviet split. It also dealt in passing with a variety of issues which cannot be taken up here, such as the 'anarchism' prevailing in the realm of birth control,[73] or the inability of China at the present stage to provide secondary education for all.[74] Regarding the problem which concerns us here, Mao declared that the 'basic' (*chi-pen-ti*) contradiction in Chinese society was that between the relations of production and the productive forces, or between the basis and the super-structure.[75] At the same time, he made plain that, in his view, class struggles had basically come to an end in China.[76]

One can find a similar emphasis on the crucial role of contradictions among the people in the official text of Mao's February 1957 speech. For example, he declared: 'It is precisely these contradictions [among the

---

[71] 1981 Resolution, annotated edn, 532.

[72] *Hsüeh-hsi wen-hsüan*, 193–5. For another version of this passage in the original February 1957 text, see *Mao Chu-hsi wen-hsien san-shih p'ien* (Thirty documents by Chairman Mao), 94–5.

[73] *Hsüeh-hsi wen-hsüan*, 209.   [74] *Ibid.* 211.   [75] *Ibid.* 212–13.

[76] *Ibid. passim*, especially p.201. See also Su Shao-chih's assessment in *Tentative views on the class situation and class struggle in China at the present stage*, 35. (Chinese text, 'Shih lun wo-kuo hsien chieh-tuan ti chieh-chi chuang-k'uang ho chieh-chi tou-cheng', in *Hsüeh-shu yen-chiu-k'an*, 1 (October 1979).

people] that are pushing our society forward'; since contradictions were, in Mao's view, the motor of change, the particular contradiction, or type of contradiction, which moves society forward ought logically to be the principal contradiction. Moreover, in the same passage, Mao went on to say:

Contradictions in socialist society are fundamentally different from those in the old societies, such as capitalist society. In capitalist society contradictions find expression in acute antagonisms and conflicts, in sharp class struggle; they cannot be resolved by the capitalist system itself and can only be resolved by socialist revolution. The case is quite different with contradictions in socialist society; on the contrary, they are not antagonistic and can be ceaselessly resolved by the socialist system itself.[77]

Such statements appear to support the view, put forward by some leading Chinese theoretical workers in recent years, to the effect that Mao's ideas of late 1956 and early 1957 implied the replacement of class struggle by contradictions among the people (which cannot, generally speaking, be regarded as a form of class struggle) as the 'principal contradiction' in Chinese society after the socialist transformation of 1955–6.[78]

An issue closely related to that of contradictions among the classes making up Chinese society is the problem of the role of the intellectuals. Mao's relatively tolerant and gradualist attitude toward the elimination of class differences in this domain was expressed in a statement of January 1957 noting that 80 per cent of university students in China were still children of landlords, rich peasants, upper-middle peasants and the bourgeoisie. 'This situation', he commented, 'should change, but it will take time.'[79] None the less, he stressed very forcefully, in the original version of his speech on contradictions among the people, the importance of making the intellectuals reform themselves, so as to do away with their self-indulgent attitudes. All they wanted, he said, was two things: a high salary, and 'an old lady' or 'an old man' (*t'ao lao p'o, t'ao lao kung*) – in other words, 'to eat and to produce children'.[80]

Mao's disdain for pleasure and status (both of which, it is hardly necessary to observe, he had abundantly enjoyed over the years) was echoed in another passage of the 27 February 1957 speech on the corrupting effects of material well-being. The Chinese, he said, had two characteristics: their standard of living was low, and their cultural level was low. Both of these traits, he said, were ambiguous:

---

[77] Mao, *SW* 5.393.
[78] Liao Kai-lung, 'She-hui-chu-i she-hui chung ti chieh-chi . . .', 246–53; Su Shao-chih, *Tentative views*, 22–6.   [79] Mao, *SW* 5.353.   [80] *Hsüeh-hsi wen-hsüan*, 207.

If China becomes rich, with a standard of living like that in the Western world, it will no longer want revolution. The wealth of the Western world has its defects, and these defects are that they don't want revolution. . . . Their high standard of living is not so good as our illiteracy (*laughter*).[81]

This strain in Mao's thought was to come to the fore and find further expression during the Great Leap Forward, as we shall see in the following section. Meanwhile, however, Mao remained on the whole, in early 1957, relatively well-disposed both toward the bourgeoisie and toward the intellectuals.

As late as 2 May 1957, an editorial in *People's daily* which, according to a well-informed Chinese specialist, 'reflected completely Comrade Mao Tse-tung's views at the time' argued: 'Following the decisive victory in socialist transformation, the contradiction between the proletariat and the bourgeoisie in our country has already been basically resolved, and the previous several thousand years of history in a system of class exploitation has been basically concluded.' As a result, the editorial stated, the principal contradiction in China was no longer that between hostile classes, but the contradiction between 'the demand to build an advanced industrial country and the reality of a backward agrarian country', and others of a similar nature.[82]

But in mid-May, Mao's attitude changed radically as a result of continuing harsh criticism, and he perceived among the members of the party 'a number of' revisionists and right deviationists, whose thinking was 'a reflection of bourgeois ideology inside the party', and who were 'tied in a hundred and one ways to bourgeois intellectuals outside the party'.[83]

Rewriting his February speech in June 1957, Mao qualified his original conclusion that class struggles were over by adding the statement: 'The large-scale, turbulent class struggles of the masses characteristic of times of revolution have basically come to an end, but class struggle is by no means entirely over.'[84] This was still a relatively soft position, but Mao progressively hardened it. Thus, in July 1957, as the Hundred Flowers campaign was being transformed into an anti-rightist movement, he asserted: 'To build socialism, the working class must have its own army of technical cadres and of professors, teachers, scientists, journalists, writers, artists and Marxist theorists. . . . This is a task that should be basically accomplished in

81 *Ibid.* 225–6.
82 'Wei shih-mo yao cheng-feng?' (Why do we want to carry out rectification?), *Jen-min jih-pao*, 2 May 1957. For the judgment quoted above regarding Mao's approval for the article, see Liao Kai-lung, 'Kuan-yü hsueh-hsi "chueh-i" chung t'i-ch'u ti i-hsieh wen-t'i ti chieh-ta' (Answers and explanations regarding some questions which have been posed in connection with study of the 'Resolution'), *Yun-nan she-hui k'o-hsueh* 2 (March 1982) 104–5 (At a meeting of party and state cadres in Yunnan on 8 October 1981.)
83 'Things are beginning to change', 15 May 1957, Mao, *SW* 5.440.   84 *Ibid.* 395.

the next ten to fifteen years.' To be sure, he added that his new army would include intellectuals from the old society, 'who would take a firm working-class stand after having been genuinely remoulded', but it was plain that most members of this army were to be young people of good class background. 'The revolutionary cause of the working class,' he added, 'will not be fully consolidated until this vast new army of working-class intellectuals comes into being.'[85]

As for the existing intellectuals, Mao warned them disdainfully:

Intellectuals are teachers employed by the working class and the labouring people to teach their children. If they go against the wishes of their masters and insist on teaching their own set of subjects, teaching stereotyped writing, Confucian classics or capitalist rubbish, and turn out a number of counter-revolutionaries, the working class will not tolerate it and will sack them and not renew their contract for the coming year.[86]

From this time forward, Mao increasingly saw 'ghosts and monsters opposed to the Communist Party and the people' everywhere.[87]

MAO'S SEARCH FOR A 'CHINESE ROAD'

As I argued in the Introduction to Part 2, the anti-rightist campaign of autumn 1957 constituted a major turning point not only in Chinese politics generally, but in the development of Mao Tse-tung's thought. The changes which took place at this time made themselves felt across the whole range of Mao's intellectual interests and political concerns, from economics to philosophy, and from China's own internal problems to relations with the Soviet Union. In substantial measure, however, the central core of these new trends in Mao Tse-tung's thinking, and the impulse which led to their emergence, can be found in his ideas about 'building socialism'.

Determinism and utopian visions: the theory of the 'Great Leap Forward'

One aspect of the sea-change in Mao's mind and thought which took place at this time was, as just noted, a sharp reversal of his attitude toward the intellectuals. By their harsh, and to his mind negative and destructive criticisms, the scholars and writers participating in the 'great blooming and contending' of early 1957 had cast doubt on Mao's own judgment in pressing ahead with these policies in the face of opposition from many of his senior comrades, and thereby, in Mao's view, undermined his prestige and

---

[85] 'The situation in the summer of 1957', July 1957, Mao, *SW* 5.479–80.
[86] 'Beat back the attacks of the bourgeois rightists', 9 July 1957, Mao, *SW* 5.469–70.
[87] *Ibid.* 444.

authority. He therefore turned savagely against them. Henceforth, apart from training new, red intellectuals of good class origin, Mao Tse-tung would rely rather on the enthusiasm and creativity of the masses.

As for those wretched bookworms who had so betrayed his confidence during the Hundred Flowers period, who needed them? Mao therefore made repeated statements, and actively promoted policies, entirely at variance with his view of 1956 that scientists were the decisive factor, stressing that 'all wisdom comes from the masses', and that 'the intellectuals are most ignorant'. In March 1958, he declared:

Ever since ancient times the people who founded new schools of thought were all young people without much learning. They had the ability to recognize new things at a glance and, having grasped them, opened fire on the old fogeys. . . . Franklin of America, who discovered electricity, began as a newspaper boy. . . . Gorki only had two years of elementary schooling. Of course, some things can be learned at school; I don't propose to close all the schools. What I mean is that it is not absolutely necessary to attend school.[88]

However pithy and forceful we may find this, and Mao's many other anti-intellectual statements of the Great Leap period, it would be wrong to take any of them as a full and balanced expression of his view on these matters. At this time, he was still striving to hold together in creative tension, and to manipulate, polarities such as mass creativity and the scientific inputs necessary to economic development, or the urban and rural sectors in Chinese society.

In December 1958, Mao wrote to Lu Ting-i endorsing a report from the Tsing-hua University Party Committee about correcting the leftist errors committed in dealing with teachers in the Physics Department, and requesting that it be reproduced for general distribution. There was a widespread feeling, said this document, that 'intellectuals are objects of the revolution during the period of the socialist revolution, and even more so during the transition to communism, because the overwhelming majority of them are bourgeois intellectuals and belong to the exploiting class. Even assistant professors who are members of the [Communist] Youth League are regarded as objects of the revolution.' The only reason for having them around at all, in this prevalent view, was to set up an object of struggle; if the professors refused to reform, and to cut their salaries voluntarily, they should be sent to an old people's home.

This view Mao (like the Tsing-hua University Party Committee) entirely rejected on the grounds that it was necessary to rally as many teachers and research workers as possible of all ranks to serve proletarian education,

---

[88] *Mao unrehearsed*, 119–20.

culture and science.[89] But nevertheless, the weight of Mao's interest, and of his hopes, had unquestionably shifted toward the masses and the countryside.

Apart from Mao's exasperation with urban intellectuals, an important factor contributing to the turn both of his thoughts, and of the main thrust of party policy, toward the countryside was the growing trend in the direction of creating larger rural organizations to cope with tasks such as mechanization and irrigation. Already in late 1955, in one of his editorial annotations to *Socialist upsurge in China's countryside*, Mao had proclaimed the superiority of big co-ops, adding: 'Some places can have one co-op for every township. In a few places, one co-op can embrace several townships. In many places, of course, one township will contain several co-ops.'[90]

During the period from the spring of 1956 to the autumn of 1957, when a campaign against 'adventurism' and other factors had led to the eclipse of some of Mao's more radical policy initiatives, this advice had, on the whole, not been put into effect. (See, in *CHOC* 14. 299–302, the discussion of political and economic developments in the run-up to the Great Leap.) In the winter of 1957–8, however, a movement for the amalgamation of the existing higher-stage cooperatives emerged. At the Chengtu Conference of March 1958, Mao threw his weight behind this development, and on 8 April 1958 the Central Committee issued a directive in the same sense, reading in part:

if the agricultural producers' cooperatives are on too small a scale, there will be many disadvantages in future concerning both organization and development. In order to adapt to the needs of agricultural production and cultural revolution, small cooperatives must, in those localities where the conditions exist, be combined into large-scale cooperatives.[91]

By a coincidence far too striking to be accidental, this directive was issued the very day after Mao's visit to the 'big co-op' at Hung-kuang in Szechwan had been announced in the press.(The visit had taken place in mid-March, while the Chengtu Conference was in session.)[92]

As already noted, the impulse toward larger-scale organization had emerged from the concern with creating a more effective infrastructure in the countryside, and above all with promoting the development of water-

---

[89] 'Chih Lu Ting-i' (To Lu Ting-i), 22 December 1958, *Selected letters*, 554–5. (For some reason, the name of the university is omitted here.) Both Mao's letter and the text of the relevant document are included in *Wan-sui* (1969) 267–9.   [90] *Socialist upsurge*, 460; Mao, *SW* 5.273–4.

[91] 1981 Resolution, annotated edn, 323–4. Mao's intervention at Chengtu in favour of *ta-she*, referred to here, does not appear in the texts of any of his three speeches at this meeting available outside China. (See *Mao unrehearsed*, 96–124.)

[92] David S.G. Goodman, *Centre and province in the People's Republic of China: Sichuan and Guizhou, 1955–1965*, 144–5.

works. It is thus not surprising that, during the very same Chengtu Conference of March 1958 at which he advocated larger cooperatives, and at the Nanning Conference which led up to it, Mao Tse-tung should have devoted a considerable amount of time to listening to conflicting views regarding the 'three gorges" plan for a giant dam to control the waters of the Yangtze, and chairing meetings to decide policy on this issue.[93]

At the early stage of the Chengtu Conference, the *ta-she* or 'big co-ops' were not yet formally invested with the administrative and military functions which were one of the distinctive aspects of the 'people's communes' as endorsed in August 1958 at Peitaiho, and one cannot say, therefore, that they were communes in all but name. They were, however, already beginning to take on some of these characteristics, and thus constituted a stage in a process of development which soon culminated in the communes.

The history of the emergence of the communes is not, of course, in itself our concern here, but the above facts are relevant to the theme of this work because they demonstrate that Mao's own thought and action contributed directly to the institutional revolution which burst upon the scene in the summer of 1958, and was to shape Chinese rural society for a quarter of a century.

The inspiration for this trend can be found not simply in Mao's identification with the rural world, but in the millenarian visions which had gripped him during the collectivization drive of 1955. These ideas found expression in the thesis, repeatedly expounded by Mao between 1956 and 1958, according to which the Chinese people could draw positive advantages from the fact that they were 'poor and blank'. 'Poor people', he wrote in April 1958, 'want change, want to do things, want revolution. A clean sheet of paper has no blotches, and so the newest and most beautiful words can be written on it, the newest and most beautiful pictures can be painted on it.'[94]

Mao was here making the same two linked points he had conveyed in different language in his speech of 27 February 1957 when he referred to the superiority of China's 'illiteracy' over the wealth of the West. To the extent that the peasants were even blanker than the Chinese people as a whole, that is, even less corrupted by material well-being, and even more innocent of the wiles of the modern world, they were evidently superior in virtue, and in revolutionary capacities.

The roots of this strain in Mao's thinking go back deep into the past, to the twenty-two years of bitter struggle in the countryside that preceded his triumphal entry into Peking. I argued in the conclusion to Part 1 that the economic policies of the late 1950s could not be characterized in terms of a

---

[93] See Li Jui, *Lun San-hsia kung-ch'eng* (On the three gorges project), 8–10, 94–9, 171, 245 and *passim*.
[94] *Hung-ch'i* (1 June 1958) 3–4; *Peking Review* 15 (10 June 1958) 6.

'Yenan model', because the concrete circumstances were too different.[95] There was, however, an existential continuity with the *spirit* of Yenan, and of the Ching-kang-shan.

This continuity is revealed with extraordinary vividness in Mao Tse-tung's speeches at the Peitaiho meeting of August 1958 which officially endorsed the formation of the people's communes. Calling repeatedly for the abolition of the wage system, and the reintroduction of the free supply system followed during the war years, Mao declared that just feeding men was no different from feeding dogs. 'If you don't aid others, and engage in a bit of communism, what's the point?' The wage system, he asserted was 'a concession to the bourgeoisie', and its result had been 'the development of individualism'. Some people, he remarked, argue that egalitarianism makes for laziness, but in fact that is the case of the grade system.[96]

This whole ethos of struggle and sacrifice Mao linked explicitly to the past of armed struggle. 'Our communism', he declared, '. . . was first implemented by the army. The Chinese party is a very special party, it fought for several decades, all the while applying communism.' Now, in the twin struggle against imperialism and the forces of nature, the goals were equally clear, and the introduction of the free supply system would in no way reduce people's motivation or commitment.[97]

Arguing that the communes contained 'sprouts of communism', Mao contrasted them with the cities, where people wanted 'regularization' (*cheng-kui-hua*), and which were full of big *yamens* divorced from the masses. Calling for desperate efforts (*p'ing-ming kan*) to make steel, Mao noted that some criticized backyard steel production as 'a rural work style' or 'a guerrilla habit'. In fact, he declared, such views were the expression of 'bourgeois ideology', which had already eliminated many good things in the party's heritage.[98]

Speaking to a reporter on 29 September 1958, Mao repeated publicly this denunciation of those who regarded mobilizing the masses for industrial production as 'irregular' or a 'rural work style'.[99] Less than a year later, in July 1959, he recognized that this had been a misguided undertaking which led to 'chaos on a grand scale' and a substantial waste of resources.[100]

Mao Tse-tung was only dissuaded from going ahead with his plan for the introduction of a military-communist style of free supply system because

---

[95] See pp. 92–3.
[96] Speeches of 21 August 1958 (morning) and 30 August 1958 (morning), *Hsüeh-hsi wen-hsüan*, 304, 306–7, 318. (This is a different collection from that cited in note 31.) At Chengtu in March 1958, Mao had opined that China would realize communism within 50 years. *Ibid.* 110.
[97] Speech of 30 August 1958, *ibid.* 318. (See also speech of 21 August, 306.)
[98] Speeches of 17 August, 21 August (morning), and 30 August (morning) 1958, *ibid.* 302, 305–7 *passim*, 318.   [99] *PTMT* 353.   [100] *Mao unrehearsed*, 144–6.

Chou En-lai produced detailed estimates, based on materials from various ministries, to show that it would be ruinously expensive as compared to the wage system.[101] It constitutes, incidentally, remarkable testimony both to Chou's steadiness of purpose, and to his prestige, that he was able to persuade Mao on this point even though he had been a primary butt of the fierce attack on those who had 'opposed adventurism' in 1956, which Mao had launched at the Nanning Conference of January 1958, and pressed home at Chengtu in March.[102] But though Mao accepted that this idea was impracticable for the moment, he continued to dream such rural utopian dreams.

And yet, Mao recognized as early as the first Chengchow Conference of November 1958 that the peasants displayed a certain attachment to their own material interests, declaring: 'The peasants after all remain peasants, throughout the period when the system of ownership by the whole people has not yet been implemented in the countryside, they after all retain a certain dual nature on the road to socialism.' At the second Chengchow Conference of February-March 1959, he reiterated this statement several times, adding that at the present stage the workers, not the peasants, still played the role of 'elder brother' in the relationship between the two.[103]

Perhaps Mao never truly resolved, either in practice or in his own mind, the dilemma of a peasantry which was simultaneously the salt of the earth, and the 'younger brother' of the working class in building socialism.

A particularly suggestive symbol of the overall pattern of socialist development which Mao Tse-tung sought to promote at the time of the Great Leap Forward was the theory of the 'permanent' or 'uninterrupted' revolution, which he defined as follows in the 'Sixty articles on work methods' of January 1958:

Our revolutions follow each other, one after another. Beginning with the seizure of power on a nation-wide scale in 1949, there followed first the anti-feudal land reform; as soon as land reform was completed, agricultural cooperativization was begun. . . . The three great socialist transformations, that is to say the socialist revolution in the ownership of the means of production, were basically completed

---

[101] Liao Kai-lung, 'Li-shih ti ching-yen ho wo-men ti fa-chan tao-lu' (The experience of history and the path of our development), *Chung-kung yen-chiu* (Taipei) (September 1981) 123. This report, delivered on 25 October 1980 at a meeting for the academic discussion of the history of the Chinese Communist Party called by the Central Party School, has been officially published in China only in a revised version, but there is every reason to believe that the original text as reproduced in Taipei is authentic. It is translated in *Issues and Studies*, October, November and December 1981; the passage cited here appears in the October issue, p.84. For the new version, see Liao Kai-lung, *Tang-shih t'an-so* (Explorations in party history), 308-65. The historical overview of the 1950s and 1960s has been significantly condensed in the official version, and does not contain details about Chou's role in persuading Mao to abandon the 'free supply system'.

[102] See, in particular, the passage in his talk of 22 March 1958, *Mao unrehearsed*, 122.

[103] *Wan-sui* (1969) 247; *Wan-sui* (1967) 12, 17, 49, etc.

in 1956. Following this, we carried out last year the socialist revolution on the political and ideological fronts [i.e., the anti-rightist campaign]. . . . But the problem is still not resolved, and for a fairly long period to come, the method of airing of views and rectification must be used every year to solve the problems in this field. We must now have a technical revolution, in order to catch up with and overtake England in fifteen years or a bit longer . . .[104]

As this passage makes plain, it was characteristic of the Great Leap Forward, as of Mao's approach to revolution generally, that economic, social, political and cultural transformation were to be carried out simultaneously. At the same time, a dramatic raising both of technical levels, and of levels of material production, was very much part of the Maoist vision in 1958. This concern found clear expression in Mao's call for a 'technical revolution', as well as in the slogan 'Overtake England in fifteen years!', which had been proclaimed in December 1957.

Twice, indeed, in the course of the radical phase of the Great Leap, Mao dated the beginnings of the process of modernization and change in China from the moment when, at the end of the nineteenth century, Chang Chih-tung embarked on his programme of industrialization. In September 1958, he measured progress in terms of numbers of machine tools; in February 1959, his criterion was the growth of the Chinese working class. In both cases, he compared China's achievements before and after 1949 in catching up with the more advanced countries of the world.[105]

This does not mean, of course, that Mao regarded industrialization, or even economic development in general, as the whole essence of revolution. In a speech at the Second Session of the Eighth Party Congress in May 1958, at which the Great Leap Forward was officially proclaimed, he asserted his resolve to press ahead with rapid economic growth, but indicated that revolution would not result from development alone:

We do not put forward the slogans 'Cadres decide everything' and 'Technology decides everything', nor do we put forward the slogan, 'Communism equals the Soviets plus electrification'. Since we do not put forward this slogan, does this mean that we won't electrify? We will electrify just the same, and even a bit more fiercely. The first two slogans were formulated by Stalin, they are one-sided. [If you say] 'Technology decides everything' – what about politics? [If you say] Cadres decide everything' – what about the masses? This is not sufficiently dialectical.[106]

Thus, although China intended to 'electrify', that is, to develop her economy (in Lenin's metaphor) just as fast as the Soviets, Mao saw this process as intimately linked to human change.

---

[104] *Wan-sui* (supplement) 32–3; translation from S. Schram, 'Mao Tse-tung and the theory of the permanent revolution', *CQ* 46 (April–June 1971) 226–7.
[105] *Wan-sui* (1969) 245, and *Wan-sui* (1967) 15.   [106] *Wan-sui* (1969) 204.

The Great Leap Forward thus involved the juxtaposition of many diverse inspirations and imperatives, the simultaneous insistence on technical revolution and political mobilization being only one instance of this. One of the most flagrant of such contradictions was that between the stress on unified party leadership, expressed in the slogan 'Politics in command!', and the fragmentation of economic initiative and control to such an extent that, as Mao later recognized, effective planning largely ceased to exist. This problem arose in large part because the system of 'dual rule', which had been re-introduced in 1956, was tilted so far in favour of the party in 1958 that effective control at every level was vested in party cadres who had no machinery at their disposal for checking, even if they had wanted to, on the wider consequences of economic decisions.

At the time, Mao suggested that this was nothing to worry about, since disequilibrium was a 'universal objective law' which acted as a spur to progress.[107] At the back of this ideological formulation lay the conviction that it was imperative to mobilize the population as a whole to play a dynamic role in economic development. This, in turn, implied not only stressing the creativity of the masses, as opposed to the experts, but attributing to the 'revolutionary people' as a whole (experts, or at least 'red' experts among them) virtually unlimited capacities to modify their own environment. Thus we find, in ideological writings of the Great Leap period manifestly reflecting Mao's viewpoint, quite extraordinary statements, such as 'There is no such thing as poor land, but only poor methods for cultivating the land', or even 'The subjective creates the objective'.[108]

It might be said that at the time of the Great Leap, a decade before the events of May 1968, Mao grasped and illustrated the slogan which the students of Paris were later to make famous: 'L'imagination au pouvoir!' The difference was, of course, that he really *was* in power. In 1958, fantasy rather than sober observation came all too often to be the criterion for defining truth and reality. In September 1958, Mao declared that the national grain output had more or less doubled, and might be expected to double again in 1959, so that soon there would be too much even to feed to the animals, and there would be a problem in disposing of it. As late as 6 November 1958 in Chengchow, he declared that the transition to communism could be completed in 15 years, though this target should not be openly published.[109]

In his speech of 9 December 1958 at the sixth plenum of the Central Committee in Wuchang, Mao Tse-tung noted that, at the informal discussions which had taken place just before the plenum, the slogan 'Seek the

---

[107] See S. Schram, article cited, *CQ* 46 (1971), especially pp. 232–6.
[108] Wu Chiang, article in *Che-hsüeh yen-chiu* 8 (1958) 25–8; extracts in *PTMT* 99, 135–6.
[109] *Wan-sui* (1969) 228; *Hsueh-hsi tzu-liao (hsu-i)*, 173.

truth from facts' had been put forward once again. He interpreted this to mean that, in planning work, it was necessary to be both hot and cold; to have lofty aspirations, and yet at the same time to carry out considerable scientific analysis. Concretely, Mao said that, when he had forecast a production of 120 million tons of steel in 1962, he had been concerned only with the demand for steel in China, and 'had not considered the problem of whether or not it was possible'. In fact, he said, such a target was neither possible nor realistic. Nor should the Chinese confuse the transition to socialism with the transition to communism, or seek to enter communism ahead of the Soviet Union.[110]

In the early months of 1959, as the 'wind of communism' blew across the land, Mao himself once again entertained unrealistic hopes. In March 1959, he told Anna Louise Strong that if steel production met the targets set for 1959, as it had done in 1958, six million tons a year could be allocated to the production of agricultural equipment, and mechanization would soon be completed.[111] By July, he had come to regard the backyard furnaces as an ill-advised adventure for which he was to blame.[112] Nevertheless, though the time-scale for achieving a decisive economic breakthough was soon revised in the direction of greater realism, the ultimate aim of rapid and decisive economic progress remained unchanged.

In order to achieve this goal, effective coordination of efforts on a national scale would be required. Mao, who in July 1959 took responsibility also for the dismantling of the planning system during the high tide of the Great Leap,[113] therefore endorsed the slogan, adopted in early 1959, 'The whole country a single chessboard'.

At the same time, while accepting the need for more effective centralized control of the industrial sector, Mao took the lead in decentralizing owner-ship and control in the communes. In March 1959, intervening to settle a sharp argument as to whether the basic level of accounting and distribution should be pushed down one level or two, Mao opted for the second and bolder solution.[114] (The unit in question was the *sheng-ch'an tui*; normally translated 'production team', this meant, in the context of 1959, what is now called the brigade, roughly the equivalent of the old APC. The intermediate solution, which Mao rejected, would have consisted in taking as the basic unit an entity equivalent to the administrative area, which was subsequently abolished. For further details, and an account of subsequent developments, see *CHOC* 14. 309–10, 378–86.)

Mao was persuaded that the system of people's communes was basically sound, and could easily be consolidated by the adjustments carried out in

110 *Wan-sui* (1969) 262, 264–5; *Miscellany*, 141–2, 144–5.
111 Anna Louise Strong, 'Three interviews with Chairman Mao Zedong', *CQ* 103 (September 1985).
112 *Mao unrehearsed*, 143.   113 *Ibid.* 142.   114 *Wan-sui* (1967) 106–7. (Letter of 15 March 1959.)

the spring and early summer of 1959.[115] Probably he thought that, by himself taking action to correct defects in the system he had devised, or in any case promoted, he would disarm potential critics in the party. If this was indeed his expectation, he was bitterly disappointed. At the Lu-shan plenum of July-August 1959, P'eng Te-huai, Chang Wen-t'ien and others openly attacked the whole range of Great Leap policies.[116]

It would be hard to overestimate the impact of the confrontation on Lu-shan, not only on Mao's attitudes towards his comrades, but on the substance of his thought. As in 1957, he had committed errors of judgment, and the experience had not chastened him, but rather rendered him more sensitive regarding his own dignity. Psychologically, the consequence was that, from Lu-shan onwards, Mao Tse-tung not only sought to punish everyone who disagreed with him, but came increasingly to regard any and every idea he put forward as the standard of orthodoxy. In other words, dissent from orthodoxy as defined by Mao became 'revisionism', if not outright counter-revolution.[117]

Synthesis or eclecticism: Chinese and Marxist elements in Mao's thought

This evocation of Mao's image of himself as ruler necessarily raises the problem of another duality which became prominent in his thought from the late 1950s onward: that of the relation between Marxism and the Chinese tradition. In May 1958, at the Second Session of the Eighth Party Congress, Mao declared that the new policies of the Great Leap Forward represented an attempt to vie with China's 'teacher' in revolution, the Soviet Union. And he added: 'We have two parents: Kuomintang society and the October Revolution.'[118] This statement, he made plain, was intended to apply to politics as well as to economics.

Of the two 'parents' acknowledged by Mao, the significance of the October Revolution requires little comment or explanation. China, he is saying, has learned about the theory and practice of making revolution, and in particular of establishing a socialist state, from Lenin, Stalin, and Soviet experience since 1917. The reference to 'Kuomintang society', on the other

---

[115] Strong, 'Three interviews', 496–7.

[116] Chang Wen-t'ien's three-hour intervention was, in fact, more systematic, and couched in more rigorous theoretical terms, than P'eng Te-huai's 'Letter of opinion'. See the analysis of Li Jui, who was present at the time, in his article 'Ch'ung tu Chang Wen-t'ien ti "Lushan ti fa-yen"' (On re-reading Chang Wen-t'ien's intervention on Lushan), Tu-shu (Reading), 8 (1981) 28–38. The text of Chang's speech has now been published in Chang Wen-t'ien hsüan-chi (Selected works of Chang Wen-t'ien), 480–506.

[117] The fullest and most accurate account of the events on Lu-shan and their significance is that of Roderick MacFarquhar, The origins of the Cultural Revolution. 2. The Great Leap Forward 1958–1960, 187–251.

[118] Wan-sui (1969) 222; Miscellany, 121.

hand, means far more than might at first be apparent. The Chinese People's Republic, he is saying, is the creation of the Chinese people as they existed in 1949, and therefore reflects the ideas, attitudes and institutions which they have developed not only during the two decades of Kuomintang rule, but throughout the whole of their long history.

To be sure, China needed a revolutionary transformation guided by Marxist theory, but this did not mean turning the country into a carbon copy of the Soviet Union. 'There are some things', said Mao in March 1959, 'which need not have any national style, such as trains, airplanes and big guns. Politics and art should have a national style.'[119] Behind this statement we can sense once again the conviction, expressed by Mao in 1938, that the assimilation of the past provides not only raw material but a 'method', for elaborating a correct line today.

By the time of the Great Leap, Mao was thus placing side by side, on the same level, the Marxist-Leninist and Soviet tradition on the one hand, and the lessons of Chinese history on the other, and even mentioning Kuomintang society first, among the two 'parents' of the current stage in the revolution. Six or seven years later, he had shifted the emphasis still further, remarking several times to comrades in the party: 'I am a native philosopher, you are foreign philosophers.'[120]

Mao's claim, in 1964 and 1965, to be a 'native' or 'indigenous' thinker by no means signified that he had abandoned Marx for Confucius. It does, however, confirm beyond any question that the traditional roots of his thinking remained important to the end of his life. But how, precisely, were the Chinese and Western elements in Mao's thought combined in the late 1950s and early 1960s? Were they fused together or integrated into a new synthesis? If so, which of the two components defined the structure of his system as a whole? Did 'Mao Tse-tung Thought' remain essentially a variant of Marxism, and hence in the last analysis a vehicle of Westernization? Was, conversely, the logic and pattern of his thought increasingly Chinese? Or was there no system, and no clear structure, but two skeletons working sometimes to reinforce one another, sometimes at cross purposes, in an unwieldy body composed of disparate elements?

There can be little doubt that, as I have already suggested, both the nature of Mao's thought, and his own perception of it, changed as the years passed. In the early years of the People's Republic, he still saw a theory of Western origin – Marxism – as the warp, and Chinese culture as the woof, of the new social and political fabric he was bent on weaving. But by the late 1950s, his interpretation of Marxist theory was beginning to evolve in directions

[119] *Wan-sui* (1967) 48.   [120] *Mao unrehearsed*, 225, 239.

which reflected simultaneously the influence of the political climate of the Great Leap, and a growing stress on modes of thought derived from the Chinese past.

In 'On contradiction', Mao Tse-tung had accepted implicitly the 'three basic laws' of Marxist and Hegelian dialectics (the unity and struggle of opposites, the transformation of quantity into quality, and the negation of the negation), but at the same time he had given a hint of a new approach to these problems by characterizing the 'law of the unity of opposites' as the 'fundamental law of thought', thus seemingly placing it in a higher category than the other two.[121] To be sure, Lenin had said, in a passage quoted by Mao in January 1957, 'In brief, dialectics can be defined as the doctrine of the unity of opposites.' But he had immediately added, 'This grasps the kernel of dialectics, but it requires explanations and development.'[122] Mao, on the other hand, was ultimately to move toward the view that the law of the unity of opposites in itself summed up the whole essence of dialectics.

In the section, 'On dialectical and historical materialism', which he contributed to the *History of the CPSU* in 1938, Stalin had enumerated four 'principal features' of the Marxist dialectical method: that phenomena are all interconnected: that nature is in a state of continuous movement and change: that development takes the form of gradual quantitative change leading to qualitative changes or 'leaps'; and that contradictions are inherent in all things, and the struggle between opposites 'constitutes the internal content of the process of development'.[123]

In his talk of January 1957 with party secretaries, Mao explicitly took issue with Stalin's views on this topic, criticizing both the philosophical inadequacy of his fourfold classification, and its political implications:

Stalin says Marxist dialectics has four principal features. As the first feature he talks of the interconnection of things, as if all things happened to be interconnected for no reason at all. . . . It is the two contradictory aspects of a thing that are interconnected. . . . As the fourth feature he talks of the internal contradiction in all things, but then he deals only with the struggle of opposites, without mentioning their unity.

Clearly the reference here is to Stalin's stress, from 1938 onwards, on class struggle, which Mao, at this stage, did not wish to exacerbate to the same degree. But he then went on to discuss other differences between his conception of dialectics and that of Stalin:

---

[121] Mao, *SW* 1.345. See also above, p. 65 and note 116 thereto. In *Dialectical materialism*, he had explicitly confirmed that Marxist dialectics as developed by Lenin comprised the three laws. (See *MTTC* 6.300.)   [122] Mao, *SW* 5.366. (Talk of 27 January 1957.)
[123] *History of the Communist Party of the Soviet Union (Bolsheviks)*, 106–10.

Stalin's viewpoint is reflected in the entry on 'identity' in the *Shorter dictionary of philosophy*, fourth edition, compiled in the Soviet Union. It is said there: 'There can be no identity between war and peace, between the bourgeoisie and the proletariat, between life and death and other such phenomena, because they are fundamentally opposed to each other and mutually exclusive.' . . . This interpretation is utterly wrong.

In their view, war is war and peace is peace, the two are mutually exclusive and entirely unconnected. . . . War and peace are both mutually exclusive and interconnected, and can be transformed into each other under given conditions. If war is not brewing in peacetime, how can it possibly break out all of a sudden? . . .

If life and death cannot be transformed into each other, then please tell me where living things come from. Originally there was only non-living matter on earth. . . . Life and death are engaged in constant struggle and are being transformed into each other all the time. If the bourgeoisie and the proletariat cannot transform themselves into each other, how come that through revolution the proletariat becomes the ruler and the bourgeoisie the ruled? . . .

Stalin failed to see the connection between the struggle of opposites and the unity of opposites. Some people in the Soviet Union are so metaphysical and rigid in their thinking that they think a thing has to be either one or the other, refusing to recognize the unity of opposites. Hence, political mistakes are made. We adhere to the concept of the unity of opposites and adopt the policy of letting a hundred flowers blossom and a hundred schools of thought contend.[124]

The following month, in the original version of 'On the correct handling of contradictions among the people', Mao repeated many of these criticisms of Stalin as a philosopher, in very similar terms. Stalin, he said, was relatively deficient (*hsiang-tang ch'üeh-fa*) in dialectics, though not completely without it. His dialectics was a 'dialectics of hemming and hawing (*t'un t'un t'u t'u pien-cheng-fa*)'. Mao's overall verdict was that Stalin had been 70 per cent a Marxist, and 30 per cent not a Marxist.[125]

The political lesson is clear enough, though, as we have seen, Mao's view on class struggle shifted dramatically six months later. The philosophical implications are, however, somewhat more obscure, or at least ambiguous. The discussion of the interrelation between life and death evokes unmistakably the old Taoist dialectics of the ebb and flow of nature. And yet, in April 1957, Mao remarked: 'Dialectics is not a cyclical theory.'[126]

How was it possible to preserve the basic feeling for the essence of the dialectical process reflected in the passages of 1957 quoted above, and in many other statements by Mao, while remaining within a modern and Marxist system of categories? Mao's solution to this dilemma was of startling simplicity – so much so that, when confronted with it, I (and to my

---

[124] Mao, *SW* 5.367–96.   [125] *Hsüeh-hsi wen-hsüan*, 212–13, 220.
[126] *Wan-sui* (1969) 104; *Miscellany*, 66.

knowledge, all other foreign students of these problems) totally failed to grasp its significance.

In the 'Sixty articles on work methods', to which he put his name in January 1958, when this directive was distributed in draft form, Mao included a sentence which, 15 years ago, I translated as follows: 'The law of the unity of opposites, the law of quantitative and qualitative change, the law of affirmation and negation, exist forever and universally.'[127] What is rendered here as 'law of affirmation and negation' (*k'en-ting fo-ting ti kui-lü*) I took to be the kind of elliptical formula commonly used in Chinese political and philosophical language, 'affirmation and negation' being intended to evoke 'affirmation, negation, and negation of the negation'. On the basis of this assumption, I subsequently wrote that, in contrast to the views he was to put forward in the mid-1960s, Mao in 1958 had 'reaffirmed' the classic formulation of the three laws by Engels.[128]

It turns out that the Chinese expression just cited should in fact be translated 'the law of the affirmation of the negation', and that it was so understood, and treated as a major theoretical innovation by Chairman Mao, in China at the time.[129]

This may seem a very abstruse point, of little interest to anyone save hair-splitting expositors of Marxist doctrine. In fact, the implications, both political and intellectual, are of considerable moment. There is, first of all, the issue of Mao's personal authority in the philosophical domain. A recent work by a scholar who was, in Yenan days, a member of Mao's small philosophical study group, declares: 'In the "Sixty articles on work methods" Comrade Mao Tse-tung changed the name of what had used to be called the law of the negation of the negation to the law of the affirmation of the negation. This is an important question which he left to us, *without providing any sort of further demonstration* (*ping wei chin-hsing keng to ti lun-cheng*), and which our philosophical circles must inquire into (*t'an-t'ao*) further.'[130]

---

[127] *CQ* 46, 228.

[128] 'Mao the Marxist', in Wilson, ed., *Mao Tse-tung in the scales of history*, 63. As early as 1976, Steve Chin had grasped that this formulation involved a significant new departure, but unfortunately he got things backwards, taking it to mean 'the negation of the affirmation'. See *The thought of Mao Tse-tung*, 60, 66–7, etc. (Preface to Chinese edition dated 1976.)

[129] See two important compilations from Mao's writings produced in 1960 for internal use: *Mao Tse-tung che-hsüeh ssu-hsiang (chai-lu)* (Mao Tse-tung's philosophical thought – extracts), 195–220; and *Mao Tse-tung t'ung-chih lun Ma-k'o-ssu-chu-i che-hsüeh (chai-lu)* (Comrade Mao Tse-tung on Marxist philosophy – extracts) (Preface dated May 1960), 150 *et seq.* Both these volumes contain extended sections bearing the title 'The law of the affirmation of the negation', though the materials for these are drawn largely from writings of the Yenan period, and of the mid-1950s, about combining the old and the new, Chinese and foreign ideas, etc. (As noted above on p. 62, the first of these volumes contains, broken up into sections by theme, the whole of the lecture notes on dialectical materialism of which Mao denied authorship in his 1965 interview with Edgar Snow.)

[130] Yang Ch'ao, *Wei-wu pien-cheng-fa ti jo-kan li-lun wen-t'i* (Some theoretical problems of materialist dialectics), 211. Hereafter *Problems of dialectics*. This was a revised version of a book originally

It is hardly necessary to elaborate on the significance of the words italicized in the previous sentence. Thus a phrase inserted by Mao Tse-tung into a directive, and never subsequently elaborated, became for two decades a new law, accepted without question by China's philosophers. The parallel with Stalin's 'contributions of genius' in biology, linguistics and other domains is unmistakable.

The trends of thought on Mao's part underlying this theoretical innovation are, however, also worthy of attention. In March 1983, Chou Yang went so far as to state explicitly that, by failing to correct Stalin's 'one-sided' view casting doubt on the 'negation of the negation' because it smacked of Hegelianism, Mao ultimately opened the door to the destructive excesses of the Cultural Revolution. The core of Chou Yang's argument is that Mao's misgivings about the old concept reflected a tendency to exaggerate the absolutely antithetical and mutually exclusive nature of successive moments in the dialectical process, and to lose sight of the fact that 'negation' meant the supersession of some elements of the thing negated, while retaining others and incorporating them into a new synthesis.[131] If that is what Mao meant, then the new theory did indeed point straight toward Cultural Revolution notions of overthrowing everything and negating everything.

Yang Ch'ao, for his part, declares that in Mao's view most of the previous phase was eliminated at each negation. He also suggests that Mao had doubts about the old formulation, and replaced it by a new concept which 'enriched its content', because he thought it implied that the end result of the whole process was a return to the *initial* affirmation, rather than a progression to a new and higher level. And he adds that Mao believed in the dialectical unity of the opposites, 'affirmation' and 'negation', just as he believed in the unity of peace and war, life and death, proletariat and bourgeoisie, and so on. All things, in Mao's view, were 'contradictory entities made up of affirmation and negation'.[132]

devoted explicitly to Mao's thought: Yang Ch'ao, *Lun Mao Chu-hsi che-hsüeh t'i-hsi* (On Chairman Mao's philosophical system). Hereafter *Mao's philosophical system*. Regarding Yang Ch'ao's participation in Mao's philosophical study group in 1939, see Wen Chi-tse, 'Mao Tse-tung t'ung-chih tsai Yenan shih-ch'i shih tsen-yang chiao-tao wo-men hsüeh che-hsüeh ti?' (How did Comrade Mao Tse-tung teach us to study philosophy during the Yenan period?), in *Ch'üan-kuo Mao Tse-tung che-hsüeh ssu-hsiang t'ao-lun hui lun-wen hsüan* (Selected essays from the national conference to discuss Mao Tse-tung's philosophical thought), 69. The other members of the group, apart from Mao himself, were Ai Ssu-ch'i, Ho Ssu-ching, Ho P'ei-yüan, and Ch'en Po-ta.

131 Chou Yang, 'Kuan-yü Ma-k'o-ssu-chu-i ti chi-ko li-lun wen-t'i ti t'an-t'ao' (An exploration of some theoretical questions of Marxism), *Jen-min jih-pao*, 16 March 1983, 4. This article, based on Chou Yang's speech on the occasion of the centenary of Marx's death, was criticized during the campaign of the winter 1983–4 against 'spiritual pollution' because of references to alienation under socialism, but there has never been any suggestion that Chou Yang's analysis of Mao's dialectics was erroneous. For the circumstances surrounding the publication and criticism of this speech, see S. Schram, *Ideology and policy in China since the Third Plenum 1978–84*, 41–56.

132 *Problems of dialectics*, 199–217, especially pp. 212–13; *Mao's philosophical system*, 247–63.

It is, perhaps, possible to combine these two perspectives, and thereby to arrive at a reasonably good understanding of what Mao was seeking to achieve by introducing this new concept. Plainly, the formulation 'affirmation of the negation' stresses the fact that, in the historical process, new things are constantly emerging. It also suggests, however, that such new things do not arise simply as a reaction against what has come before ('negation of the negation'), but that they are affirmed or asserted by historical actors: classes, or those leaders and parties that claim to speak for classes. In other words, 'affirmation of the negation' evokes both the ceaseless change which is the essence of 'permanent revolution' (not surprisingly, since the two terms were used side by side in the 'Sixty articles' of January 1958), and the role of the will. Or, to put it another way, it corresponded to a further shift in emphasis from the basis to the superstructure.

In terms of the concrete political significance of Mao's ideas, the concept of the affirmation of the negation can perhaps best be seen as the symbolic expression of the 'poor and blank' hypothesis discussed above. In other words, it is a way of saying that the negative can be transformed into the positive, or that a situation comprising many negative factors can, in the course of a process of transformation baptized 'affirmation' instead of 'negation' (of the negation), be turned into a new situation, rich with promise for the future. To the extent that we accept Chou Yang's analysis, this 'affirmation' would consist in the chiliastic hope of a rapid and total change, rather than a gradual and incrementalist strategy building on what has already been achieved.

Then, in the 1960s, Mao went beyond simply renaming and in some degree redefining the negation of the negation to repudiating this basic Marxist concept altogether. On 18 August 1964, in the course of a conversation on philosophy with K'ang Sheng, Ch'en Po-ta and others, K'ang asked the chairman to 'say something about the problem of the three categories'. Obviously he knew that Mao had new ideas to put forward, as indeed the chairman proceeded to do:

Engels talks about the three categories, but as for me I don't believe in two of those categories. (The unity of opposites is the most basic law, the transformation of quality and quantity into one another is the unity of the opposites quality and quantity, and the negation of the negation does not exist at all.) The juxtaposition, on the same level, of the transformation of quality and quantity into one another, the negation of the negation, and the law of the unity of opposites is 'triplism', not monism. . . . Affirmation, negation, affirmation, negation . . . in the development of things, every link in the chain of events is both affirmation and negation. Slave-holding society negated primitive society, but with reference to feudal society it constituted, in turn, the affirmation. Feudal society constituted the negation in relation to slave-holding society but it was in turn the affirmation with reference to capitalist society. Capitalist society was the negation in relation to feudal society, but it is, in turn, the affirmation in relation to socialist society.[133]

The following year, at the Hangchow Conference of December 1965, Mao summed up his view very succinctly once again, on the eve of the Cultural Revolution:

It used to be said that there were three great laws of dialectics, then Stalin said there were four. In my view there is only one basic law and that is the law of contradiction. Quality and quantity, positive and negative . . . content and form, necessity and freedom, possibility and reality, etc., are all cases of the unity of opposites.[134]

In the past, some Western scholars, including both Frederic Wakeman and myself, have seen in this development a turn, or reversion, on Mao's part toward a more traditional approach to dialectics.[135] Whether or not one accepts such a view of this point, there can be no doubt that in the 1960s the influence of traditional Chinese thought across the board came increasingly into prominence in Mao Tse-tung's thought as a whole.

One important index of Mao's evolving attitude toward traditional Chinese culture was manifestly his evaluation of Confucius. Mao, who denounced teachers of Chinese literature during the May Fourth period as 'obstinate pedants' who 'forcibly impregnate our minds with a lot of stinking corpse-like dead writings full of classical allusions',[136] had come to take the view, as early as 1938, that the classical heritage had a positive as well as a negative aspect, and that it was therefore necessary to deal selectively with it. Though he had no doubts about the reactionary and harmful character of Confucianism as an answer to the problems of the twentieth century, Mao alluded with approval to various attitudes defined by tags from the Confucian classics, such as Confucius' practice of going about and 'inquiring into everything',[137] his attitude of 'not feeling ashamed to ask and learn from people below',[138] and the recommendation from the *Mencius*: 'When speaking to the mighty, look on them with contempt.'[139] (See also p.73 above, regarding the link between theory and practice in Confucius' thought.)

It was in 1964, however, that Mao's turn back to the Chinese classics for inspiration led him to a surprisingly favourable view of Confucius. While criticizing the sage for his contempt for manual labour, and for his lack of

---

[133] *Mao unrehearsed*, 226. [134] *Ibid.* 240.
[135] Wakeman, *History and will*, 323–6; Schram, 'Mao the Marxist', 63–4.
[136] 'The great union of the popular masses'; my translation from *CQ* 49 (Jan.–March 1972) 80–1.
[137] 'Oppose book worship', in *Selected readings*, 34. (*Confucian analects*, 7, ch. 2; Legge, *The Chinese classics*, 1.195.) [138] Mao, *SW* 4.378. (*Confucian analects* 5, ch. 14; Legge, 1.178.)
[139] *Mao unrehearsed*, 82. (*Mencius* 6, part 2, ch. 34; Legge, 2.496.)

interest in agriculture, Mao declared in February 1964, at the Spring Forum on Education: 'Confucius was from a poor peasant family; he herded sheep, and never attended middle school or university either. . . . In his youth, he came from the masses, and understood something of the suffering of the masses. Later, he became an official in the state of Lu, though not a terribly high official . . .'[140]

The following August, in his philosophical conversations with K'ang Sheng and Ch'en Po-ta, Mao quoted with approval a passage from the *Shih-ching*, commenting: 'This is a poem which accuses heaven and opposes the rulers. Confucius, too, was rather democratic . . .'[141]

Perhaps the most distinctive expression of a 'Chinese national style' in Mao's approach to politics is to be found in his emphasis on the political relevance of moral values, and more generally on the educational function of the state. In January 1958, Mao included in the directive which constituted the blueprint for the Great Leap Forward a call to train new, Communist intellectuals, in the following terms:

The various departments of the Centre, and the three levels of the province, the special area and the *hsien*, must all compete in training '*hsiu-ts'ai*'. We can't do without intellectuals. The proletariat must definitely have its own *hsiu-ts'ai*. These people must understand relatively more of Marxism-Leninism, and they must also have a certain cultural level, a certain amount of scientific knowledge and of literary training.[142]

The deliberate use of the term *hsiu-ts'ai* or 'cultivated talent', the popular name for the lowest-level graduates of the imperial examination system (*sheng-yüan*), with all of its traditional connotations, cannot be dismissed as a mere pleasantry. No doubt Mao intended the parallel to be taken with a pinch of salt, but there is also implicit in it the deep-seated conviction, which lay at the heart of the Confucian orthodoxy, that people are educated in order to assume political responsibilities, and that having been educated, it is their duty to take up the burdens of power.

Another echo of the past can be found in Mao's statement, in May 1958, at the Second Session of the Eighth Party Congress, that 'for the layman to lead the expert' (*wai-hang ling-tao nei-hang*) is a universal law. To be sure, he noted that this question had been raised in the previous year by the rightists, who had created a tremendous disturbance, claiming that laymen could not lead experts.[143] In other words, his formula was a refutation of the view, which Mao had already dismissed in the 'Sixty articles', that 'we are petty

---

[140] *Mao unrehearsed*, 208.   [141] *Mao unrehearsed*, 215.
[142] *Wan-sui* (supplement), 37 (Article 47 of the 'Sixty Articles').
[143] *Wan-sui* (1969) 210–11; *Miscellany*, 110–11.

intellectuals, incapable of leading the big intellectuals'.[144] But apart from the resentment of the normal school graduate against the 'bourgeois academic authorities' who had criticized him in the spring of 1957, it is hard not to see, in the argument advanced by Mao in this same speech of May 1958 to the effect that 'politicians handle the mutual relations among men', a reaffirmation of the moral basis of politics and society.

A few months later, at the Peitaiho meeting of August 1958, Mao declared, in discussing the question of rule by law (as advocated by Han Fei-tzu) and rule by men (as advocated by the Confucians):

You can't rely on law to rule the majority of the people; for the majority of the people you have to rely on cultivating [the right] habits . . . I took part in establishing the Constitution, but I don't remember it. . . . Every one of our [party] resolutions is a law; when we hold a meeting, that's law too. Public security regulations will only be respected if they rely on cultivating habits. . . . Our various systems of constitutional instruments (*hsien-chang chih-tu*) are concocted for the most part, to the extent of 90 per cent, by the bureaux. Basically, we do not rely on all that, we rely mainly on our resolutions . . . we do not rely on civil or criminal law to maintain order. The National People's Congress and the State Council have their stuff (*t'a-men na-i-t'ao*), while we have this stuff of ours.[145]

Apart from the implications of this passage regarding the relation between the Chinese Communist Party and the administrative machine, Mao here conveys very forcefully his feeling for the traditional role of the state as supreme educator.

In April 1964, Mao discussed problems of reform through labour with the Minister of Public Security, Hsieh Fu-chih. 'In the last analysis,' said Mao, 'what is most important – transforming people, the production output of those engaged in reform through labour, or both of them equally? Should we attach importance to men, to things, or to both? Some comrades think only things, not men, are important. In reality, if we do our work with men well, we will have things too.' To this, Hsieh replied: 'I read out the "Double Ten Articles" [a common locution at the time for the First Ten Articles of May 1963, plus the later Ten Articles of September 1963, on the Socialist Education Campaign] to the prisoners of the Shou-shih produc-tion team of the First Prison of Chekiang Province. . . . Afterwards, the overwhelming majority of the prisoners who had not confessed before now admitted their guilt, and many obstinate prisoners also underwent a conversion.'[146]

I would not go so far as to suggest that reading a directive on the

---

[144] My translation, from *CQ* 46 (April–June 1971), 227.
[145] Speech of 21 August, *Hsüeh-hsi wen-hsüan*, 310.   [146] *Wan-sui* (1969) 493; *Miscellany*, 347.

'Socialist Education Campaign' in the countryside to political prisoners was strictly equivalent to convoking the population in the old days to listen to the reading of the imperial edicts, but surely there is a certain underlying continuity in the conviction that moral exhortation is an important dimension of political leadership. Perhaps it was implicit in Mao's view that intellectuals in the new society should be Marxist or 'proletarian' in their political outlook, 'bourgeois' in the sense that they must be the bearers of the modern knowledge developed under capitalism, and 'feudal' to some extent in their conception of their own role.

As for the problems of the structure of power discussed in the first section of Part 2, the relation between Marxism-Leninism and the Chinese tradition was perhaps, in this domain, an even more ambiguous one. The blend of Confucianism and Legalism which defined, on the whole, the orthodox view of the state in late imperial times was hierarchical and authoritarian, and so too was Leninism, to a very high degree. To this extent there was convergence. Moreover, if Mao saw in politics the 'leading thread' which always had priority over economics, and ultimately shaped the pattern of social change, he was following in this not only Lenin, but also the monistic and state-centred vision of the social order which had prevailed in China for two thousand years.[147] At the same time, there were profound differences between Mao's ideas and those of the Chinese past, as regarded both the persons and institutions who were seen as the wielders of the transformative power of correct thought, and the goals of political action.

In view of the overriding emphasis on centralism in Mao's thinking about the state, which was, as we saw in a previous section, starkly consistent in all of his writings from the 1940s to the 1960s, it is not surprising that he should have spoken out repeatedly in praise not only of the first Ch'in emperor, but of other strong rulers in the Chinese past as well. 'King Chou of the Yin dynasty [commonly known as the "Tyrant Chou"], who was well versed in both literature and military affairs, Ch'in Shih-huang and Ts'ao Ts'ao have all come to be regarded as evil men,' he wrote in 1959. 'This is incorrect.'[148] And in a famous passage from one of his speeches to the Second Session of the Eighth Party Congress in May 1958, Mao had hailed Ch'in Shih-huang as a 'specialist in stressing the present and slighting the past', quoting with approval Li Ssu's proposal, endorsed by the emperor, that 'those who make use of the past to disparage the present

---

[147] On this theme, see my prefaces to *The scope of state power* and *Foundations of state power*, and the latter volume, *passim*, especially the contributions of Jacques Gernet and Benjamin Schwartz.

[148] From Mao's critique of 1959 of Stalin's *Economic problems of socialism in the USSR*, in *Wan-sui* (1967), 163; *Miscellany*, 197.

should be exterminated together with their whole families [*i ku fei chin che tsu*]'. He had also boasted that the Chinese Communist Party had executed a hundred times as many counter-revolutionary intellectuals as Ch'in Shih-huang, who had buried 'only 460 Confucian scholars'.[149]

And what, if anything, did Mao Tse-tung take from that other tradition, often seen as the ideology of the failures and misfits of the imperial system, Taoism? As already noted, events in the Chinese People's Republic, under Mao's leadership, were marked by a succession of campaigns, interspersed with periods of repose, to make a pattern of what Skinner and Winckler have called 'compliance cycles', and which Mao himself characterized as alternating 'hard fighting' and 'rest and consolidation' in a 'wavelike form of progress'.[150]

Angus Graham has remarked that the Lao-tzu 'advises Doing Nothing as a means of ruling, not as an abdication of ruling'.[151] Some curious parallels can be observed between aspects of Mao's role as Chairman during the last two decades of his life, when he first retired to the 'second line', and then, although reasserting his authority, remained in seclusion except for the first Red Guard rallies, and the principles asserted in the chapter of the *Chuang-tzu* entitled 'The way of heaven':

those who of old reigned over the empire, though wise enough to encompass heaven and earth would not do their own thinking, though discriminating enough to comprehend the myriad things would not do their own explaining, though able enough for all the work within the four seas would not do their own enacting. . . . Emperors and kings do nothing, but the world's work is done . . . This is the Way by which to have heaven and earth as your chariot, set the myriad things galloping, and employ the human flock.[152]

Looking at the pattern of Mao's thought and action throughout his career, and especially in the period after 1949, it seems evident that he was, in the last analysis, more strongly influenced by the 'great' than by the 'little' tradition.[153]

These para-traditional ideas regarding the role of the ruler were to grow still more in importance during Mao's last decade, and constitute, with the leftist attitudes he increasingly displayed in economic and political matters, one of the roots of the Cultural Revolution. A third, and in many respects crucial dimension of the situation was, however, the unfolding of Sino-Soviet relations, and Mao's response to these developments.

[149] *Wan-sui* (1969) 195.   [150] *Mao unrehearsed*, 106–7.   [151] Angus Graham, *The book of Lieh-tzu*, 10.
[152] Angus Graham, *Chuang-tzu*. The seven inner chapters and other writings from the book *Chuang-tzu*, 261.
[153] For further discussion of this point, and a refutation of Wolfgang Bauer's ideas to the contrary, see Schram, 'Party leader or true ruler?'

CAUSES AND CONSEQUENCES OF THE SINO-SOVIET SPLIT

From the very inception of the Chinese Communist Party, Soviet influence upon its development was, of course, many-sided and profound. Moscow was at once the locus of authority and the source of inspiration for the world communist movement from the 1920s to the 1940s and beyond. Mao's response to these two dimensions of the Soviet role was markedly different. The validity of the Soviet model he called into question only progressively, and relatively late. The notion that China was not merely a junior partner in the cause of communism, but should subordinate herself entirely to a worldwide revolution organization and lose her own identity in the process, he was, on the contrary, never at any time willing to accept.

In a sense, the whole of this dimension of the problem is summed up in Mao's reply to Edgar Snow when, in 1936, Snow asked him whether, in the event of a Communist victory, there would be 'some kind of actual merger of governments' between Soviet China and Soviet Russia. 'We are not fighting for an emancipated China in order to turn the country over to Moscow!' Mao shot back at him, adding: 'The Chinese Communist Party cannot speak for the Russian people, or rule for the Third International, but only in the interests of the Chinese masses.'[154]

The evolution of relations between the Soviet and Chinese Communist Parties, and between Mao and Stalin, during the Yenan period falls outside the scope of Part 2. It does seem appropriate, however, to note, by way of introduction to what happened after 1949, Mao's own assessment of Stalin's behaviour during the crucial years of civil war, beginning in 1945. Recalling, at a meeting of the Central Committee of the Chinese Communist Party in September 1962, that since 1960 the Chinese had been distracted from their internal tasks by the need to 'oppose Khrushchev', he commented: 'You see that among socialist countries and within Marxism-Leninism, a question like this could emerge.' Then, turning back to earlier events, he continued:

In fact its roots lie deep in the past, in things which happened very long ago. They did not permit China to make revolution: that was in 1945. Stalin wanted to prevent China from making a revolution, saying that we should not have a civil war and should cooperate with Chiang Kai-shek, otherwise the Chinese nation would perish. But we did not do what he said. After the victory of the revolution he next suspected China of being a Yugoslavia, and that I would become a second Tito. Later, when I went to Moscow to sign the Sino-Soviet Treaty of Alliance and Mutual Assistance, we had to go through another struggle. He was not willing to sign a treaty. After two months of negotiations he at last signed. When did Stalin

154 *PTMT* 419.

begin to have confidence in us? It was the time of the Resist America, Aid Korea campaign, from the winter of 1950. He then came to believe that we were not Tito, not Yugoslavia.[155]

In June 1949, on the eve of victory in the civil war, Mao none the less proclaimed that solidarity with the Soviet Union would be the cornerstone of the new China's foreign policy, which he summed up as follows: 'unite in a common struggle with those nations of the world which treat us as equals and unite with the peoples of all countries. That is, ally ourselves with the Soviet Union, with the People's Democracies and with the broad masses of the people in all countries, and form an international united front.'

Replying to an imaginary interlocutor to whom he attributed the comment: 'You are leaning to one side,' he elaborated on the reasons for this policy:

Exactly. The forty years' experience of Sun Yat-sen and the twenty-eight years' experience of the Communist Party have taught us to lean to one side, and we are firmly convinced that in order to win victory and consolidate it we must lean to one side. In the light of the experiences accumulated in these forty years and these twenty-eight years, all Chinese without exception must lean either to the side of imperialism, or to the side of socialism. Sitting on the fence will not do, nor is there a third road.[156]

Although this was the clearly enunciated foreign policy line in 1949, Stalin's attitude did not always make it easy, or agreeable, for Mao to carry it out. When Mao went to Moscow in December 1949, it took him, as he himself later recalled, two months of negotiations, 'amounting to a struggle', to get Stalin to offer China even that minimum of assistance and support which Mao regarded as essential. One dimension of the problem was, of course, the clash between the national interests of China and the Soviet Union, and the place of these two states in the larger unity known in the 1950s as the 'socialist camp'. Mao explained his own approach to these matters during the Moscow negotiations of 1950 in a speech of March 1958:

In 1950 I argued with Stalin in Moscow for two months. On the questions of the Treaty of Mutual Assistance, the Chinese Eastern Railway, the joint-stock companies and the border we adopted two attitudes: one was to argue when the other side made proposals we did not agree with, and the other was to accept their proposal if they absolutely insisted. This was out of consideration for the interests of socialism.[157]

Behind these discords lay, of course, not merely Stalin's lack of enthusiasm for the emergence of another communist great power which might ultimately be a rival to the Soviet Union, or at least demand the right to have its

---

[155] *Mao unrehearsed*, 191.   [156] Mao, *SW* 4.415.   [157] *Mao unrehearsed*, 101.

say as to how the 'interests of socialism' should be pursued on the world scene, but twenty years of conflict between Mao and Stalin as to the way in which the Chinese revolution should be carried out. Referring to the events of the 1920s and 1930s, Mao said, in his important speech of 30 January 1962:

Speaking generally, it is we Chinese who have achieved understanding of the objective world of China, not the comrades concerned with Chinese questions in the Communist International. These comrades in the Communist International simply did not understand, or we could say they utterly failed to understand, Chinese society, the Chinese nation or the Chinese revolution. For a long time even we did not have a clear understanding of the objective world of China, let alone the foreign comrades![158]

'Understanding the objective world of China' meant, of course, grasping the special circumstances of a revolution under Communist leadership in a vast and overwhelmingly peasant country, and devising a pattern of struggle based on agrarian reform and guerrilla warfare from rural bases. But it also meant working out new methods for transforming society and developing the economy once the struggle for power had been carried to a victorious conclusion. The crucial years during which Chinese and Soviet perceptions of these realities gradually diverged to the point of sharp, if as yet undeclared conflict extended from the beginning of the first five-year plan in 1953 until the Great Leap Forward of 1958–60.

The problem of the relation between foreign and domestic developments during this period is a complex one, and there was undoubtedly action and reaction in both directions. The Chinese probably soon became aware, after the upheaval in Poland and Hungary in the autumn of 1956, that Moscow would henceforth be in a position to offer less economic assistance, because it was necessary to spend more on Eastern Europe in order to stabilize the situation there. To this extent, the emphasis on 'self-help' in Chinese policy beginning especially in 1958 did not reflect a purely arbitrary decision on Mao's part, but also constituted a response to the realities of the international situation. There was also the behaviour of the 'ugly Russian', who was plainly no more appealing than the 'ugly American' who served in certain other countries during the same period as adviser and technical specialist. But apart from these diplomatic and psychological aspects of Sino-Soviet economic and technical cooperation, reliance on foreign experts for leadership in China's programme of economic development also raised more basic

---

[158] *Mao unrehearsed*, 172. The officially published text does not underscore quite so strongly the point that the foreign comrades were even more incapable of understanding the Chinese revolution. (See *Peking Review* 27 (1978) 14.)

problems of the role of the Chinese people themselves in shaping their own future.

Mao's overall approach to the various interrelated aspects of the problem of a Chinese road to socialism is clearly and forcefuly projected in a passage from his speech of 30 January 1962. In the first few years after 1949, he said,

the situation was such that, since we had no experience in economic construction, we had no alternative but to copy the Soviet Union. In the field of heavy industry especially we copied almost everything from the Soviet Union, and we had very little creativity of our own. At that time it was absolutely necessary to act thus, but at the same time it was also a weakness – a lack of creativity and lack of ability to stand on our own feet. Naturally this could not be our long-term strategy. From 1958 we decided to make self-reliance our major policy, and striving for foreign aid a secondary aim.[159]

Mao's formulation here strongly emphasizes considerations of national dignity; wholesale imitation of foreign experience, he says, however necessary for a time, simply 'could not be' the long-term strategy of the Chinese people. In 1958, when the economic and social experiments of the communes and the Great Leap Forward were first implemented, Mao stated bluntly that he was aware of the resentment which the Soviets might feel at China's refusal to follow them blindly – and could not care less. In a discussion of the need to smash 'blind faith' in the Soviet example, specifically in the military field, he said: 'Some people mentioned that when the Soviet comrade advisers saw that we were not copying their [combat regulations], they made adverse comments and were displeased. We might ask these Soviet comrades: do you copy Chinese regulations? If they say they don't, then we will say: if you don't copy ours, we won't copy yours.'[160]

Mao's insistence on breaking with the Soviet model was not, however, motivated simply by considerations of pride; for several years prior to 1958 he had been having increasing doubts about the value of Russian methods in the Soviet Union itself, as well as about their applicability to China. In the speech of April 1956 'On the ten great relationships', which marked the beginning of his attempt to sketch out in systematic form the ideas underlying the Chinese road to socialism, Mao declared:

We have done better than the Soviet Union and a number of Eastern European countries. The prolonged failure of the Soviet Union to reach the highest pre-October Revolution level in grain output, the grave problems arising from the glaring disequilibrium between the development of heavy industry and that of light industry in some Eastern European countries – such problems do not exist in our country ... The Soviet Union has taken measures which squeeze the peasants very

[159] *Mao unrehearsed*, 140–1.   [160] *Mao unrehearsed*, 126–7.

hard ... The method of capital accumulation has seriously dampened the peasants' enthusiasm for production. You want the hen to lay more eggs and yet you do not feed it, you want the horse to run fast and yet you don't let it graze. What kind of logic is this?[161]

Despite these misgivings about the Soviet experience of economic development, and despite his own criticism of Stalin's obsession with class struggle, and of Stalin's weaknesses as a dialectician, Mao Tse-tung had serious reservations regarding both the manner and the substance of the enterprise of de-Stalinization launched by Khrushchev in 1956. It is time to consider more systematically his response to these events.

De-Stalinization and 'modern revisionism'

The problem of the Chinese reaction to the Soviet Twentieth Congress, which was for so long the object of speculation and controversy on the basis of fragmentary texts released by one side or the other, can now be examined in the light of a much more abundant, though still not altogether complete documentation. As early as April 1956, the Central Committee of the Chinese Communist Party had decided on the assessment of 30 per cent for mistakes and 70 per cent for achievements in looking at Stalin's career as a whole. Mao declared in 'On the ten great relationships' that the editorial of 5 April 1956 had been written 'on the basis of this evaluation', though the figures do not actually appear there.[162] Despite Stalin's wrong guidance of the Chinese revolution, Mao thought the 30–70 assessment was 'only fair'.[163]

Half a year later, in the aftermath of the Hungarian and Polish events, Mao made his famous remarks, at the second plenum on 15 November 1956, regarding the 'sword of Stalin' and the 'sword of Lenin'. In Mao's view, even the first of these should not simply be discarded, in the name of opposition to 'so-called Stalinism'. While criticizing Stalin's mistakes, he should at the same time be protected. As for the 'sword of Lenin', that is, the insistence on the model of the October Revolution as opposed to the 'parliamentary road', Mao argued that it should under no circumstances be abandoned.[164]

This trend of thought was continued in the *People's daily* editorial of 29 December 1956, 'More on the historical experience of the Dictatorship of the Proletariat', which placed greater emphasis both on Stalin's merits and

---

[161] Mao, *SW* 5.185 and 291. For the reasons explained above in Section 1, this official text of Mao's 'On the ten great relationships' is more explicit in its criticism of the Soviets than that reproduced by the Red Guards and translated in *Mao unrehearsed*.
[162] *The historical experience*, 18–19.   [163] Mao, *SW* 5.304.   [164] *Ibid.* 341–2.

on the continuance of class struggle under socialism than that of the previous April. In his speech of 27 February 1957 on contradictions among the people, on the other hand, Mao Tse-tung spelled out his views about Stalin, and about related issues, both theoretical and concrete, in a somewhat different spirit.

I have already quoted, in the first section of Part 2, a passage about Stalin's propensity to exterminate his critics. Following on from this, Mao developed, under the heading of eliminating counter-revolutionaries, a comparison between China and the Soviet Union as regarded the use and abuse of revolutionary violence:

How has the work of eliminating counter-revolutionaries been carried out after all in our country? Very badly, or very well? In my opinion, there have been shortcomings, but if we compare ourselves with other countries, we have done relatively well. We have done better than the Soviet Union, and better than Hungary. The Soviet Union has been too leftist, and Hungary too rightist.

China, too, he acknowledged, had at times committed leftist errors, but mostly in the base areas during the Kiangsi period, under Soviet influence; these had been rectified by the directive of 1942 against killings and excessive arrests. Even after that, there had been some shortcomings, but nothing like the Soviet Union when Stalin was in power:

He didn't deal with this matter well at all (*t'a na-ko tung-hsi kao-te pu-hao*). He had two aspects. On the one hand, he eliminated genuine counter-revolutionaries; this aspect was correct. On the other hand, he wrongly killed a large number of people (*hsü to jen*), important people, such as delegates to the Party Congress. . . .

Here Mao alluded to the figures for percentages killed given by Khrushchev in his secret speech, before confirming that in 1950–2, 700,000 had been executed in China, a measure which he characterized as 'basically correct'.[165]

Apart from criticizing Stalin's policy of sending to a camp or killing anyone who dared to say anything negative about the party or the government, Mao also commented once again, as he had done in his talk of January 1957 to party secretaries, on Stalin's deficiencies as a Marxist theoretician. This time, however, he went farther, and claimed philosophical originality for himself as compared to Marx and Lenin, as well as to Stalin:

Contradictions among the people, and how to resolve this problem, is a new problem. Historically, Marx and Engels said very little about this problem, and though Lenin referred to it, he only just referred to it (*chien-tan t'an-tao*). He said that

---

[165] *Hsüeh-hsi wen-hsüan*, 197–8. The Soviet Union is not even mentioned in the corresponding section of the official revised text (Mao, *SW* 5.396–9) – not surprisingly, since this was first published in June 1957, when any such negative comments would have been quite out of the question.

in a socialist society antagonisms died away, but contradictions continued to exist; in other words ... the bourgeoisie had been overthrown, but there continued to be contradictions among the people. [Thus] Lenin said there were still contradictions among the people, [but] he didn't have time to analyse this problem systematically. As for antagonism, can contradictions among the people be transformed from non-antagonistic to antagonistic contradictions? It must be said that they can, but in Lenin's day there was as yet no possibility of investigating this probem in detail. There was so little time allotted to him. Of course, after the October Revolution, during the period when Stalin was in charge, for a long time he mixed up these two types of contradictions.[166]

Lenin's failure to develop the concept of contradictions among the people Mao excused by the lack of experience in those early days of the revolution.[167] Stalin's mistakes, on the other hand, Mao attributed to his inherently inadequate understanding of dialectics.[168]

Summing up regarding the criticism of Stalin at the Twentieth Congress, Mao declared that this business had a dual nature. On the one hand, to smash blind faith in Stalin, and to take the lid off, was a 'liberation movement' (*i-ko chieh-fang yün-tung*). But, on the other, Khrushchev's manner of doing it, without analysis, and without taking account of the consequences in the rest of the world, was wrong. We have, said Mao, complained of this in face-to-face discussions with the Soviets, saying that they were great-nation chauvinists.[169]

When he visited Moscow for the second time, in November 1957 to attend the conference of Communist and workers' parties, Mao remarked that he still had a 'belly full of pent-up anger, mainly directed against Stalin', though he would not elaborate on the reasons, because it was all in the past. He then proceeded, in characteristic fashion, to do precisely that: 'During the Stalin era, nobody dared to speak up. I have come to Moscow twice and the first time was depressing. Despite all the talk about "fraternal parties" there was really no equality.' Now, he said, we 'must admit that our Soviet comrades' style of work has changed a lot'. Consequently, he expressed the opinion that 'first of all, we must now acknowledge the Soviet Union as our head and the CPSU as the convenor of meetings, and that, secondly, there is now no harm in doing so'.[170] While the available record of the Moscow

---

166 *Hsüeh-hsi wen-hsüan*, 194. For a comparison of Mao's ideas regarding non-antagonistic contradictions with those of Lenin and Stalin, see S. Schram, *Documents sur la théorie de la 'révolution permanente' en Chine*, xxxii–xxxviii. In the official text of the 27 February 1957 speech, Mao's judgment on his predecessors is turned into its opposite; Lenin, it reads, 'gave a very clear exposition of this law'. (Mao, *SW* 5.392–3.)   167 *Hsüeh-hsi wen-hsüan*, 211–21.   168 *Ibid.* 212–13.

169 *Ibid.* 223–4. (The text as printed in this collection actually says 'our great-nation chauvinism', but I take *wo-men* to be a misprint for *t'a-men*. Alternatively, Mao might have indicated that when he criticized Khrushchev's handling of the problem of Stalin, the Soviets denounced *China's* great-nation chauvinism, i.e. her insistence on having a voice in such matters.)

170 Speech of 14 November 1957, translated by Michael Schoenhals in *The Journal of Communist Studies* II (2), June 1986.

meetings suggests a reasonably cordial atmosphere between Mao and Khrushchev, a formulation such as this clearly does not indicate a degree of veneration for Soviet ideological or political authority which would make it in any way surprising that, within a year, signs of conflict were to emerge. A major factor in this deterioration of relations was, of course, Moscow's reaction to the new economic policies of the Great Leap Forward.

The Soviets, not surprisingly, saw only the heterodoxy of some of Mao's new methods, and not the basic consistency of many of his policies and aims with the logic of Leninism. They took a particularly dim view of the people's communes, set up in the summer of 1958, which Khrushchev ridiculed first privately, and soon afterwards in public as well.

Undoubtedly, the Soviets were also shocked and irritated by what they saw as the extravagant and boastful claims of the Chinese in the domain of industrial production. They must have been particularly taken aback when one of the most extreme of these, the call to overtake England in fifteen years in the output of steel and other major industrial products, was first put forward by Mao under their very noses, at the November 1957 meeting of Communist and workers' parties.[171]

Mao's new approach to internal problems, accompanied as it was by a greater reluctance to rely on Soviet assistance, implied in itself a loosening of the ties between China and the Soviet Union. As late as December 1956, Mao had reaffirmed unequivocally the policy of 'leaning to one side' which he had first put forward in 1949:

The principal components of the socialist camp are the Soviet Union and China. China and the Soviet Union stand together. This policy line is correct. At present, there are still people who have doubts about this policy. They say, 'Don't stand together.' They think that China should take a middle course and be a bridge between the Soviet Union and the United States. This is the Yugoslav way, a way for getting money from both sides. Is this way of doing things good or not? I don't think it is good at all, it is not advantageous to our people. Because on one side is powerful imperialism, and this China of ours has suffered from imperialist oppression for a long time. If China stands between the Soviet Union and the United States, she appears to be in a favourable position, and to be independent, but actually she cannot be independent. The United States is not reliable, she would give you a little something, but not much. How could imperialism give you a full meal? It won't . . .[172]

In 1958, however, there took place a sharp deterioration in the relations between Mao and Khrushchev going far beyond what was implied by the logic of the Great Leap policies. This growing estrangement was not

<hr/>

[171] See Mao's speech of 18 November 1957, as translated in Schoenals. These events are also discussed in Hu Hui-ch'iang, 'Ta lien kang-t'ieh yun-tung chieh-k'uang' (A brief account of the campaign to make steel in a big way), *Tang-shih yen-chiu tzu-liao* (Materials for research on party history), 4, 762.
[172] *Wan-sui* (1969) 62–3.

simply, or even primarily, the result of disagreement about de-Stalinization, though, as we have seen, Mao had strong reservations about the way in which Khrushchev had carried out that operation, without consulting him. For, at the same time, Mao nourished strong resentment against Stalin for his high-handed treatment of the Chinese, and he therefore approved – up to a point – Khrushchev's effort to cut him down to size. 'Buddhas', he said in March 1958,

are made several times lifesize in order to frighten people . . . Stalin was that kind of person. The Chinese people had got so used to being slaves that they seemed to want to go on. When Chinese artists painted pictures of me together with Stalin, they always made me a little bit shorter, thus blindly knuckling under to the moral pressure exerted by the Soviet Union.

And in April 1958, he declared: 'This Comrade Stalin of ours had something of the flavour of the mandarins of old . . . In the past, the relations between us and the Soviet Union were those between father and son, cat and mouse.'[173]

But nevertheless, he objected, he said in March 1958 at Chengtu, to Khrushchev's action in 'demolishing Stalin at one blow'. Stalin's errors should be criticized, but it was necessary to recognize that he also had a correct side, and that correct side 'we ought to revere and continue to revere for ever'.

Despite his reservations on this point, Mao still held up Khrushchev, at the same conference in Chengtu in March 1958, as an example of those excellent and vigorous revolutionaries who emerge from the local party organizations:

Comrades working in the provinces will sooner or later come to the Centre. Comrades at the Centre will sooner or later either die or leave the scene. Khrushchev came from a local area. At the local level the class struggle is more acute, closer to natural struggle, closer to the masses. This gives the local comrades an advantage over those at the Centre.[174]

It is fair to say, I think, that never again, after the middle of 1958, would Mao have spoken of Khrushchev in such basically positive terms as these. A decisive episode in the deterioration of relations between the two men was, of course, the foreign policy crisis (or crises) of the summer of 1958. Khrushchev's attempt to solve the Middle Eastern conflict of July 1958 without the participation of Peking was clearly a major source of annoyance. Even more important, perhaps, was Mao's conviction that the Soviet leader was trying to dictate China's foreign policy.

On 29 July 1959, as the confrontation with P'eng Te-huai at the Lu-shan

---

[173] *Mao unrehearsed*, 99; also *Wan-sui* (1969) 183.   [174] *Mao unrehearsed*, 114–55.

meeting of the Central Committee was approaching its climax, Mao wrote a brief annotation to three documents regarding foreign criticism of the communes, including press reports of Khrushchev's remarks on the subject in the United States. Three days later, he sent a copy of these materials and of his accompanying comment to an old comrade, with a note saying in part:

The Khrushchevs oppose or are dubious about these three things: letting a hundred flowers bloom, the people's communes, and the Great Leap Forward. I think they are in a passive position, whereas we are in an extremely active position. What do you think? We must use these three things to fight the whole world, including a large number of opponents and sceptics within the party.[175]

Obviously Mao was both angry and contemptuous at the suggestion that his methods for building socialism were not compatible with Marxist orthodoxy. At the same time, his resentment at slurs against the communes, and more broadly at Khrushchev's meddling in the internal affairs of the Chinese Communist Party (through his criticisms of the communes, his relations with P'eng Te-huai, and so on) was greatly exacerbated by the anxiety which he felt because the Soviet reservations were shared in some degree within China.

There followed, in the autumn of 1959, the incident of the Tass communiqué, and then a series of other clashes with the Soviets, which Mao summarized briefly as follows in his speech at the tenth plenum:

in September 1959 during the Sino-Indian border dispute, Khrushchev supported Nehru in attacking us and Tass issued a communiqué [in this sense]. Then Khrushchev came to China and, at our Tenth Anniversary Celebration banquet in October, he attacked us on our own rostrum. At the Bucharest conference in 1960 they tried to encircle and annihilate us. Then came the conference of the Two Communist Parties [of China and of the Soviet Union], the Twenty-Six-Country Drafting Committee, the Eighty-One-Country Moscow Conference, and there was also a Warsaw Conference, all of which were concerned with the dispute between Marxism-Leninism and revisionism . . .[176]

Mao's use in this context of the term 'encircle and annihilate' (*wei ch'ao*), which was that employed by Chiang Kai-shek in the 1930s to characterize the campaigns of extermination launched by him against the Communists, vividly reflects the degree of hostility which Mao perceived in his erstwhile comrades. But, though he reacted to this hostility with anger, he remained wholly imperturbable in the face of it. In a speech of March 1960, he expounded the reasons for his confidence:

After all, who are the people of the so-called great anti-China [movement or chorus]? How many are there? There are merely imperialist elements from certain

---

[175] Letter to Wang Chia-hsiang, in *Mao Chu-hsi tui P'eng, Huang, Chang, Chou fan-tang chi-t'uan ti p'i-p'ang*, 14. [176] *Mao unrehearsed*, 190–1.

Western countries, reactionaries and semi-reactionaries from other countries, and revisionists and semi-revisionists from the international communist movement. The above three categories of people can be estimated to constitute a small percentage, say 5 per cent, of mankind. At the most, it cannot be more than 10 per cent. ... So far as we are concerned, their anti-China activities are a good thing, and not a bad thing. They prove that we are true Marxist-Leninists, and that we are doing our work pretty well. ... The hatred which has grown up between the United States and us is somewhat greater, but they do not engage in anti-China activities daily either. Not only is there now a brief pause between two waves of anti-China activities, but also there may be a pause of longer duration in the future. ... [If] the entire party, and the entire people really unite as one, and we can catch up with or overtake them in gross output and per capita output of our main items of production, then such pauses will be prolonged. This is to say that this will compel the Americans to establish diplomatic relations with us, and do business with us on an equal basis, or else they will be isolated.[177]

The improvement in Sino-American relations which Mao predicted in 1960 was not to materialize for another decade. Meanwhile, China's relations with the Soviet Union rapidly moved toward a climax. A month after Mao made the speech just quoted, the Chinese opened a massive ideological offensive with the publication of an editorial entitled 'Long live Leninism!' and a series of other texts, ostensibly directed against the 'revisionists' mentioned by Mao as members of the 'great anti-China chorus', that is, at the Yugoslavs, but in fact aimed at the Soviet 'semi-revisionists', who were soon to become openly the principal villains in Mao's book. A decisive turning point was reached in January 1962, when Mao Tse-tung called in effect, at the 7,000-cadres meeting, for the overthrow of the existing Soviet regime.

In a passage from his remarks on this occasion (published as a 'directive' in 1967) Mao said:

The Soviet Union was the first socialist country, and the Soviet Communist Party was the party created by Lenin. Although the party and state leadership of the Soviet Union have now been usurped by the revisionists, I advise our comrades to believe firmly that the broad masses, the numerous party members and cadres of the Soviet Union are good; that they want revolution, and that the rule of the revisionists won't last long.[178]

Although this speech was not publicly divulged at the time it was delivered, the Soviet leaders assuredly soon grasped the fact that Mao considered them beyond the pale. In any case, the rupture between Moscow and Peking was made abundantly manifest in the public polemics of 1963–4. Even though authorship of the nine Chinese replies to the Soviets, from 6 September 1963 to 14 July 1964, has been attributed to Mao, I shall not

[177] Wan-sui (1969) 316–18.   [178] Mao unrehearsed, 181.

review their contents here. What is relevant in this context is how rapidly Mao himself gave ideological and policy substance to the anti-Soviet rhetoric generated beginning in early September.

In late September 1963, the Politburo held an enlarged meeting. On 27 September, Mao put forward in this context a 'Directive on opposing revisionism in Sinkiang'. The first point, he said, was to do economic work well, so that the standard of living of the population was improved until it surpassed not only the level which had existed under the Kuomintang, but that 'in the Soviet Union under revisionist domination' (*hsiu-cheng-chu-i t'ung-chih hsia ti Su-lien*). Less grain should be requisitioned, and in order to heighten the favourable contrast with the situation across the border, the supply of cotton cloth, tea, sugar and so on should be 'a bit more ample than in other areas'.

Against this background, Mao then enunciated the second point:

(2) We must put politics in command, and strengthen ideological and political education. We must carry out very well anti-revisionist education directed at the cadres and people of every nationality . . . Cadres of the Han nationality should study the languages and literatures of the minority nationalities, they must pay attention to dealing well with relations among nationalities, and to strengthening solidarity among them. We must educate cadres and people of the Han nationality strictly to observe the party's policy toward nationalities, to uphold a class viewpoint, and to implement a class line . . . In the anti-revisionist struggle, we must have participation by units of the army and of the militia made up of national minorities, in order to guarantee the success of the anti-revisionist struggle.

The third point for attention was the education of the local Han population to respect the customs and habits of the local minorities. Some idea of what this signified is conveyed by the fact that under this heading Mao called for assistance to the Han workers sent to Sinkiang in resolving their 'marriage and other difficulties'. The fourth point was constant attention to the situation on the border, and intensifying the 'anti-revisionist struggle on the border'. The fifth point was vigilance against subversion and sabotage, as well as military incursions, by the 'Soviet modern revisionists'. The last point, finally, was 'integrated leadership' (*i-yuan-hua ling-tao*) of the anti-revisionist struggle.[179]

Mao Tse-tung was, in fact, convinced that China was rapidly catching up with the Soviet Union in terms of standard of living, not only in Central Asia, but in the country as a whole. 'Khrushchev,' he told Anna Louise Strong in January 1964, 'has said that we have one pair of trousers for every five people in China, and sit around eating out of the same bowl of watery

---

[179] *Mao Chu-hsi kuan-yü kuo-nei min-tsu wen-t'i ti lun-shu hsüan-pien* (Selections from Chairman Mao's expositions regarding problems of nationalities within the country), 40–1.

cabbage soup. Actually, when he said that, his own economic situation was getting worse, and he said it for the Soviet people to show how well off they were. Now they are getting shorter on trousers and their soup is getting more watery. Actually, the livelihood of the people in the Soviet Union now is not much better than that of our own people.'[180]

Whether or not Mao actually believed this, he was assuredly persuaded that the Soviet Union sought to use its primacy in the socialist camp to promote its own selfish economic interests. In his reading notes of 1960 on the Soviet textbook of political economy, Mao had attacked Moscow's policy of economic specialization within Comecon, designed to keep certain countries in the position of suppliers of agricultural raw materials to their more advanced neighbours, and in particular to the USSR.[181] This point continued to rankle, and in his January 1964 interview with Anna Louise Strong, Mao declared: 'The problem with the socialist countries is that Khrushchev wants them to stick to a one-sided economy producing to meet the needs of the Soviet Union. . . . It's hard to be the son of a patriarchal father.'[182]

Thus, in the late 1950s and early 1960s, Mao Tse-tung voiced an increasingly assertive nationalism as a response not only to the boycott of China by the imperialists, but to Soviet great-power chauvinism. Linked to this trend, and to the evolution of Sino-Soviet relations generally, was a growing radicalism, manifesting itself above all in an emphasis on class struggle. This turn toward the left was, as I argued above in the second section of Part 2, a natural outgrowth of the Great Leap policies, but further impetus was given to it by Mao's revulsion at Khrushchev's 'goulash communism'. Moreover, having been struck by the emergence of revision-ism within the Soviet Union, Mao Tse-tung began to discern the existence of similar phenomena within China itself. Thus yet another factor was injected into the complex process which ultimately culminated in the Cultural Revolution.

The enemy within: Mao Tse-tung's growing obsession with class struggle

As I noted at the end of the first section of Part 2, Mao drastically changed his position regarding the nature of the contradictions in Chinese society during the summer of 1957. The consequences of this shift for economic policy have already been explored, and some of its implications in the philosophic domain have also been evoked. Now, having reviewed the interaction between trends in Mao's thought after 1957 and the Sino-Soviet

---

[180] Strong, 'Three interviews', 504.   [181] *Wan-sui* (1967) 226–7; *Miscellany*, 296.
[182] Strong, 'Three interviews', 504.

conflict, it is time to consider how Sinocentrism, a radical interpretation of Marxism, and leftist sentiments engendered by nostalgia for the heroic virtues of the past, came together to lead Mao toward unprecedented experiments.

A central element in the growing radicalization of Mao Tse-tung's thought and political stance in the early 1960s was, of course, his increasingly strident and persistent emphasis on the existence and importance of class struggle within Chinese society. I shall therefore begin by reviewing briefly the evolution of Mao's ideas regarding classes and class struggle from the Greap Leap to the eve of the Cultural Revolution.

The first systematic formulation of his new approach was contained in Mao's speech of 9 October 1957 at the third plenum. Abandoning the position which had been adopted a year earlier at the Eighth Congress, and which, as we have seen, he had himself reiterated in February 1957, to the effect that the basic contradiction in China at the present stage was between the productive forces and the relations of production, Mao asserted:

the contradiction between the proletariat and the bourgeoisie, between the socialist road and the capitalist road, is undoubtedly the principal contradiction in contemporary Chinese society . . . Previously the principal task for the proletariat was to lead the masses in struggles against imperialism and feudalism, a task that has already been accomplished. What then is the principal contradiction now? We are now carrying on the socialist revolution, the spearhead of which is directed against the bourgeoisie, and at the same time this revolution aims at transforming the system of individual production, that is, bringing about cooperation; consequently the principal contradiction is between socialism and capitalism, between collectivism and individualism, or in a nutshell between the socialist road and the capitalist road. The resolution of the Eighth Congress makes no mention of this question. It contains a passage which speaks of the principal contradiction as being that between the advanced socialist system and the backward social productive forces. This formulation is incorrect.[183]

It is, of course, the formulation just quoted which is now seen in China as incorrect. Right or wrong, however, it was the emphasis on class struggle, against the bourgeoisie and between the 'two roads', which was to characterize Mao's thought for the rest of his life. Within this broad orientation, there were, however, to be significant twists, turns and fluctuations during the ensuing nineteen years, both in the vigour and harshness with which Mao Tse-tung promoted class struggle, and in his analysis of the existing class relationships.

On the eve of the Great Leap, Mao spelled out his view regarding the class structure of Chinese society in rather curious terms, stating that 'the reciprocal relations between people' were 'determined by the relationship

[183] Mao, *SW* 5.492–3.

between three big classes': (1) 'imperialism, feudalism, bureaucratic capital-ism, the rightists, and their agents', (2) 'the national bourgeoisie', by which he said he meant all the members of this class except the rightists; and (3) 'the left, that is to say the labouring people, the workers, the peasants'. To this last category Mao added, more or less as an afterthought, the parenthetical remark: 'In reality there are four classes – the peasants are a separate class.'[184]

In his speech of 6 April 1958 to the Hankow Conference, Mao corrected one anomaly – the failure to single out the particular role of the peasantry – but continued to include the 'imperialists' among the classes existing in China. On this occasion, he put the matter as follows:

there are four classes within the country, two exploiting classes and two labouring classes. The first exploiting class consists of imperialism, feudalism, bureaucratic capitalism and the remnants of the Kuomintang, as well as 300,000 rightists. The landlords have now split up, some of them have been reformed, and others have not been reformed. The unreformed landlords, rich peasants, counter-revolutionaries, bad elements and rightists resolutely oppose communism. They are the Chiang Kai-shek and the Kuomintang of the present day, they are the class enemy, like Chang Po-chün. The rightists in the party are just the same. . . . If you add up all these people, they come to roughly 5 per cent of the population, or about 30 million. . . . This is a hostile class, and still awaits reform. We must struggle against them, and at the same time take hold of them. . . . If we succeed in transforming 10 per cent of them, this can be accounted a success. . . . After a few years, when they demonstrate a sincere change of heart and are genuinely reformed, their exploiting class hats can be removed.[185]

The second exploiting class, made up of the national bourgeoisie, including the well-to-do middle peasants in the countryside, Mao described as a vacillating and opportunistic class. As for the 'two labouring classes, the workers and the peasants', Mao remarked: 'In the past, their minds were not as one, and they were not clear about ideology or about their mutual relations.' And he added: 'The workers and peasants work and till the land under the leadership of our party, but in the past we did not properly handle the problem of their mutual relations.'

In the aftermath of the Great Leap Forward, Mao's previous approach to the problem of class, which combined objective and subjective criteria, was modified by the addition of a new dimension: the notion that privileged elements among the cadres and intellectuals constituted an embryonic class. This trend was linked to the generational change referred to above, for it had long been understood that, because they were accustomed to a certain standard of living, intellectuals of bourgeois origin must be paid high salaries. This was extensively discussed in the Chinese press in 1956–7, and in January 1957 Mao himself defended what he called 'buying over' at a

[184] *Mao unrehearsed*, 112–13.   [185] *Wan-sui* (1969) 180–1; *Miscellany*, 85–6.

'small cost' the capitalists plus the democrats and intellectuals associated with them.[186] Obviously the same considerations did not apply to the newly trained young people, who did not have such expensive tastes, and who might be assumed to have a higher level of political consciousness.

I have already noted Mao's advocacy, at the Peitaiho meeting of August 1958, of the 'free supply system'. His speech on this occasion was not, of course, openly published at the time, but much of the substance of his thinking was conveyed in an article by Chang Ch'un-ch'iao reproduced in *People's daily* in October 1958. Chang's article, which had originally appeared in Shanghai in September, did not, in fact, represent simply an accidental convergence between his views and Mao's, but was the result of a clever political manoeuvre. K'o Ch'ing-shih, the leftist Mayor of Shanghai, who was present at the Peitaiho meeting, had read out to Chang Ch'un-ch'iao over the telephone his notes of Mao's speech, and this had provided the inspiration for Chang's piece. Mao's decision, on reading the article, to have it reprinted in Peking was therefore evidence both of his own susceptibility to flattery, and of the functioning, already at this time, of a Shanghai link, if not a Shanghai network.[187]

In the editorial note which he wrote to accompany Chang's article when it appeared in *People's daily*, Mao said the views expressed were 'basically correct', but he judged the article 'one-sided', and 'incomplete' in its explanation of the historical process.[188] But even though Mao thought Chang was in too much of a hurry to eliminate the 'ideology of bourgeois right', the issue evoked by this term remained posed in his speeches and writings from this time forward. In brief, Mao regarded the inequalities resulting from compensation according to work, even under a socialist system, as qualitatively similar to the 'bourgeois right' or bourgeois legal norms defined by Marx with reference to capitalist society, and it was this which provided the theoretical basis for his view that the party, because it contained the greatest number of high cadres attached to their privileges, was a nest of bourgeois or bourgeois-minded elements.[189]

---

[186] Mao, *SW* 5.357.

[187] Information regarding the role played by K'o Ch'ing-shih from conversation of 23 April 1986 with Hu Hua, confirmed by Kung Yü-chih in a conversation of 24 April 1986.

[188] Chang Ch'un-ch'iao, 'P'o-ch'u tzu-ch'an-chieh-chi fa-ch'üan ssu-hsiang' (Eliminate the ideology of bourgeois right), *Jen-min jih-pao*, 13 October 1958.

[189] For the most authoritative recent Chinese analysis of this trend in Mao's thought, see Shih Chung-ch'üan, 'Ma-k'o-ssu so shuo ti "tzu-ch'an chieh-chi fa-ch'üan" ho Mao Tse-tung t'ung-chih tui t'a ti wu-chieh' (The 'bourgeois right' referred to by Marx, and Comrade Mao Tse-tung's misunderstanding of it), *Wen-hsien ho yen-chiu* (1983) 405–17, and the revised openly published version of this in *Hung-chi'*, 11 (1985) 12–17. This article, like many other recently published accounts, asserts unequivocally that Mao played the central role in introducing the concept of 'bourgeois right' into Chinese political discourse from the Great Leap onwards. The term commonly rendered into English as 'bourgeois right' has as its *locus classicus* Marx's *Critique of the Gotha Programme*, where he

I have already stressed the importance of the Lu-shan plenum of 1959 as a turning point toward an ever greater emphasis on class struggle. Condemning P'eng and his allies as anti-Marxist 'bourgeois elements' who had infiltrated the Chinese Communist Party,[190] Mao declared that the struggle at Lu-shan had been a class struggle, 'the continuation of the life-and-death struggle between the two great antagonists of the bourgeoisie and the proletariat in the process of the socialist revolution during the past decade', and predicted that such struggle would last 'for at least another twenty years'.[191] (In the event, Mao very nearly saw to it that it did.)

Discussing Mao Tse-tung's 'errors regarding the problem of class struggle' in the period just before the Cultural Revolution, Teng Li-ch'ün has pointed to another source for Mao's increasing radicalism: 'In reality, after 1958, he basically paid no attention to economic work. This affected his estimate of the situation regarding classes and class struggle.'[192] The above statement should not be taken literally to mean that Mao henceforth took no interest in anything related to the economy. After all, it was in 1960 that he organized the study of the Soviet textbook of political economy, and Mao is now said to have taken personal charge of the drafting of the 'Sixty articles' on the communes in March 1961.[193] Teng Li-ch'ün's point, therefore, was that, while Mao continued to talk about the political and ideological dimensions of the economic system, he took little serious interest in economics or in economic reality. In this sense, his conclusion is undoubtedly justified.

Mao's growing conviction, from 1958–60 onwards, that the bureaucratic tendencies which not only he but Liu Shao-ch'i and others had long

makes use of it in criticizing the notion of a 'fair distribution of the proceeds of labour'. (Marx and Engels, *Selected works*, 317–21.) *Recht* means, in German, both right, in the sense of entitlement to the rewards of one's labour (or of human rights), and legal order. Marx is in effect referring, in the passage in question, to both these dimensions, as he makes plain when, after stating that 'equal right is still in principle bourgeois right', he goes on to note: 'Right by its very nature can consist only in the application of an equal standard . . .' In other words, right (or rights) in the sense of entitlement is defined by a system of legal or quasi-legal norms. The Chinese have further compounded this confusion by rejecting the translation of the term used by Mao, *tzu-ch'an chieh-chi fa-ch'üan* (meaning literally 'bourgeois legal rights'), since 1979, in favour of *tzu-ch'an chieh-chi ch'üan-li*, which points rather toward the rights of the individual subject. In any case, Mao's concern was primarily with the fact that, as he saw it, the strict application of the socialist principle of 'to each according to his work' failed to take into account the social needs of the individual, and was therefore in some degree heartless, just as the capitalist system of wage labour was heartless.

190 Speech of 11 September 1959 to the Military Affairs Committee, *Mao unrehearsed*, 147–8.
191 'The origin of machine guns and mortars', 15 August 1959, *Chinese Law and Government*, I, no.4 (1968–9) 73.
192 Teng Li-ch'ün, answering questions about the Resolution of 27 June 1981 at an academic discussion held on 11 and 12 August 1981, in the context of a national meeting on collecting materials for party history, in *Tang-shih hui-i pao-kao chi*, 145.
193 Yao K'ai, 'K'ai-shih ch'üan-mien chien-she she-hui-chu-i ti shih-nien' (The ten years which saw the beginning of the all-round construction of socialism), in *Hsüeh-hsi li-shih chüeh-i chuan-chi* (Specialized collection on the study of the resolution on [party] history), 121.

denounced in the Chinese Communist Party were not simply the result of a defect in 'work style' but reflected an incipient change in the class character of the party and its cadres, was inspired to a significant extent by his observations regarding the Soviet Union. But the comments he made in 1960 regarding the emergence of 'vested interest groups' in a socialist society after the abolition of classes were obviously intended to apply to China as well.

Indeed, there are scholars in China today who take the view that Mao's analysis of Soviet 'revisionism' had as its primary purpose the forging of a weapon against those in the Chinese Communist Party who did not share his ideas. That is probably putting it too strongly; Mao undoubtedly did have an acute distaste for Khrushchev's Russia and all it had come to stand for in his eyes. In fact he even traced the defects in the Soviet system back to its very origins. After the October Revolution, he asserted, the Soviets had failed to deal properly with the problem of 'bourgeois right'. As a result, a pattern of stratification reminiscent of the tsarist era had emerged; most party members were the children of cadres, and ordinary workers and peasants had no chance of advancement.[194] He also noted that the Soviets had failed to smash bourgeois freedom, and thereby to promote proletarian freedom; China's political and ideological revolution had been more thorough.[195] None the less, Mao's most acute concern was with the threat that such unwholesome tendencies might take root in China. Already in 1960 he attributed to the Chinese bearers of such contagion two traits which were to remain central to his ideas on this theme in later years. On the one hand, they were attached to their privileges, founded in the principle of distribution 'to each according to his work' – in other words, to the 'ideology of bourgeois right'. And, at the same time, they behaved like overlords. 'This animal, man, is funny,' said Mao, 'as soon as he enjoys slightly superior conditions he puts on airs.'[196]

In January 1962, in a speech mainly stressing the need to continue the struggle against the old reactionary classes (landlords and bourgeoisie), which he said were 'still planning a comeback', Mao stated explicitly that, in a socialist society, 'new bourgeois elements may still be produced'.[197] And, in August 1962, at a preliminary meeting of the Central Committee in Peitaiho, prior to the tenth plenum, Mao declared:

In the book *Socialist upsurge in China's countryside* [which he had himself edited] there is an annotation saying that the bourgeoisie has been eliminated, and only the

---

194 *Hsüeh-hsi wen-hsüan*, 305. (Speech of 21 August 1958, in the morning.)
195 *Ibid.* 311. (Speech of 21 August 1958, in the afternoon.)
196 *Wan-sui* (1967) 192. For an earlier reference to 'putting on airs like overlords', see Mao's speech of November 1958 on Stalin's *Economic problems of socialism in the USSR* in *Wan-sui* (1967) 117–18.
197 *Mao unrehearsed*, 168.

influence of bourgeois ideology remains. This is wrong, and should be corrected. ... The bourgeoisie can be born anew; such a situation exists in the Soviet Union.[198]

As it stands, this statement that the bourgeoisie can be 'born anew' leaves open the question of whether Mao means the old bourgeoisie can be reborn, or whether he is referring to the reincarnation of the soul or essence of the bourgeoisie in a new form, adapted to the conditions of a socialist society. Probably he was talking about the second of these things – what Djilas and others have called the 'new class' – though to my knowledge, Mao himself never used that term. He seemed unable to make up his mind, however, as to whether these 'new bourgeois elements' were merely isolated individuals, corrupted by the advantages drawn from the misuse of their status, or whether *all* cadres, because of the privileges and power they enjoyed, were prone to take on this character.

In the early 1960s, he appeared to lean in the first direction, by stressing the corrupting effects of money, and advantages bought with money. Thus, while continuing to acknowledge that material incentives were necessary in Chinese society at the present stage, he argued that they should be subordinated to 'spiritual incentives' in the political and ideological domains, and that individual interests should be subordinated to collective interests.[199]

In his speech of 30 January 1962 to a central work conference, Mao related the 'five bad categories' to the social origins of the individuals in question: 'Those whom the people's democratic dictatorship should repress', he declared, 'are landlords, rich peasants, counter-revolutionary elements, bad elements and anti-communist rightists. The classes which the counter-revolutionary elements, bad elements and anti-communist rightists represent are the landlord class and the reactionary bourgeoisie. These classes and bad people comprise about 4 or 5 per cent of the population. These are the people we must compel to reform.'[200]

At the tenth plenum of September-October 1962, Mao put forward the slogan, 'Never forget the class struggle!' and personally revised the communiqué of the plenum, which summed up his thinking.[201] Like his speech five years earlier, at the third plenum, and the confrontation on Lu-shan, this occasion marked yet a further turn toward a policy of promoting 'class struggle'. The nature and locus of the classes being struggled against

---

[198] *Wan-sui* (1969) 424.
[199] *Wan-sui* (1967) 206, 210. From Mao's 'reading notes' of 1960 on the Soviet textbook of political economy. These are now known to be, not notes written by Mao himself, but an edited version of his remarks at sessions with other top leaders for the detailed discussion of the Soviet work, prepared by Hu Sheng and Teng Li-ch'ün. See Shih Chung-ch'üan, 'Tu Su-lien "Cheng-chih ching-chi hsüeh chiao-k'o shu" ti t'an-hua' (Talks on reading the Soviet textbook of political economy), *Mao Tse-tung ti tu-shu sheng-huo* (Mao Tse-tung's reading activities), 148–78. Hereafter *Mao's reading*. Although they thus contain some errors, and some comments which are in fact by other participants, on the whole they convey Mao's views. Hu Sheng and Kung Yü-chih confirmed this in conversations of January 1988.   [200] *Mao unrehearsed*, 169–70.   [201] 1981 Resolution, annotated edn, 359.

remained, however, fundamentally ambiguous. In his speech of January 1962, Mao had referred to 'classes and bad people'. In other words, though the counter-revolutionaries and other 'bad elements' were said by Mao to 'represent' the landlords and the reactionary bourgeoisie, they did not necessarily come from these classes. Two passages from speeches by Mao during the period from the summer of 1962 to the spring of 1963, when the 'Socialist Education Campaign' was in the process of taking shape, stress more heavily the class origins of deviations within the party, but at the same time underscore the continuing importance, in Mao's view, of transformation through education. In his talk of 9 August at Peitaiho, Mao said:

The composition of the party membership (*tang-yuan ti ch'eng-fen*) includes a large number of petty bourgeois, a contingent of well-to-do peasants and their sons and younger brothers, a certain number of intellectuals, and also some bad people who have not yet been properly transformed; in reality, [these last] are not Communist Party members. They are called Communist Party members, but they are really [members of the] Kuomintang. . . . As for the intellectuals and sons and brothers of landlords and rich peasants, there are those who have been transformed by Marxism (*Ma-k'o-ssu-hua le ti*), there are those who have not been transformed at all, and there are those who have not been transformed to a satisfactory level. These people are not spiritually prepared for the socialist revolution; we have not educated them in good time.[202]

In May, 1963, on the eve of the promulgation of the first directive regarding the Socialist Education Movement (the 'First ten points'), Mao defined the class composition of the party quite differently, but discussed the problem of 'transformation' in very similar terms:

With respect to party composition, the most important class components are workers, poor peasants and farm labourers. Consequently, the main class composition is good. However, within the party there is a large number of petty bourgeois elements, some of whom belong to the upper stratum of the urban and rural petty bourgeoisie. In addition, there are intellectuals, as well as a certain number of sons and daughters of landlords and rich peasants. Of these people, some have been transformed by Marxism; some have been partly, but not totally transformed by Marxism-Leninism; and some have not been transformed at all. Organizationally they may have joined the party, but not in terms of their thought. They are not ideologically prepared for the socialist revolution. In addition, during the last few years some bad people have wormed their way in. They are corrupt and degenerate and have seriously violated the law and discipline. . . . This problem requires attention, but it is relatively easy to deal with. The most important problem is the petty-bourgeois elements who have not been properly reformed. With respect to intellectuals and the sons and daughters of landlords and rich peasants we must do more work. Consequently, we must carry out education, and yet more education, for party members and cadres. This is an important task.[203]

---

[202] *Wan-sui* (1969) 426.   [203] *Tzu-liao hsüan-pien* ([Peking], January 1967), 277.

It is evident from these two quotations that, although objective social origins remained important for Mao, inward transformation through political education was likewise a crucial aspect of the problem of class taken as a whole. The tension between these two elements in Mao's thought was well illustrated by his directive of 9 May 1963, incorporated into the First Ten Points. In this text, while stressing the need to transform human beings into 'new people' (*hsin-jen*) by participation in labour and in scientific experiment, Mao also conjured up the spectre of an offensive spearheaded by the landlords and rich peasants (together with counter-revolutionaries, bad elements, and demons), which might cause China to change colour and become fascist.[204]

In May 1964, as the Socialist Education Campaign unfolded, Mao declared, at a meeting with four vice-premiers:

We must definitely pay very close attention to class struggle. The 'four clean-ups' in the countryside is a class struggle, and the 'five antis' in the cities is also a class struggle. . . . Class status (*ch'eng-fen*) must also be determined in the cities. As for how such class lines should be drawn, criteria must be formulated when we come to do this work. We cannot take account only of [inherited] class status (*wei ch'eng-fen lun*). Neither Marx, Engels, Lenin nor Stalin had working-class family origins (*ch'u-shen*).[205]

A directive on drawing class distinctions, undated but almost certainly from late 1964, discusses explicitly the relation between subjective and objective criteria:

It is necessary to draw class distinctions. . . . Of the two, [objective] class status (*chieh-chi ch'eng-fen*) and the behaviour of the person in question (*pen-jen piao-hsien*), it is the behaviour of the person in question which is most important. The main thing in drawing class distinctions is to ferret out the bad elements.

We must moreover clearly distinguish between family origins (*ch'u-shen*) and the behaviour of the person in question. The emphasis must be placed on behaviour; the theory that everything depends on class status alone (*wei ch'eng-fen lun*) is wrong, the problem is whether you take the stand of your class of origin, or whether you adopt a different class stand, that is, on the side of the workers and the poor and lower-middle peasants. Moreover, we must not be sectarian, but must unite with the majority, even including a portion of the landlords and rich peasants, and their children. There are even some counter-revolutionaries and saboteurs who should be transformed; it suffices that they be willing to be transformed, and we should be willing to have them, one and all.[206]

[204] For a conveniently available translation of this whole directive, see Richard Baum and Frederick C. Teiwes, *Ssu-ch'ing: The Socialist Education Movement of 1962–1966*, 58–71. (The passage by Mao is on pp.70–1.) This text was first openly published in the Ninth Chinese Reply to the Soviet open letter; see *PTMT* 367.   [205] *Miscellany*, 351; *Wan-sui* (1969) 494–5.
[206] *Miscellany*, 351; *Wan-sui* (1969) 602–3. (For the dating of this text, see the discussion in volume 2 of the index to Mao's post-1949 writings published in 1981 by the Research Institute of Humanistic Studies, Kyoto University: Kyōto Daigaku Jimbun Kagaku Kenkyūsho. *Mō Takutō chosaku nempyō. Goi sakuin* (Glossary and index), p.47.)

It can be argued that, in Mao's later years, certain pairs of opposites which had hitherto co-existed in dynamic and creative tension became dissociated, thus unleashing forces that ultimately propelled his thought and action into destructive channels. In several crucial and interrelated repects, this unravelling of the previous synthesis began with the tenth plenum. Increasingly, Mao came to perceive the relation between the leaders, with their privileges, and the rest of society, as an antagonistic contradiction rather than a contradiction among the people. The consequence which inevitably flowed from this insight was that the party, considered as an entity which included virtually all of these privileged power-holders, must not be simply tempered and purified in contact with the masses, but smashed, at least in large part.

Apart from the relation between the party, or privileged elements in the party, and the masses, the very complex process of dissociation or disagregation of the structure of Mao Tse-tung's thought which took place beginning in the 1960s involved a number of other polarities. I have already dealt at some length with the interaction between Marxism and the Chinese tradition, and also with the issue of the relation between the Soviet model and Chinese experience.

The Sino-Soviet conflict also played an important role in shaping Mao Tse-tung's philosophical thought by contributing to the context in which the key idea of 'One divides into two' emerged. On 26 October 1963, Chou Yang delivered to the Chinese Academy of Sciences a speech entitled 'The fighting task confronting workers in philosophy and the social sciences'. This speech, which was published, by an altogether too striking coincidence, on Mao's 70th birthday (26 December 1963), plainly represented Mao Tse-tung's own thinking. In it, Chou Yang surveyed the history of the workers' movement from Marx's own day to the present in terms of the axiom 'One divides into two'.[207]

Mao himself had, in fact, used this expression in a speech of 18 November 1957 at the Moscow meeting, although on that occasion his emphasis was not on divisions within the socialist movement but on the fact that all societies, including socialist society, 'teem' with contradictions, and on the fact that there is good and bad in everyone. 'One divides into two,' he concluded. 'This is a universal phenomenon, and this is dialectics.'[208]

Very soon after Chou Yang's speech of 1963, the slogan 'One divides into two' came to evoke above all, in Mao's own usage, the need to struggle against 'capitalist roaders' in the Chinese Communist Party. In other words,

---

[207] *Peking Review* 1 (1964) 10–27, especially p.14; Chinese in *Hung-ch'i*, 24 (1963) 1–30. (The expression *i fen wei erh* appears on pp.4–5.) On Mao's involvement with this report, see also *Ideology and policy*, 44–5.   [208] Mao, *SW* 5.516.

it was by implication, a call for class struggle. (It was also, as discussed in *CHOC* 14. 466–67, the rallying-cry for the purge and persecution of Yang Hsien-chen and other partisans of the opposing formulation, 'Two combine into one'.)

This principle, Mao declared, constituted 'the heart of dialectical materialism'. He drew from it the conclusion that the electron, like the atom, would ultimately be split.[209] But above all, he was persuaded that social categories and political forces would continue to split, now and forever.

In the last analysis, Mao's conflict with others in the leadership revolved, of course, around the fundamental political and economic strategy which should be adopted for building socialism. The domain of culture was, however, a crucial battleground as well. In the early 1960s, Mao perceived certain developments in literature and philosophy not only as the expression of unwholesome tendencies, but as a weapon for attacking the very foundations of socialism through the agency of the superstructure. It is thus no accident that Mao should have first expressed his anxieties in cogent form precisely at the tenth plenum, simultaneously with his call for class struggle:

Writing novels is popular these days, isn't it? The use of novels for anti-party activity is a great invention. Anyone wanting to overthrow a political regime must create public opinion and do some preparatory ideological work. This applies to counter-revolutionary as well as to revolutionary classes.[210]

The clear implication of this statement was that 'counter-revolutionary classes' were still at work in China, thirteen years after the conquest of power, seeking to overthrow the dictatorship of the proletariat, and that constant struggle in the realm of the superstructure was necessary in order to keep them in check. There is here present in embryonic form the idea of 'continuing the revolution under the dictatorship of the proletariat', which was to loom so large during the Cultural Revolution decade. In view of the ambiguity of Mao's notion of class at this time, this development clearly represents a further manifestation of the accent on the superstructure, and on subjective forces, which had characterized Mao's thought from the beginning.

Just as Mao's call for class struggle at the tenth plenum had led to the Socialist Education Campaign, so this statement gave the impetus to a movement for literary rectification, and encouraged Chiang Ch'ing to

---

[209] Strong, 'Three interviews', 499–500. For a detailed discussion of Mao's thinking about natural dialectics in general, and this question in particular, see Kung Yü-chih, 'Mao Tse-tung yü tzu-jan k'o-hsüeh' (Mao Tse-tung and the natural sciences), *Mao's reading*, 83–114.

[210] *Mao unrehearsed*, 195. A similar concern with the influence of the media, and with the superstructure as a crucial realm of political struggle, had already been expressed by Mao in his 'reading notes' of 1960. See *Wan-sui* (1969) 342–3; *Miscellany*, 266.

launch the reform of the Peking opera. These policies and their consequences have been described and analysed in *CHOC* 14. 460–3. Here it will suffice to mention briefly two directives by which Mao continued to pour oil on the fire. In December 1963, he complained that the 'dead' still ruled in many departments of art, literature and drama. 'The social and economic base has already changed,' he declared, 'but the arts as part of the superstructure, which serve this base, still remain a great problem today. . . . Isn't it absurd that many Communists are enthusiastic about promoting feudal and capitalist arts, but not socialist art?' In June 1964 his judgment was even harsher. The Chinese Writers' Association, he said, 'for the past fifteen years has *basically* [Mao's italics] . . . not implemented the party's policy'. Instead of uniting with the workers and peasants, they had acted as bureaucrats and overlords, going to the brink of revisionism. Unless they mended their ways, they would become another Petöfi Club.[211] In other words, they would be outright counter-revolutionaries, and would be treated as such.

At the same time, in 1963–4, Mao showed greatly increased scepticism regarding the role of intellectuals in revolution and development. Without carrying his distrust of intellectuals to the point of characterizing them, like the gang of four, as the 'stinking ninth category', Mao therefore moved toward education policies infinitely more extreme than those of the Great Leap Forward. 'We shouldn't read too many books,' he said in February 1964. 'We should read Marxist books, but not too many of them either. It will be enough to read a dozen or so. If we read too many we can move toward our opposite, become bookworms, dogmatists, revisionists.'[212]

In all of these various domains – art and literature, philosophy, education – Mao attacked leading intellectuals not so much because they were privileged elements exploiting the masses (though he could make a good case to show that they were), but because they failed to share his utopia of struggle, and to obey wholeheartedly his directives.

In the summer of 1964, Mao referred scathingly to material corruption throughout the party. 'At present', he said, 'you can buy a branch secretary for a few packs of cigarettes, not to mention marrying a daughter to him.'[213]

The reference here to lower-level cadres would suggest that at that moment, shortly before Liu Shao-ch'i produced his 'revised later ten points', Mao did not wholly disagree with the view that the Socialist Education Campaign should be directed at the grass roots, as well as at the higher echelons. He was, however, particularly exercised about the atti-

---

[211] These are two of the 'five militant documents' on art and literature published in May 1967. For a translation (somewhat modified here) of the directives of 12 December 1963 and 27 June 1964, see *Peking Review* 23 (1967) 8. [212] *Mao unrehearsed*, 210. [213] *Mao unrehearsed*, 217.

tudes and behaviour of the privileged urban elite. In a talk of June 1964 on the third five-year plan, he remarked:

Don't strive for money all the time, and don't spend it recklessly once you've got it. . . . In accordance with our policy, bourgeois intellectuals may be bought when necessary, but why should we buy proletarian intellectuals? He who has plenty of money is bound to corrupt himself, his family, and those around him. . . . In the Soviet Union, the high-salaried stratum appeared first in literary and artistic circles.[214]

As is well known, the final confrontation between Mao Tse-tung and Liu Shao-ch'i took place in December 1964, when Mao, dissatisfied with what he perceived as the distortion and watering-down of his original strategy for the Socialist Education Campaign, put forward a new 23-article directive which Liu, Mao later claimed, refused to accept. On this occasion, he made a number of observations regarding the 'new bourgeoisie' in which power, rather than money, began to appear as the decisive factor.

It is perhaps worth noting in passing that, although the problem of status and wage differentials was obviously of very acute concern to Mao, he displayed toward it even at this time a relaxed and humorous attitude scarcely to be found in the writings of the glum and fanatical ideologists of the gang of four. 'This business of eating more and possessing more is rather complex!' he declared. 'It is mainly people like us who have cars, and houses with central heating, and chauffeurs. I earn only 430 yuan, and I can't afford to hire secretaries, but I must. . . .'[215]

It is hard to resist reading this passage in the light of Mao's remark, earlier in the same year of 1964, 'Hsuan-t'ung's salary of a little over 100 yuan is too small – this man is an emperor.'[216] One has the impression that for Mao, there existed, in addition to 'worker', 'poor peasant', 'son of revolutionary martyr' and so on, yet another *ch'eng-fen*: that of ruler. As for those who did not share this status with him, and with the former emperor, they could not be allowed to grow attached to their privileges.

In a discussion of 20 December 1964, he thus castigated once again those 'power holders' among the cadres who were primarily concerned about getting more wage points for themselves, and agreed that the 'hat' of 'new bourgeois elements' should be stuck on 'particularly vicious offenders' among them. He warned, however, against overestimating their number, and said they should be referred to as elements or cliques, not as 'strata' – still less, obviously, as a fully-formed class.[217] A week later, on 27 December

---

[214] *Wan-sui* (1969) 498–9.   [215] *Wan-sui* (1969) 587.
[216] *Mao unrehearsed*, 198. (Remarks at the Spring Festival Forum on Education.) Hsüan-t'ung was the reign title of the last Manchu emperor, a boy at the time of his abdication in 1912, and also known as Pu-yi (P'u-i) when he was emperor of the Japanese puppet state of Manchukuo from 1932 to 1945. He was still living in Beijing in 1964.   [217] *Wan-sui* (1969) 582–8.

1964, Mao declared that there were 'at least two factions' in the Chinese Communist Party, a socialist faction and a capitalist faction; these two factions thus incarnated the principal contradiction in Chinese society.[218]

Such formulations, and Mao's determination to direct the spearhead of the Socialist Education Campaign against 'those in authority taking the capitalist road', led, of course, directly to the confrontation with Liu and others in the party, and to the Cultural Revolution.

THE IDEOLOGY OF THE CULTURAL REVOLUTION

Before addressing ourselves to the substance of Mao's thinking during the Cultural Revolution, it may be useful to ask ourselves precisely why he launched this movement, and what was the relationship between this decision and the 'unravelling' of the Great Leap and post-Great Leap synthesis evoked above. Did he adopt extreme lines of conduct because his thinking had become skewed or distorted, or did he think as he did because he was obsessed with certain existential problems — above all, with the desire to punish and ultimately to destroy his critics?

As I have already suggested, especially in discussing his changing ideas on dialectics, and on class struggle, there were, in my view, elements of both these processes at work, but the predominant factor was the second one. In other words, the political and psychological roots of his ideas were notably more important than the intellectual ones. As a Chinese author has put it, Mao was so thoroughly persuaded that his own views were the only correct exposition of Marxism-Leninism that anyone who failed to agree with him automatically became a revisionist in his eyes. As a result, 'The more it proved impossible to put his ideas into practice, the more he saw this as the reflection of class struggle . . . and of the emergence of "counter-revolutionary revisionist elements" within the party.'[219]

Dictatorship, rebellion, and spiritual transformation

Among the multifarious ideological and policy innovations of the Cultural Revolution, it was the radical calling into question of the party, and of authority in all its forms (except that of the Chairman) which attracted the

---

[218] *Wan-sui* (1969) 597–8.

[219] Wang Nien-i, 'Mao Tse-tung t'ung-chih fa-tung "wen-hua ta ko-ming" shih tui hsing-shih ti ku-chi' (Comrade Mao Tse-tung's estimate of the situation at the time when he launched the 'Great Cultural Revolution'), *Tang-shih yen-chiu tzu-liao* 4, 772. For a more extended discussion of the psychological roots of the Cultural Revolution, see my article 'Party leader or true ruler?', 221–4, 233–7. Also, S. Schram, 'The limits of cataclysmic change: reflections on the place of the "Great Proletarian Cultural Revolution" in the political development of the People's Republic of China', *CQ* 108 (December 1986) 613–24.

most attention at the outset of this upheaveal. In retrospect, it is clear that Mao's repudiation of leadership from above was not so sweeping as it appeared at the time. Nevertheless, he did go very far.

In his comments of 1960 on the Soviet textbook, Mao had declared: 'No matter what, we cannot regard history as the creation of the planners, it is the creation of the masses.'[220] And yet, he had always held, down to the eve of the Cultural Revolution, the view that the masses could exercise this role of making history only if they benefited from correct leadership. As the great confrontation with the party approached, in December 1965, he went a step farther, proclaiming that democracy meant 'dealing with the affairs of the masses through the masses themselves'. There were, he added, two lines: to rely entirely on a few individuals, and to mobilize the masses. 'Democratic politics', he said, 'must rely on everyone running things, not on a minority of people running things.' At the same time, however, he called once more for reliance on 'the leadership of the party at the higher level and on the broad masses at the lower level'.[221] It was only with the actual onset of the Cultural Revolution in March 1966 that Mao sounded a much more radical note, suggesting that the masses could dispense with centralized party leadership:

The Propaganda Department of the Central Committee is the palace of the King of Hell. We must overthrow the palace of the King of Hell and set the little devils free. I have always advocated that whenever the central organs do bad things, it is necessary to call upon the localities to rebel, and to attack the Centre. The localities must produce many Sun Wu-k'ungs to create a great disturbance in the palace of the King of Heaven. . . .[222]

Two months later, these 'Monkey Kings' burst upon the scene, using Mao's own rhetoric, including the slogan 'To rebel is justified!' which he had coined in 1939, attributing it – irony of ironies – to Stalin.[223] 'Daring to . . . rebel is . . . the fundamental principle of the proletarian party spirit,' proclaimed the Red Guards of Tsing-hua University Middle School. 'Revolutionaries are Monkey Kings. . . . We wield our golden rods, display our supernatural powers, and use our magic to turn the old world upside down, smash it to pieces, pulverize it and create chaos – the greater the confusion the better! We are bent on creating a tremendous proletarian uproar, and hewing out a proletarian new world!'[224] The 'old world' these Red Guards wanted to smash was, of course, that controlled by the party; they did not propose to rectify it, but to dissolve it in the chaos of the Cultural Revolution, and replace it by a completely new order.

[220] Wan-sui (1967) 206.
[221] Wan-sui (1969) 630. (Talk of 21 December 1965 with Ch'en Po-ta and Ai Ssu-ch'i.)
[222] Wan-sui (1969) 640.   [223] MTTC 7.142; translated in PTMT 427–8.
[224] Jen-min jih-pao, 24 August 1966; translated in Peking Review 37 (1966) 2–21.

Mao himself never proclaimed such a goal. At a Central Work Conference on 23 August, he remarked, 'The principal question is what policy we should adopt regarding the so-called disturbances (*so-wei luan*) in various areas. My view is that we should let disorder reign for a few months (*luan t'a chi-ko yüeh*). . . . Even if there are no provincial party committees, it doesn't matter; aren't there still district and *hsien* committees?'[225]

The phrase 'for a few months' should probably be taken literally, to mean three or four months, or six at the outside. That in itself would have made the Cultural Revolution more like a conventional rectification campaign. Nevertheless, by accepting the prospect that for a time the party might survive only in the form of local-level committees, the central organs having been effectively smashed and put out of action, Mao was at the very least taking the risk of destroying the political instrument to which he had devoted more than four decades of his life, in order to purge it of his enemies.

When events moved in such a direction, in late 1966 and early 1967, that the threat to the very existence of the party became acute, Mao was forced to choose between Leninism and anarchy. He had no hesitation in preferring the former. Speaking in February 1967 to Chang Ch'un-ch'iao and Yao Wen-yüan, Mao noted that some people in Shanghai had demanded the abolition of 'heads', and commented: 'This is extreme anarchism, it is most reactionary. If instead of calling someone the "head" of something, we call him "orderly" or "assistant", this would really be only a formal change. In reality, there will still always be heads.'[226] Discussing the objections to setting up communes as organs of government, as Chang and Yao had just done in Shanghai, Mao queried: 'Where will we put the party? . . . In a commune there has to be a party: can the commune replace the party?'[227] The history of the ensuing nine years made it abundantly clear that in the chairman's view it could not.

Another contradiction which became acute at this time was that between Mao's consistently held view that the party should command the gun, and the gun should never be allowed to command the party, and the increasingly dominant role of the People's Liberation Army in Chinese politics from 1960 onwards. This trend had begun, of course, as an essentially tactical manoeuvre on Mao's part to develop a power base in Lin Piao's PLA because he felt the party to be slipping from his grasp, and not because of any innovation or brusque mutation in his thought. The pursuit of these tactics, however, soon led Mao in directions which, whatever his own orginal intentions, had major theoretical implications.

The most important of these developments was the establishment, in the

---

[225] *Wan-sui* (1969) 653.   [226] *Mao unrehearsed*, 277.   [227] *Wan-sui* (1969) 670–1; *Miscellany*, 453–4.

course of the 'Learn from the PLA' campaign launched in February 1964, of political departments, modelled on that of the army, in industrial enter-prises, schools, and other units throughout the country. Not only did the army provide the model for these departments; it also provided the person-nel, as Mao himself had decided in advance. On 16 December 1963, he wrote to Lin Piao, Ho Lung, Nieh Jung-chen, and Hsiao Hua, saying in part:

In every branch of state industry people are now proposing to emulate the People's Liberation Army from top to bottom (that is, from the ministry down to the factory or to the mine), to set up everywhere political departments, political offices and political instructors, and to put into effect the Four Firsts and the Three-Eight work style. I too propose that several groups of good cadres be transferred from the Liberation Army to do political work in the industry ministries. . . . It looks as though we just can't get by without doing this, for otherwise we will be unable to rouse the revolutionary spirit of the millions and millions of cadres and workers in the whole industrial sector (and commerce and agriculture to). . . . I have been considering this question for several years. . .[228]

Such colonization of other organizations by the army rather than the party was without precedent in the history of the world Communist movement. Of equally great symbolic importance was the fact that by 1964 the People's Liberation Army was becoming increasingly the ideological and cultural mentor of the Chinese people. It was the army which compiled and published, in May 1964, the first edition of the 'Little red book', *Quotations from Chairman Mao.* Moreover, Mao himself, though he is not known to have participated in the work of compiling this breviary, had a share in the authorship of it, for the preface was drawn in large part from a resolution of the Military Affairs Commission of October 1960 which he had personally rewritten and approved at the time.[229] Thus the stage was set for the dialectic between anarchy and military control during the period 1966–72, and for the further and final unravelling of the polarities of Mao Tse-tung's thought.

By no means the least of the paradoxes of the Cultural Revolution period lay in the role of youth. On the one hand, Mao called on the Red Guards, at the outset of the movement, to serve as the vanguard, as he and his own generation of students had burst upon the stage of history in 1919; and yet, on the other hand, the policies of 1966 and after involved downgrading sharply the role of this very educated elite. Part of the explanation is to be

[228] *Tzu-liao hsüan-pien,* 287; translated in S. Schram, 'New texts by Mao Zedong, 1921–1966', *Communist Affairs* 2.2 (1983) 161.

[229] The resolution of 20 October 1960 is translated in J. Chester Cheng, ed., *The politics of the Chinese Red Army:* a translation of the *Bulletin of Activities* of the People's Liberation Army, 66–94. The passage corresponding to the preface to the *Quotations* appears on p.70; on p.33 of the same volume, it is noted that the resolution has been revised 'by Chairman Mao himself'.

found in the undisciplined and self-indulgent behaviour of the Red Guards, for which Mao castigated them in the summer of 1968, before sending them to the countryside, beginning in December 1968, to learn 'proletarian class consciousness' from the peasants. But this paradox also reflects a deeper ambiguity, in Mao's thinking and policies, regarding the role in building socialism of expertise, and of the highly trained people who are the bearers of expertise.

Theoretically, all these contradictions should have been subsumed in a larger unity under the slogan 'Red *and* expert'. In fact, the emphasis was shifted so far, in the aftermath of the Cultural Revolution, in the direction of politics as a substitute for, rather than as a complement to, knowledge and skills, that the whole foundation for the enterprise of modernization to which, as we have seen, Mao was committed, was substantially undermined.

The fountainhead for many of these excesses was Mao's directive of 21 July 1968, which reads as follows:

It is still necessary to have universities; here I refer mainly to the need for colleges of science and engineering. However, it is essential to shorten the length of schooling, revolutionize education, put proletarian politics in command and take the road of the Shanghai Machine Tools Plant in training technicians from among the workers. Students should be selected from among workers and peasants with practical experience and they should return to practical work in production after a few years' study.[230]

Mao commented on this text, or perhaps on the talk from which it is drawn, in his conversation of 28 July 1968 with Red Guard leaders. On this occasion, he showed himself less exclusively concerned with technical knowledge for practical purposes, but in some respects even more sceptical about the value of formal education. 'Should we continue to run universities?' he said. 'Should universities continue to enrol new students? To stop enrolling new students won't do either. You should make some allowances for [the context of] that talk of mine. I spoke of colleges of science and engineering, but I by no means said that all liberal arts colleges should be closed.' Mao then went on, however, to say that if liberal arts colleges were unable to show any accomplishments, they should be overturned. In any case, he argued, courses in senior middle schools merely repeated those in junior middle schools, and those in universities repeated those in senior middle schools. The best method, he held, was independent study in a library, as practised by Engels, and by Mao himself in his youth, or setting

---

[230] *PTMT* 371. For the example of the Shanghai Machine Tools Plant, see *Peking Review* 37 (1968) 13–17.

up a 'self-study university' (as Mao had done in 1921). 'The real universities are the factories and the rural areas,' he concluded.[231]

Some account must be taken, in interpreting these remarks, of the fact that Mao had at the same time a very stern and indeed harsh message to convey to his Red Guard interlocutors, namely that the party was over and the activities in which they had been indulging for the past two years would no longer be tolerated. In these circumstances, it was understandable that he should sweeten the pill by expressing agreement with them on some things. Thus he also went on to say that examinations were a waste of time. 'All examinations should be abolished, absolutely abolished. Who examined Marx, Engels, Lenin and Stalin? Who examined Comrade Lin Piao? Who examined me? Comrade Hsieh Fu-chih, call all the students back to school.'[232]

The students were indeed to be called back to school, and though the academic discipline of examinations was (for the moment at least) to be abolished, social discipline was to be forcefully restored. Explaining to the Red Guard leaders why he was obliged to put a stop to the bloody internecine conflicts which had already claimed thousands of victims, Mao declared:

The masses just don't like civil wars. . . . For two years, you have been engaged in the Great Cultural Revolution, that is, in struggle-criticism-transformation, but at present you are neither struggling nor criticizing nor transforming. It's true that you are struggling, but it is armed struggle. The people are unhappy, the workers are unhappy, the peasants are unhappy, Peking residents are unhappy, the students in most schools are unhappy. . . . Can you unite the realm in this way?

'If you are unable [to handle the problem]', he warned, 'we may resort to military control, and ask Lin Piao to take command.'[233] That was, of course, exactly what Mao did do, but whatever the Soviets, and/or leftists of various persuasions may think, military dictatorship was not his ideal. He 'resorted to military control' because there was no other instrument, apart from the People's Liberation Army, capable of putting down factional fighting conducted not merely with bricks and slingshots, but with rifles and even with mortars and other heavy weapons. As soon as circumstances appeared to permit it once again, he undertook to re-establish the primacy of the party over the 'gun'. Justifying this step in his talks of August-September 1971 with military commanders, he suggested that the PLA was not the best instrument for exercising leadership in complex political and economic matters. 'I approve of the army's traditional style of quick and decisive action,' he said. 'But this style cannot be applied to questions of

---

[231] *Wan-sui* (1969) 693, 706, 695; *Miscellany*, 475, 488, 471.
[232] *Wan-sui* (1969) 714; *Miscellany*, 496.   [233] *Wan-sui* (1969) 698, 688, *Miscellany*, 481, 470.

ideology, for which it is necessary to make the facts known and reason with people.' The main thrust of these talks was, in fact, the re-establishment of unified party leadership, and the subordination of the army to the party. 'Now that the regional party committees have been established,' said Mao, 'they should exercise unified leadership. It would be putting the cart before the horse if matters already decided by regional party committees were later turned over to army party committees for discussion.'[234]

The Ninth Congress of the Chinese Communist Party in April 1969 was presented at the time, and was widely seen outside China as marking the conclusion of the Cultural Revolution. In retrospect, and despite the symbolic significance of the formal disgrace of Liu Shao-ch'i on this occasion, the over-arching continuity of events from 1966 to 1976 was such that it is probably more accurate to speak, as the Chinese have done since the third plenum of 1978, of the 'Cultural Revolution decade'. None the less, the phase inaugurated by the Ninth Congress did see the emergence of significant new themes and formulations in the thought of Mao Tse-tung.

Marx and Ch'in Shih-huang – the ambiguous legacy

Thus far, I have used the term 'Cultural Revolution' as a convenient label for the period beginning in 1966, without inquiring further into its meaning. Before proceeding further in the analysis of the ideological content of the so-called 'Great Proletarian Cultural Revolution', as it continued to unfold after 1969, let us now consider the appropriateness of the expression.

Leaving aside the adjective 'great', of which the force is purely rhetorical or emphatic, was it 'proletarian'? Was it 'cultural'? Was it a revolution? Plainly Mao believed it to be all three of these things. To my mind, it was in truth none of them. The question of why Mao thought it *was* is, however, central to any understanding of his thought during his last decade.

In reality Mao's reasons for attributing to the movement he launched in 1966 each of these three qualities overlap to such a significant extent that they stand or fall together. In other words, either it was proletarian, socialist and revolutionary, or it cannot appropriately be characterized by any of these terms.

If we consider the three attributes in the order in which they are commonly placed, 'proletarian' might signify, to begin with, 'related to the urban working class'. In that sense, the upheaval of 1966 was assuredly not proletarian. The shock troops of the movement, during its first and formative stage, were students rather than workers. And though so-called

---

[234] *Mao unrehearsed*, 296.

'revolutionary rebels' among the workers subsequently played a significant role in political events, their intervention scarcely reflected the qualities of discipline, and of orientation toward technological modernization which Marx attributed to the urban proletariat.

The Cultural Revolution might, in a slightly looser sense, be legitimately called 'proletarian' if it contributed to industrial development, and thereby to expanding the working class, and laying the material foundations for a society dominated by the proletariat. That was assuredly not the case, either. In December 1968, when Mao issued his directive ordering educated young people to go to the countryside to be re-educated by the poor and lower-middle peasants, this was interpreted to signify that the sons and daughters of urban workers would receive 'a profound class education' from the poor peasants in the countryside.[235] And while, as I have stressed repeatedly, Mao never ceased to call for rapid economic development, arguing even that the policies of the Cultural Revolution would produce economic and technical miracles, he showed increasing anxiety about the consequences of economic development.

In August 1958 at Peitaiho, he had called for the revival of the spiritual heritage of Yenan, but nevertheless, at that time the emphasis was overwhelmingly on economic goals. In April 1969, on the other hand, at the first plenum of the new Ninth Central Committee, he spoke with nostalgia of the very high proportion of comrades killed during the struggle for power, and went on to say:

For years we did not have any such thing as salaries. We had no eight-tier wage system. We had only a fixed amount of food, three mace of oil and five of salt. If we got 1½ catties of millet, that was great . . . Now we have entered the cities. This is a good thing. If we hadn't entered the cities Chiang Kai-shek would be occupying them. But it is also a bad thing because it caused our party to deteriorate.[236]

Though Mao concludes that it was, after all, right to enter the cities, his sentiments toward the consequences of modernization and economic development were, thus, profoundly ambiguous.

If the Cultural Revolution did not reflect either the role or the ideals of the urban working class, there remains only one sense in which it might qualify as proletarian: by its conformity to 'proletarian' ideology as defined by Mao. We have already noted the three-fold framework in which Mao Tse-tung had begun to view classes in the late 1950s and early 1960s. During the Cultural Revolution, while objective class origins were never regarded as *irrelevant*, high and generally decisive importance was attributed to subjective factors as the main criterion of class nature.

[235] *Peking Review* 52 (1968) 6–7.   [236] *Mao unrehearsed*, 288.

Lenin, for his part, had written in orthodox Marxist vein: 'The funda-mental criterion by which classes are distinguished is the place they occupy in social production . . .' In November 1966, Mao's evil genius, K'ang Sheng, said that Lenin's definition had proved inadequate, for class differ-entiation also fell under political and ideological categories, and in 1970 K'ang stated more precisely:

The existence of the capitalist class is particularly manifest in relations of economic exploitation. In socialist society, although there are economic contradictions among the various classes, the existence of classes shows itself ideologically and politically.[237]

Leaving aside for the moment the question of just where and how the existence of classes in this sense 'showed itself' in China at this period, it is evident that to define class in ideological terms brings, in effect, the matter of the 'proletarian' character of the movement launched by Mao in 1966 into the cultural domain. In other words, this 'revolution' was proletarian only to the extent that it was also cultural.

The notion, propagated at the time by some naive observers, that the events of 1966 constituted a 'cultural revolution' in the same sense as the May Fourth movement, and indeed the legitimate continuation of the May Fourth movement, was altogether absurd. The bitter joke current in China in the years after Mao's death, '*Wen-hua ko-ming shih ko wen-hua ti ming*' (The Cultural Revolution was about doing away with culture), is nearer the mark. This upheaval did grow, none the less, as we have seen, out of Mao's reaction to certain cultural phenomena, and from beginning to end it was marked by the stress on psychological transformation which had long characterized his thought.

To mention only a few manifestations of this tendency, there was the slogan of a 'great revolution which touches people to their very souls', thereby initiating a subjective process leading to a new political identity. There was the whole range of ideas and policies summed up by the slogan 'Fight self, oppose revisionism', with the implication that 'bourgeois' tendencies were to be found even in the hearts of veteran revolutionaries, if not in that of the chairman himself. Above all, there was the idea of 'continuing the revolution under the dictatorship of the proletariat', by ruthless struggle in the superstructure, which Mao endorsed, though (unlike 'permanent revolution') he did not explicate the term himself.

However violent the resulting battles, and however frenzied the enthusi-asm they unleashed, can these events properly be called a revolution? The word revolution may refer either to the conquest of power by a different

[237] Su, 18–19.

class or political faction, or to the use which is made of power, once attained, to transform society. China had, in Mao's view, been carrying out socialist revolution in this second sense since 1949, and especially since 1955. The concrete economic dimension of 'building socialism', which had been prominent in his vision of the Great Leap, did not figure very extensively in Mao's scheme of things during his last decade. Even the transformation of attitudes came, in the end, to play a relatively limited role. The dominant concern was rather with the 'seizure of power' from the 'bourgeoisie'.

Such an enterprise was possible in a country which had been ruled for seventeen years by a 'dictatorship of the proletariat' only thanks to the redefinition of the class enemy from whom power was to be seized as the 'bourgeois elements' and 'capitalist roaders' in the party – that is, all those who had ventured to disagree with Mao Tse-tung about anything from material incentives to literature and philosophy. So, in the last analysis, the Cultural Revolution was a 'revolution' only by virtue of an ideological and cultural definition of its target and goal.

Ironically, the Cultural Revolution, which had opened with manifestos in favour of the Paris Commune model of mass democracy, closed with paeans of praise to that most implacable of centralizing despots, the first Ch'in emperor. This decade saw the rise and fall of Lin Piao and of the influence of the PLA, as well as the fall, rise, and renewed partial eclipse of the party in favour of the 'Legalist leading group around the emperor (or around the empress)'.[238]

Apart from Lin Piao's probable reluctance to accept the renewed subordination of the army to the party, the reasons for his fall are of little interest here. (See, for a detailed account of these matters, CHOC 15, ch. 4.) This affair, though it throws light on the functioning of the Chinese political system, is scarcely relevant to the analysis of Mao Tse-tung's thought. The 'Campaign to criticize Lin Piao and Confucius', on the other hand, is not merely a fascinating puzzle for Pekingologists; it also had significant theoretical implications.

One crucial aspect of the campaign in this respect was the veritable cult of Ch'in Shih-huang which developed in 1973–4. It is only an apparent paradox that the 'Shanghai radicals' should have propagated such an ideal of centralized rule by an autocratic leader, for anarchy and despotism are two maladies of the body politic which engender one another.

In the Great Leap period, as we have seen, Mao had not hesitated to praise Ch'in Shih-huang, and to evoke him as a precursor. But this does not

---

[238] Liang Hsiao, 'Yen-chiu Ju-Fa tou-cheng ti li-shih ching-yen' (Study the historical experience of the struggle between the Confucian and Legalist schools), *Hung-ch'i* 10 (1974) 60; *Peking Review* 2 (1975) 11.

necessarily mean that he took, then or later, the same view of the historical significance of the Ch'in unification of the empire as did the ideologists of 1973–5. At that time, Chairman Mao was said to have expounded, in his speech of 1958, quoted earlier, 'the progressive role of revolutionary violence, and exposed the reactionary essence of attacks on Ch'in Shih-huang as attacks on revolutionary violence and the dictatorship of the proletariat'.[239] The conclusion, which is never stated outright, but is clearly implicit in materials of the mid-1970s, is that the Ch'in Shih-huang analogy should, as it were, be turned inside out. Lin Piao had criticized Mao as a despot; right-minded people should, on the contrary, see Ch'in Shih-huang as a revolutionary leader and the Ch'in autocracy as a kind of proto-proletarian dictatorship.

The analogy obviously requires that there should have been a change in the 'mode of production', that is, in the ruling class, and not merely a change in the organization of the state, with the founding of the dynasty. The transition from slave-holding society to feudalism, which Mao himself had earlier placed (in the original version of 'The Chinese Revolution and the Chinese Communist Party') in the eleventh century BC, was therefore brought forward to the fifth, or even the third century BC. Conceivably, Mao might have changed his mind on this point since 1939, and in any case the views put forward in 1972–4 had long been held by some Chinese historians. It is quite another matter to suggest, however, even if there *was* a change in the ruling class at the end of the third century BC, that the 'new rising landlord class' was consciously reshaping Chinese society, taking Legalist ideology as its guide, in the same sense that the Communists, armed with Marxism-Leninism Mao Tse-tung Thought, are doing so today. Such a view was totally un-Marxist, and historically absurd, and there is no evidence that Mao ever espoused it.

The only justification for this line of argument would appear to reside in a desire to demonstrate that China had revolutionary power, and revolutionary ideology, before anyone else. In other words, in putting forward the Ch'in Shih-huang analogy, Yao Wen-yüan and the other theoreticians of the gang of four were, in reality, disciples of Lin Piao, baptizing 'class struggle' an exceedingly old-fashioned Chinese view of politics as a succession of palace coups. Mao's position was subtler, and despite his pride in China's cultural heritage, less narrowly nationalistic.

Nevertheless, the mid-1960s had seen, as stressed above, a further unravelling of the polarity between Marxism and the Chinese tradition in

---

[239] Chin Chih-pai, 'P'i-K'ung yü lu-hsien tou-cheng' (Criticism of Confucius and two-line struggle), *Hung-ch'i* 7 (1974) 32; *Peking Review* 33 (1974) 11 (and note 2).

Mao Tse-tung's thought, in the context of a general trend toward the dissociation of opposite insights held in creative tension.

As I have already suggested, it can be argued that the changes in Mao's philosophical outlook at this time resulted from the resurgence of Chinese influences in his thinking, and in particular from a drift toward a quasi-Taoist understanding of the relation between opposites in terms of ebb and flow, such that the direction of historical change was no longer built into the structure of the dialectical process. But Mao's pessimism about the prospects for revolution also grew out of his fear of 'restoration' in China and the Soviet Union. It was because the pursuit of the more moderate course which he had himself worked out with Chou En-lai only a year or two earlier conjured up once more in his mind the spectre of 'revisionism' that Mao had endorsed, in 1973, the '*p'i-Lin p'i-K'ung*' campaign of which Chou was the real target. It was the same bugbear which led him to support wholeheartedly the 'Campaign to study the theory of the proletarian dictatorship' launched by Chang and Yao in the spring of 1975.[240]

Joseph Esherick draws a distinction between Lenin, who 'always identified the primary threat of capitalist restoration with the spontaneous capitalist tendencies of the "small-producer economy"', and Mao, who saw the main danger of restoration in the emergence of a new class in the party and state bureaucracy.[241] This approach leads him to put forward the idea of the new bourgeoisie as a potential hereditary ruling class in a socialist society which has taken the road of revisionism and 'restoration'. He calls attention to a striking passage in Mao's comments of 1960 on the Soviet textbook regarding the defects of the children of cadres:

The children of our cadres are a source of great concern. They have no experience of life and no experience of society, but they put on very great airs, and have very great feelings of superiority. We must teach them not to rely on their parents, nor on revolutionary martyrs, but to rely entirely on themselves.[242]

Recalling Mao's disparaging comments in the 1960s, to Snow and others, about the defects of China's youth, Esherick argues that, in Mao's view, these sons and daughters of cadres might inherit the status and privileges of their parents, thus constituting a 'vested interest group' which, by perpetuating itself over several generations, would transform itself into a class.[243]

The difficulty with this argument is that it fails to provide any serious analysis of the relation between such a bureaucratic stratum and the rest of society, or any real justification for calling it a class. I do not mean to suggest

[240] Liao Kai-lung, 'Li-shih ti ching-yen', 147; English in *Issues and Studies* (November 1981), 98.
[241] Joseph W. Esherick. 'On the "Restoration of capitalism": Mao and Marxist Theory', *Modern China*, 5.1 (January 1979) 57–8, 71–2.   [242] *Wan-sui* (1969) 351.   [243] Esherick, 66–8.

that an argument cannot be made for focusing on control rather than ownership of the means of production, and treating existing socialist systems as forms of 'state capitalism', ruled by a 'new class' or 'new bourgeoisie' defined in this context. From Djilas to Bahro, a great many people have done just that during the past three decades. Moreover, on the basis of all the available evidence, it appears that Mao himself leaned in this direction in his later years. Not only did he accept K'ang Sheng's view that, in a socialist society, classes manifested themselves 'ideologically and politically' rather than in terms of relation to the means of production, but he actually did subscribe to the view, put forward in 1975–6, that in China the bourgeoisie was to be found primarily, or decisively, in the party. Moreover, he accepted the logical conclusion from such a premise, namely that these 'new bourgeois elements' exploited the workers and peasants through the mechanism of the socialist system, that is, of the state apparatus.[244]

Even if we conclude, however, that Mao held such a view in the early 1970s, he did not produce a systematic argument to justify it – indeed, by that time he was probably incapable of doing so. Nor, in my opinion, have those Western scholars who have written on these issues done so on his behalf.[245]

On the problem of the relation between the old and the new bourgeoisie, Chang and Yao, while discussing at considerable length the selfish and corrupt behaviour of privileged strata among the leading cadres, in terms derived from Mao, treat these 'extremely isolated persons' rather as the tools of those remnants of the 'overthrown reactionary classes' who desire the restoration of capitalism in the literal sense. If the role of 'bourgeois right' and material incentives is not restricted, writes Yao Wen-yuan,

capitalist ideas of making a fortune and craving for personal fame and gain will spread unchecked; phenomena like the turning of public property into private property, speculation, graft and corruption, theft and bribery will increase; the capitalist principle of the exchange of commodities will make its way into political and even into party life, undermining the socialist planned economy; acts of capitalist exploitation such as the conversion of commodities and money into

---

[244] This statement regarding Mao's position during his last years corresponds to the view commonly expressed by responsible theoretical workers, at the Chinese Academy of Social Sciences and elsewhere, in conversations conducted in April and May 1982. See also Liao Kai-lung, 'Li-shih ti ching-yen', 135–6; English in *Issues and Studies* (November 1981), 84–5.

[245] The study by Richard Kraus, *Class conflict in Chinese socialism*, is a far more important contribution to the subject in general than Esherick's article. On many aspects of the problem of the relation between stratification based on class origins, and 'class as political behaviour', Kraus offers extremely subtle and illuminating analyses. I believe that he errs, however, as does Esherick, in arguing that in his later years Mao defined class primarily in terms of the privileges, and the control of the means of production, derived by cadres from their relationship to the state.

capital, and labour power into a commodity, will occur. . . . When the economic strength of the bourgeoisie has grown to a certain extent, its agents will demand political rule, demand the overthrow of the dictatorship of the proletariat and the socialist system, demand a complete changeover from socialist ownership, and openly restore and develop the capitalist system . . .[246]

This analysis is likewise ill worked out, and even more difficult to reconcile with reality than that in terms of a new bureaucratic elite controlling the means of production. Was the pre-1949 bourgeoisie really so powerful in China a quarter of a century after the revolution? Above all, how could the 'new class elements' within the party, who revelled in their power and perquisites under the existing order, willingly participate in the restoration of actual capitalism, involving the private ownership of the means of production? Surely they must have realized that, in such a system, they would be very ill-equipped to compete with the 'real' capitalists of yore, and would soon lose their privileged position? And yet, both of the perspectives just evoked regarding the role of the 'new class' in Chinese society build explicitly on tendencies apparent in Mao's own writings from the late 1950s onward.

To a large extent, Mao's primary concern was with the resurgence in China, after the revolution, of 'bourgeois' attitudes such as attachment to money, pleasure and privilege. Such deviations would, in his view, be encouraged by inequality of material rewards – hence his support, qualified or not, for the campaign of 1975 against 'bourgeois right'. But in the last analysis he was more concerned with the struggle to transform 'hearts' or 'souls'. If he focused his attention on 'bourgeois elements' in the party, this was partly because such people enjoyed more of the privileges likely to corrupt them, and more of the power and influence which would enable them to corrupt others.

At the same time, it should be stressed that in Mao's view the source of corruption was not merely the rewards of power, but power itself. In one of the very last directives published in his lifetime, Mao was quoted in May 1976 as saying that revolutions would continue to break out in future because 'junior officials, students, workers, peasants and soldiers do not like big shots oppressing them'.[247] There is no way of verifying the authenticity of this text, but it sounds very much like the irrepressible Mao. Although he remained committed to the need for leadership, and for a strong state, he was plainly sceptical that anyone – except the emperor himself – could be trusted with power.

I have stressed repeatedly that the remarkable and extreme tendencies in

[246] Yao Wenyuan, *On the social basis of the Lin Piao anti-party clique*, 7–8.
[247] *Peking Review* 21 (1976) 9.

Mao's thought and behaviour during his last years were based, to a substantial extent, on his conclusions regarding the measures necessary to ensure the thoroughgoing and systematic realization of Marxist ideals or principles such as struggle against the class enemy, the reduction of the differences between town and countryside, and the creation of a more egalitarian society. But although such ideas of Western origin, however, oddly interpreted, remained a significant component of his thought, there is no denying the increasingly large place occupied in Mao's mind, and in the Chinese political system, by Chinese and traditional influences.

Apart from the cult of Ch'in Shih-huang, discussed above, a notable manifestation of this trend was the stress on devotion to the Leader and his Thought, symbolized by the value of 'loyalty' (*chung*). Not only were 'proletarian revolutionaries' such as the Red Guards to learn by heart the 'Little red book', so they could repeat a suitable saying on every occasion and thereby demonstrate their mastery of Mao Tse-tung Thought. They were also to be 'boundlessly loyal to Chairman Mao', and this quality above all others was the touchstone for distinguishing genuine from sham revolutionaries in the China of the late 1960s and the early 1970s.

In the *Tso-chuan* under the ninth year of Duke Ch'eng, it is written: '*Wu ssu, chung yeh.*' Loosely translated, this can be taken to mean, 'He who is selfless is truly loyal [to the ruler].' The Chinese, in Mao's last years, read this equation both backwards and forwards. On the one hand, he who was genuinely selfless, who was willing to serve the people like Lei Feng as a 'rustless screw', was a true and loyal disciple of Chairman Mao and a genuine proletarian revolutionary. But conversely, he who was loyal to Mao Tse-tung and Mao Tse-tung Thought became, by that very fact, selfless and proletarian, and endowed with all the other revolutionary virtues.[248] In this respect, as in the use of the parallel with Ch'in Shih-huang, Mao truly moved, at the end of his life, from expressing Marxist ideas in a language accessible to the Chinese people to a somewhat eclectic position in which traditional values and ideas played an increasingly large part.

IN SEARCH OF MAO TSE-TUNG'S IDEOLOGICAL LEGACY

The term 'Mao Tse-tung Thought', or 'Mao Tse-tung's Thought', has at least three different meanings. First of all, it can be used to signify what Mao himself actually thought, in the course of his long life, as evidenced by contemporary sources for the writings of each period. Secondly, it may

---

[248] For a discussion of the significance of *chung*, and more broadly of the nature of Mao's rule in his last days, see my article 'Party leader or true ruler?', 223–5, 233–43.

have the sense given to it in China from the 1950s until Mao's death (or indeed until the third plenum, in December 1978), that is, it may refer to the orthodox doctrine at any given time, as laid down in the post-1951 edition of the *Selected works*, and in other speeches and writings openly published, including the extracts issued during the Cultural Revolution period as 'supreme directives'. Thirdly, it can be used as the Chinese use it today, to designate that portion of the total corpus of Mao Tse-tung's writings still regarded as correct, complemented by works in which Chou En-lai, Liu Shao-ch'i, Chu Te and others further developed some of Mao's ideas, but without those writings by Mao reflecting the 'errors of his later years'.

In Part 2 of this book I have continued the attempt begun in Part 1 to trace the development of Mao Tse-tung's thought in the first sense, from 1917 to 1976. I have also dealt with the problem of changing patterns of orthodoxy grounded in Mao's writings, which did not exist for the period prior to 1949 because there was no official canon and no such orthodox interpretation of 'Mao Tse-tung Thought'. Now, in conclusion, I propose to sum up the essence of Mao's theoretical contribution, but to do so on a rather different basis from that currently adopted in China.

It is often suggested that the approach of the present leaders of China to Mao Tse-tung's thought is altogether arbitrary, manipulative and cynical – in other words, that they characterize as 'correct' those ideas of Mao's which will serve to justify the policies they have laid down on a quite different basis. That is, in my opinion, far too simple a view. Apart from the need to adopt enough of Mao's ideological heritage to demonstrate that they are his legitimate successors, those engaged in defining and elaborating 'Mao Tse-tung Thought' today are for the most part veterans of decades of revolutionary struggle under Mao's leadership, who cannot but have internalized and built into their own thinking many ideas and practices from the era of Mao Tse-tung. It is therefore not implausible to accept that the current attempt at a redefinition of Mao's Thought has the aim which is attributed to it, namely to determine what portions of his heritage are correct, in the dual sense of being good Marxism, and of being adapted to China's needs.

Even if this is the case, however, the goals, and therefore the logic and the criteria of the ongoing Chinese reassessment are different from those of this book, and consequently my evaluation cannot follow theirs. In the Conclusion to this study as a whole, which follows Part 2, I shall deal with the enduring significance of Mao Tse-tung and his thought, as it appears to us today. Here, my concern is rather with what constitutes the essence of Mao's thinking about problems of socialist development, from 1949 to 1976.

In the past, I have referred to the substance of Mao Tse-tung's positive contribution to the theory of building socialism as 'mainstream Maoism', and have suggested that it could be found in the period 1955–65, and more precisely in the early 1960s.[249] In other words, I have defined 'mainstream Maoism' as the rational kernel of the 'Chinese Road to Socialism' devised by Mao, minus the excesses of the Great Leap and the Cultural Revolution. On further reflection, I find this usage less than satisfactory. As I have argued above, the progression from 1958 to 1966 was in many respects inexorable, and the leftist tide which carried everything before it in the course of both these radical experiments might well be regarded as more characteristic of Mao's last quarter-century (if not of his life as a whole) than the relatively prudent and realistic position he adopted in the early 1960s, and again in the early 1970s.

'In all things, one divides into two,' said Mao in March 1964. 'I, too, am a case of one divides into two.'[250] That is, perhaps, the first and most fundamental thing that needs be said by way of conclusion. On the one hand, Mao's thought from beginning to end, and especially his thought of the 1950s and 1960s, was an uneasy juxtaposition of disparate ideas and imperatives. And secondly, the provisional and unstable synthesis which he had managed to forge between these elements began to unravel and fly apart with the onset of the Cultural Revolution.

If we look at Mao's economic ideas during and after the Great Leap Forward as formulated at the time, we must recognize, in my opinion, that they are far less one-sided and simplistic than they have commonly been made out to be in recent years, in interpretations based on the Cultural Revolution reconstruction of the 'struggle between two lines'. We find him placing stress equally on moral *and* material incentives, on redness *and* expertise, and on large- and small-scale industry. The policy of 'walking on two legs', which was in some respects the heart of his whole economic strategy, was a policy of walking as fast as possible on both legs, and not of hopping along on the leg of small-scale indigenous methods alone.

And yet, there are aspects of Mao Tse-tung's approach to development, even after he had retreated from the extravagant illusions of the summer of 1958, which reflect a fundamental ambiguity toward the implications of industrialization and technical progress. One of these, to which I devoted considerable attention earlier, was his attitude toward the intellectuals. Another was his conception of the political process, and of the relation between the leaders and the masses.

In 1960, discussing the Soviet Constitution, Mao Tse-tung said that this Constitution gave the workers the right to work, to rest, and to education,

---

[249] See in particular S. Schram, *Mao Zedong: a preliminary reassessment*, p. 71.
[250] *Wan-sui* (1969) 477; *Miscellany*, 343. (Remarks at a briefing.)

but that it gave the people no right to supervise (*cheng-li*) the state, the economy, culture or education, whereas these were the most basic rights of the people under socialism.[251] A parallel passage in the 'Reading notes' uses the term *kuan-li*, instead of *cheng-li*.[252] Although there is a significant nuance between these two expressions, both are relatively ambiguous, and their ambiguity reflects, once again, the contradictions we have already noted in Mao's theory and practice of the 'mass line'. *Kuan-li*, the term which appears in Mao's own words as reproduced by the Red Guards, may mean manage, run, administer, or supervise; *cheng-li*, employed by Liao Kai-lung in his paraphrase, signifies put in order, straighten out or arrange. The first is obviously more concrete, evoking an organizational context rather than simply a process. Both are equally vague as to whether the workers, or toilers (*lao-tung che*) are intended by Mao essentially to keep track of what is going on, and to make sure that political authority is exercised in accordance with their wishes, or whether he means they should actually *run* things themselves.

One of the English translations of Mao's 'Reading notes' has 'run' and 'manage' for *kuan-li*; the other has 'administer' and 'take charge'.[253] I have preferred 'supervise', which does not imply that the workers, collectively, are all actually taking charge to the same degree, because such a reading corresponds better to Mao's thought in 1960 as I understand it. This choice is, admittedly, arbitrary, but no more so than that of the other translators. The ambiguity is in fact there, in Mao's own language, and in his thought.

Another case in point is the passage of 1965 quoted above, asserting that democracy means 'dealing with the affairs of the masses through the masses themselves' (*ch'ün-chung ti shih-ch'ing yu ch'ün-chung lai kuan-li*).[254] For the character *yu* can mean either *by* the masses, in the sense that they are the effective agents, or *through* the masses, in other words that the matter is laid before them and they are consulted. I have translated 'through', because the clear statement, in the same text of December 1965, about the need for party leadership from above confirms that, at this time, Mao still held to the view, which he had repeatedly stated, that centralism was even more important than democracy. And yet, by 1965, his approach to these matters was clearly beginning to shift.

During the period before and after the Great Leap, the emphasis on centralism took the form of an insistence on the crucial and decisive role of party leadership. As noted in the first section of Part 2, Mao revived the

---

251 Liao Kai-lung, 'Ch'üan-mien chien-she she-hui-chu-i ti tao-lu' (The road to building socialism in an all-round way), *Yün-nan she-hui k'o-hsüeh* (Yun-nan Social Sciences), 2 (1982) 2.
252 *Wan-sui* (1969) 342–3.   253 Mao Tsetung, *A critique of Soviet economics*, trans. 61; *Miscellany*, 266.
254 *Wan-sui* (1969) 630.

concept of *i-yuan-hua* or integrated party control, which had been so much stressed in Yenan.

Generally speaking, Mao's view during the Great Leap period was that integration or *i-yuan-hua* had to be carried out not merely at the national level, but in the localities. Otherwise, even the 'small power' referred to in the 1953 jingle could not be dispersed without leading to confusion. And the agent of integration could only be the party committee at each level. Party control, whether at the Centre or in the localities, involved, as Mao made clear in 1958, first taking decisions on matters of principle, and then subsequently checking on their implementation.

With the approach of the Cultural Revolution, this whole philosophy was undermined because Mao Tse-tung called into question in theory, and then denied in practice, the legitimacy and political rectitude of the party which was supposed to exercise the function of 'integration'. One of the first and most dramatic hints of what was to come is to be found in the famous passage from the Ninth Reply to the Soviets, dated 14 July 1964, stating that if cadres were to be 'corrupted, divided, and demoralized' by the class enemy (made up of 'the landlords, rich peasants, counter-revolutionaries, bad elements and monsters of all kinds'), then 'it would not take long ... before a counter-revolutionary restoration on a national scale inevitably occurred, the Marxist-Leninist party would undoubtedly become a revisionist party or a fascist party, and the whole of China would change its colour'.[255]

Although Mao reasserted, in his conversations of February 1967 with Chang and Yao, that there had to be a party as a leading nucleus, and although he continued to strive to combine in some fashion the need for leadership with the anti-elitism and the encouragement of initiative from below which had constituted the justification (if not the principal motive) for the Cultural Revolution, this whole enterprise was distorted and vitiated by the fact that the right of the masses to 'rebel' against the party hierarchy and state bureaucracy was guaranteed only by a figure exercising personal authority of a kind which soon came to be officially likened to that of the first Ch'in emperor.

It is in this light that one must interpret the calls by Wang Hung-wen at the Tenth Party Congress[256] and by Chang Ch'un-ch'iao at the National People's Congress in January 1975[257] for the 'integrated [*i-yuan-hua*] leadership' of the party over the state structure, and over everything else. For by

[255] *Hung-ch'i* 13 (1964) 31–2; *Peking Review* 29 (1964) 26. (Originally from a note by Mao on a document of 9 May 1963 regarding cadre participation in productive labour in Chekiang.)
[256] *Hung-ch'i* 9 (1973) 22, 27; *Peking Review* 35/36 (1973) 25, 28.
[257] *Hung-ch'i* 2 (1975) 17; *Peking Review* 4 (1975) 19.

this time, neither Chang, nor indeed Mao himself were so much interested in the relation between organizations as in imposing Mao Tse-tung's personal authority. Henceforth, truth and authority resided not in the party, but in Chairman Mao, the leader invested by history with the mission of educating the Chinese people and guiding them toward communism.

Throughout his career, from the Ching-kang-shan and Yenan to the 1960s, Mao Tse-tung treated democracy and centralism as two indissolubly linked aspects of the political process, one of which could not be promoted without reference to the other. The Cultural Revolution saw the emergence of two quite different concepts. Democracy was replaced by 'rebellion'; centralism was replaced by *chung*, or personal loyalty to the great leader and helmsman. No doubt Mao Tse-tung saw these tendencies as bound together in a dialectical unity, like democracy and centralism, which he had not in principle repudiated. Nevertheless, he allowed a situation to develop in which the 'heads', of which he himself acknowledged the necessity, at all levels of society and the economy, could not in fact function as heads because, although they were held accountable they had no power to take decisions. The alliance between the leader and the masses took the form, on the national level, of an unstructured plebiscitary democracy, sadly reminiscent of earlier examples. At lower levels, it produced a mixture of arbitrary rule by *ad hoc* committees, military control, apathy and confusion.

The roots of these last developments go back to the 1960s, and in particular to Mao's repeated statements, beginning in 1963, asserting the axiom 'One divides into two.' For it is only if the party is in reality symbolized by and incarnated in one man that the two principles of *i-yuan-hua* or 'making monolithic', and *i fen wei erh*, or the divisibility of all things (and the propensity of their components to struggle with one another) can coexist. In other words, the Communist Party could split, and yet remain one, capable of carrying out its mission of integration, only if its oneness and integrity were the emanation of Chairman Mao, who (despite his remark quoted earlier) did not split, but remained permanently in charge, even though his thoughts teemed with contradictions.

Another duality central to the interpretation of Mao's thought was, as I have stressed throughout this account, that between Marxism and the Chinese heritage. The fact that, in Mao's later years, the leader had come to be the focus of loyalty and the fount of truth is not in harmony with Marxist theory, or indeed with Mao's own reminder, in 1971, of the words of the Internationale denying the existence of 'supreme saviours'.[258] This does not, in itself, make of his rule a species of oriental despotism, nor does it

[258] *Mao unrehearsed*, 297.

even signify that the ideology to which he lent his name was primarily Chinese rather than Western. There were, after all, sufficient Western or Westernizing sources for the cult of the leader – including Stalin's red fascism, as well as the original doctrines of Hitler and Mussolini. Moreover, in the complex process of acculturation, if new Western ideas can be made to serve old Chinese goals and values, Chinese forms can also be turned to purposes defined by foreign doctrines.[259] The final balance is therefore not easy to draw up, but the problem merits a few final reflections.

Between the mid-1950s and the mid-1960s, Mao Tse-tung moved from the rejection to the acceptance of Chang Chih-tung's principle, 'Chinese learning as the substance, Western learning for practical application.' In his 'Talk to music workers' of August 1956, he adopted the relatively balanced view he had expounded since 1938, namely that China must learn many things from the West, while remaining herself. Marxism, he declared, was 'a general truth which has universal application'. This 'fundamental theory produced in the West' constituted the foundation or '*t'i*' of China's new regime, though it must be combined with the concrete practice of each nation's revolution.[260] In December 1965, at Hang-chow, on the other hand, he said in effect that Chang Chih-tung was right: 'We cannot adopt Western learning as the substance . . . We can only use Western technology.'[261]

Even though Mao declared in the same speech, as noted earlier, that he was a 'native philosopher', such remarks should not be understood to mean that Mao no longer proposed to take anything from Marxism, or from the West. They were rather an emphatic way of saying that China's revolutionary doctrine today must be rooted in her culture, and in her past, if borrowings from the West were to be put to good use. The problem is not, however, one which can fruitfully be approached in purely intellectual terms, through the dissection of Mao's theoretical formulations. Deeply rooted feelings also come into it, and colour even his political or ideological statements.

In March 1958 at Chengtu, Mao declared: 'First classes wither away, and then afterward the state withers away, and then after that nations (*min-tsu*) wither away, it is like this in the whole world.'[262] Talking to Edgar Snow on 18 December 1970, Mao put the matter as follows:

What is a nation (*min-tsu*)? It includes two groups of people (*liang pu-fen jen*), one group consists of the upper strata, the exploiting classes, a minority. These people know how to speak [effectively], and to organize a government, but they don't

---

[259] On this theme, see 'Party leader or true ruler?'.   [260] *Mao unrehearsed*, 85–6.
[261] *Ibid.* 234–5.   [262] *Mao Chu-hsi kuan-yü kuo-nei min-tsu wen-t'i*, 8.

know how to fight, or to till the land, or to work in a factory. More than 90 per cent of the people are workers, peasants, and petty-bourgeoisie; without these people, it is impossible to constitute a nation (*tsu-ch'eng min-tsu*).[263]

Mao's remarks of 1970 illustrate once again his tendency, in his later years, to see class struggle as a conflict between a small group of 'big shots' and the people as a whole. But they also underscore, as does his comment of 1958, the fundamental importance he attached to the nation as a primary form of social organization.

Although Mao unquestionably always regarded China as the 'central place', and Chinese culture as the 'central flower' (*chuang-hua*), I would by no means suggest that we should draw from the trait the conclusion, commonly put forward by the Soviets and their supporters, as well as by Trotskyites and other leftists of various persuasions, that Mao was, after all, nothing but an old-fashioned Chinese nationalist with very little Marxism about him.

The fact remains that, during the Cultural Revolution decade especially, the synthesis toward which Mao had been bending his efforts for many decades largely fell apart, at least as regarded his own ideas and attitudes. Moral and political criteria drawn from the *Tso-chuan* and similar sources thus loomed very large in 1976, when Mao, as he put it to Edgar Snow, 'saw God', or 'saw Marx' (or perhaps both of them), and a new era opened under his successors.

If we look, however, not at these last sad anti-climatic years, but at the soberer elements in Mao's thought, as he developed it from 1935 to 1965, it constitutes, in my opinion, in the last analysis rather a revolutionary ideology of Western origin, and a vehicle of Westernization.

The ambiguous relation between this Westernizing thrust and Mao Tse-tung's indisputable sinocentrism is illustrated by his view regarding what has been called the 'dialectics of backwardness'. In the 'Reading notes' of 1960, which are one of the quintessential expositions of 'mainstream Maoism', a section is devoted to the topic 'Is revolution in backward countries more difficult?' Needless to say, Mao concluded that it was not. The poisons of the bourgeoisie were, he said, extremely virulent in the advanced countries of the West after two or three centuries of capitalism, and affected every stratum of society, including the working class. Lenin's dictum, 'The more backward the country, the more difficult its transition from capitalism to socialism' was therefore incorrect:

---

[263] *Ibid.* 6–7. (This quote is from the official Chinese record of the talks; to my knowledge, Snow never made use of this passage in his own writings.)

In reality, the more backward the economy, the easier, and not the more difficult, the transition from capitalism to socialism. The poorer people are, the more they want revolution. . . . In the East, countries such as Russia and China were originally backward and poor. Now not only are their social systems far more advanced than those of the West, but the rate of development of the productive forces is far more rapid. If you look at the history of the development of the various capitalist countries, it is again the backward which have overtaken the advanced. For example, the United States surpassed Britain at the end of the nineteenth century, and Germany also surpassed Britain in the early twentieth century.[264]

On the one hand, this argument clearly reflects the emphasis on the human and moral dimension of politics, which is, as I have stated repeatedly here, so much a part of the Chinese tradition. Indeed, Mao also asserted, in the context of the passage just quoted, that the greatest difficulty, once the revolution had succeeded in these advanced and highly mechanized countries, would lie in 'the transformation of the people (*jen-min ti kai-tsao*)'. But, at the same time, these words of Mao's eloquently express his profound conviction, fuelled by a century of national humiliation, and strengthened and confirmed by victory in political and military struggle, that a situation of backwardness and inferiority must not be endured, and need not be endured.

During the last two decades of his life, Mao showed a remarkable capacity for setting aside this emotional imperative when the situation became really difficult, as it did in the aftermath of the Great Leap Forward in particular, and accepting the need to deal realistically with the problems facing the country's economy. As soon as conditions appeared to be improving even slightly, however, as in the autumn of 1962, Mao immediately threw caution to the winds, and once again gave free rein to his utopian aspirations, and to the radical policies designed to turn these visions into reality.

It is this contradictory and protean character of Mao's heritage, and not simply the undoubted disagreements among the current Chinese leadership as to the road which should be followed, which have made it so difficult for his successors to arrive at a detailed, rigorous, and adequate assessment of Mao Tse-tung's historical role. The same ambiguity means that any attempt to sum up his thought as a whole, whether by a Chinese or by a foreigner, can only be provisional and subject to qualification. None the less, the task, though seemingly impossible, must somehow be attempted.

---

[264] *Wan-sui* (1969) 333–4; *Miscellany*, 258–9.

CONCLUSION

In the Introduction, I argued that the most general, and probably the most lasting expression of Mao Tse-tung's contribution to the Chinese revolution was his thought. This view also implies, conversely, that one cannot sum up Mao's thought without summing up his life as well.

Few would deny Mao Tse-tung the major share of the credit for devising the pattern of struggle based on guerrilla warfare in the countryside that ultimately led to victory in the civil war, and thereby to the overthrow of the Kuomintang, the distribution of land to the peasants, and the restoration of China's independence and sovereignty. These achievements must be given a weight commensurate with the degree of injustice prevailing in Chinese society before the revolution, and with the humiliation felt by the Chinese people as a result of the dismemberment of their country by the foreign powers. 'We have stood up,' said Mao in September 1949. These words will not be forgotten.

Mao's record after 1949 is more ambiguous. The official Chinese view is that his leadership was basically correct until the summer of 1957, but from then on mixed at best, and frequently quite wrong. It cannot be disputed that Mao's two major policy innovations of his later years, which were also the two major innovations in his thought, the Great Leap Forward and the Cultural Revolution, were ill-conceived and led to disastrous consequences. His goals of combatting bureaucracy, encouraging popular participation and stressing China's self-reliance were generally laudable, but the methods Mao used to pursue them, though bold and imaginative, were in these instances very largely self-defeating.

One might say that Mao Tse-tung was better at conquering power than at ruling the country and developing a socialist economy. That would be true, but not quite fair or adequate as a judgment. The problems of transforming Chinese culture, and modernizing the Chinese economy, with which Mao grappled after 1949 were more intractable, and in any case more complex, than those he faced in earlier periods. On the Ching-kang-shan, or in Yenan, it was a matter of win or lose, live or die. The alternatives after 1949 were less clear cut, and the issue of the struggle could not be finally resolved, in a day or even in a decade.

At the same time, it must be acknowledged that limits were set to Mao's potential for creating a new, socialist China by the very qualities which had made him great as a military and political leader during the struggle for power. Already before 1949, his image of himself as ruler had begun to take the form of a strange hybrid of Leninist and Chinese elements, the latter drawn both from the 'Great' and the 'Little' traditions. Such a figure – part emperor, part peasant rebel, and part revolutionary leader – was a very effective mobilizing symbol in the struggle for power. It was not, perhaps, so suitable for promoting the true economic, cultural and technological revolution China needed after 1949.

Similarly, Mao's closeness to the peasantry made him sensitive to the needs of the great mass of the population which would be re-shaped by socialism, but did not allow him the necessary detachment with respect to ideas and values immanent among the peasantry. In these and other ways, Mao mirrored too well the China of the first half of the twentieth century to constitute a reliable guide in solving the problems of the late twentieth century.

And yet, in other fundamental respects, he did not become out of date, and has not become out of date even today. Most crucial of these was, no doubt, his single-minded attachment to making China flourish, and restoring her place in the world. In one sense, the national revolution was carried to completion in Mao's lifetime, the final act being the visit by an American president to the ruler of China in the Forbidden City. The road to true equality with the other great powers remains a long one, but Mao's determination that China should pursue it, and pursue it in her own way, is still honoured. Revolution is still seen as an ongoing process. And politics – though it is a different kind of politics – remains the key.

Although this book is about what Mao Tse-tung thought and did in his own lifetime, the problems of the Maoist era can today be viewed from a perspective which adds new dimensions to our understanding. On the one hand, the consequences of his ideas and policies have become more clearly visible. On the other, the contrast between the 1960s and the 1980s further illustrated the range of possibilities for the application of Marxism in China, and thereby helps us to determine what is peculiar and specific, and what is of more lasting significance, in the experiments which took place under Mao's guidance.

Many things divide the China of Teng Hsiao-p'ing today from that of Mao Tse-tung two decades ago, but one thing has not changed a jot: the goal of learning from the West, and from Marxism in particular, in order to find a way of modernizing while remaining themselves. Mao talked of devising a 'Chinese Road to Socialism'; Teng prefers to speak of building

'Socialism with Chinese Characteristics'. The logic of these two enterprises is in some ways significantly different, but in each case involves both *using* Marxism to guide the revolution in China, and at the same time *adapting* it to the circumstances, and to the culture, of the Chinese people.

To put it rather baldy, the distinction between the way Marxism is applied in China today, and the way it was applied by Mao Tse-tung, lies in the fact that Mao was concerned above all with the dialectic between class struggle and building socialism, while Teng Hsiao-p'ing takes as the axis of his policy the dialectic between political reform and economic development. Mao believed that only unrelenting struggle in the superstructure could keep human beings on the correct course toward a new and selfless society, and that all the gains of the revolution since the bitter days of guerrilla warfare in the countryside could be forfeited in an instant if vigilance were relaxed before the goal was achieved. Teng, in contrast, argues that true socialism can only be built on a highly developed economy, and he has stated repeatedly that the necessary foundation can be created only toward the middle of the next century. In biblical language, one might say that Mao's view was 'Seek ye first the kingdom of socialism, and riches shall be added unto you,' while Teng's view is that he who builds on ideology alone builds upon sand.

The problem of applying Marxism to China in either of these perspectives is particularly delicate because of the ingrained Europocentric bias of the Marxist tradition. For Marx, Europe was the pre-eminent world, which stood in the forefront of humanity's advance. There were many variations in the views of European Marxists about Asia, during the century after Marx first hailed the progressive effects of the Western impact, but one constant thread runs through them all: Asia needed European tutelage if it was ever to emerge from its torpor and become an active participant in world history. The guiding hand of Europe might display itself through colonial conquest. It might also operate through comradely advice from European revolutionaries to their Asian brethren, once socialism had triumphed in Europe. From Engels and Kautsky to Stalin and Khrushchev, however, such counsels were distinctly avuncular in tone, directives from on high, rather than advice between equals.

The need for European or Soviet tutelage was explicitly denied by the Chinese only in the late 1950s, though Mao in fact made plain much earlier his commitment to the independence and autonomy of the Chinese revolution. In repudiating any notion of foreign guidance, however, Mao by no means rejected the postulate of European primacy in initiating the two great revolutions in which the Chinese wished to participate: the industrial revolution, and the socialist revolution. His view was rather that, while

Europe as a whole (including North America) was the first to carry out industrialization, and scientific socialism was invented by Marx and first implemented by Lenin and Stalin, the Chinese could surpass their teachers on both these fronts. They could industrialize in fifty to a hundred years, instead of the three centuries required by the Europeans; they would carry out a more rapid and more thoroughgoing social revolution than the Soviet Union.

None the less, the fact remained that Marxism was an ideology which had come from wholly outside the Chinese cultural universe. The difficulty of making Marxist revolution in such a society lies in the fact that the heritage of the past must be simultaneously burst asunder, if there is to be revolution, and reaffirmed, if the national dignity is to be maintained. It is almost exactly a half century since Mao Tse-tung first addressed these issues by calling for the 'sinification of Marxism' in October 1938. In Part 1 of this book, I analysed in detail the text in which he did so; the ensuing developments, reviewed in Part 2, illustrate concretely the implications of Mao's initial formulation.

In essence, sinification involved for Mao three dimensions or aspects: communication, conditions and culture. The first of these is the clearest and least controversial. In calling for a 'new and vital Chinese style and manner, pleasing to the eye and to the ear of the Chinese common people', Mao was making the valid but previously neglected point that, if Marxism is to be understood and accepted by the people of any non-European country, it must be presented in language which is intelligible to them, and in terms relevant to their own problems. But how, in Mao's view, was the reception of Marxism in China determined by mentality (or culture), and experience (or concrete circumstances)? Above all, how were both the culture of the Chinese people, and the conditions in which they lived, to be shaped by the new revolutionary power set up in 1949?

As we have seen in Part 2, the Chinese Communist Party, and Mao himself, found it necessary to copy a great deal from the Soviets in the new circumstances created by the fact that the Chinese Communist Party was henceforth a ruling party. They did not, of course, copy the Soviets blindly, even in the early 1950s, but the imprint of Soviet thinking, and of Soviet methods, was very marked. It is symbolized by the extremely high proportion of textbooks and theoretical works published in China in the 1950s which were translated from the Russian.

From 1955, when he brought about a 'high tide' of agricultural collectivization, until his death in 1976, Mao sought to define and follow a Chinese road to socialism. In pursuing this aim, he unquestionably took Marxism as his guide, though he also did strange things to it on occasion, as well as seeking inspiration, as he had advocated in 1938, from the lessons and the values of Chinese history. The essence of Mao's contribution to applying Marxism in China was commonly regarded, not so long ago, as residing in the pattern of economic development which began to emerge in 1955, crystallized in 1958 with the Great Leap Forward, and continued, with some fluctuations in the political climate, until 1978. This 'Maoist model' looks backward toward Yenan, and forward to the Cultural Revolution.

When I say the Great Leap experience must be seen in relation to the earlier period, I do not mean it was essentially the same. In Part 1 I indicated my disagreement with those who hold that 'Maoist economics' was born in Yenan. I noted in particular that, in those days, there was no 'walking on two legs', combining the large and the small, the modern and the traditional, whereas this idea lay at the heart of the Great Leap strategy.

The ideological heritage of Yenan was, on the other hand, very clearly present during Mao's last two decades. The 'mass line', with its emphasis on listening to people at the lower levels, though not necessarily doing what they asked, remained in honour. The most important element of continuity lay, however, in the emphasis on struggle, sacrifice and austerity as supreme moral values, and in the importance accorded to the virtues of the peasantry.

As we have seen, in the mid-1950s Mao turned back again to his rural roots, declaring in December 1955: 'Chinese peasants are even better than English and American workers.' The existential continuity of Mao's thinking during the Great Leap period with the spirit of Yenan, and of the Ching-kang-shan, was revealed with extraordinary vividness in his speeches at the Pei-tai-ho meeting of August 1958, when he called repeatedly for the abolition of the wage system, and the reintroduction of the free supply system followed during the war years. The wage system, he asserted, was a 'concession to the bourgeoisie', and its result had been 'the development of individualism'. The alternative moral values he sought to promote Mao linked explicitly to the past of armed struggle. 'Our communism,' he declared, '. . . was first implemented by the army. . . . The Chinese Party is a very special party, it fought for several decades, all the while applying communism.' Arguing that the communes contained 'sprouts of communism', Mao contrasted them with the cities, where people wanted 'regularization' (*cheng-kui-hua*), and which were full of 'big *yamens* divorced from the masses'.

And yet, as we have seen, Mao recognized half a year later, at the Chengchow conference of February–March 1959, that the peasants displayed a certain attachment to their own material interests, declaring: 'The peasants after all remain peasants, throughout the period when the system of ownership by the whole people has not yet been implemented in the countryside.' At the present stage, he added, the workers, not the peasants, still played the role of 'elder brother' in the relationship between the two. Perhaps, as I suggested above, Mao never truly resolved, and integrated into his understanding of Marxism, the dilemma of a peasantry which was simultaneously the salt of the earth and the 'younger brother' of the working class in building socialism.

I said that Mao's thought of the Great Leap period looked in some respects back toward Yenan, and in other ways forward to the Cultural Revolution. There were, assuredly, very fundamental differences between these two great radical upheavals, the most important being that the party, which had been placed in command in 1958, was smashed in 1966. The origins of the Cultural Revolution can, however, be traced to two trends which emerged in 1958–9: the new high tide of the Mao cult, and the leftist political and ideological climate, manifested above all in the ever shriller emphasis on class struggle.

Looking at Mao's last two decades as a whole, it would be wrong to conclude that, at any time in this period, he interpreted Marxism in such a way as wholly to subordinate the role of the basis to that of the superstructure. Twice, indeed, in the course of the radical phase of the Great Leap, Mao dated the beginnings of the proces of modernization and change from the moment when, at the end of the nineteenth century, Chang Chih-tung launched China's first programme of industrialization. None the less, Mao's view, which he had put forward in 1937, even before Stalin's exposition of similar ideas, regarding the primacy, at certain times or periods, of politics and culture over the economic foundation, was increasingly to the fore in his later years. Not only did he hold that it was imperative to mobilize the population as a whole to play a dynamic role in economic development, and to give full play to their creativity; he also attributed to the revolutionary people virtually unlimited capacities to modify themselves and their environment.

The question was frequently debated, from 1966 onwards, whether the extraordinary phenomenon of the 'Great Proletarian Cultural Revolution' constituted the natural culmination of Mao's previous ideas and actions. Some people, especially at the outset, were inclined to dismiss it as merely a senile aberration. Others, including, of course, those in the West who sought inspiration and guidance from Mao and his thought, saw the Cultural Revolution policies not only as the apogee and supreme achievement of Mao's career, but as the goal toward which all his previous activity had been tending.

In my opinion, both the above judgments are wrong. I see the Cultural

Revolution not as *the* necessary and ineluctable culmination of Mao's approach to revolution, but as one possible, and entirely logical outcome of his life. He was pushed in this direction by his vehement and impulsive temperament, by his tendency to carry ideas to extremes, and also by the vendetta which he had been pursuing, for the better part of a decade, against his critics in the party. These factors were strengthened by his consciousness of his own mortality, and his determination to effect a decisive change in China in his own lifetime. He was restrained – or should have been restrained – by his longstanding commitment to the need for taking account of objective reality, and by his attachment to the party as an indispensable leadership tool, even if he did not have for it the same veneration as a more orthodox Leninist such as Liu Shao-ch'i. In other words, he was not fated to end like this, but neither is it surprising that he did.

There can be little doubt that Mao Tse-tung sincerely believed he had defined a new and distinctive Chinese road to socialism, which marked a clear break with many aspects of the Soviet interpretation of Marxism. Ten or twenty years ago, it was widely accepted that he had. Today, while recognizing his achievements, Mao's successors acknowledge also the historical limitations on his contribution.

Many people outside China are persuaded, of course, that the re-examination of Mao's career, and the re-evaluation of his thought, during the past decade amounts in fact to a process of 'de-Maoization', or at the very least to maintaining outward respect for the man and his thought, while hollowing them out and depriving them of any real substance. That view is, in my opinion, incorrect. In March 1979, *People's Daily* published an article containing the sentence: 'What China is doing is not de-Maoization, but de-sacralization.'[1] That is, I think, a fair assessment, even though recent trends, symbolized by the casting down of graven images of the Chairman in 1988, have led to further fading of the awe which used to surround his person.

In an effort to explore this issue further, let me make some comments about what are today seen as positive and negative elements in Mao's heritage. The three main points put down to Mao's credit in the Resolution of 27 June 1981, which still defines the official position regarding his role, and in many articles and commentaries before and since, are the emphasis on independence and self-reliance, the 'mass line', and the slogan 'Seek the truth from facts', which Mao, of course, put forward in Yenan (basing himself on an ancient Chinese source, Pan Ku's *History of the Han Dynasty*). This formula is taken today to evoke Mao's interpretation of Marxist epistemology, as laid down in 'On practice', which Teng Hsiao-p'ing has

[1] See the article by Tung T'ai, 'Tui-tai "wai-lun" ti ching-yen chiao-hsun' ('The lessons to be learned from our experience in dealing with "foreign theories" [about China]'), *Jen-minjih-pao*, 9 March 1979.

encapsulated since 1978 in the slogan 'Practice is the sole criterion for testing truth.' Self-reliance remains in honour, though the Chinese under Teng Hsiao-p'ing propose to maintain and consolidate their independence by joining the world and learning from it, rather than by standing aloof from it. The 'mass line', too, is still frequently cited as a symbol of the democratic tradition of the Chinese Communist Party, but democracy is seen less as a 'work style' and more as something requiring institutional-ization, than in Mao's day.

As for negative factors, the most important is undoubtedly seen as the overestimation of the 'role of man's subjective will'.[2] The 'errors of Mao's later years' are also blamed on his promotion of the cult of his own personality, as well as on his obsession with class struggle, but the issue of voluntarism is regarded as the most fundamental. All four of the points just enunciated are closely interrelated, both in logic and in Teng Hsiao-p'ing's own view of the matter. Most obvious, perhaps, is the polarity between 'seeking the truth from facts' and the exaggeration of the people's capacity to change the world by an act of will.

Mao won victory in 1949 in large part because he had grasped that, given the real balance of forces in the 1920s and 1930s, the Chinese revolution could only be a protracted one, and rapid triumph through an urban uprising of the proletariat was impossible. Then, in a curious and ironic paradox, after Mao had opposed his patience and realism to the impatience and doctrinaire illusions of the 'orthodox' faction in the party, the roles were reversed. Now it was Mao who, unwilling to wait for the development of the productive forces, sought to leap into socialism, or even to commu-nism, overnight.

All of the errors which Mao Tse-tung then proceeded to commit, in the Great Leap Forward and after, are now seen in China as a betrayal of his own principles of learning from practice and keeping a firm grip on reality. Similarly, the closeness to the people symbolized by the 'mass line' is viewed as the essence of the democratic tradition of the Chinese Communist Party, and one of Mao Tse-tung's great original contributions. 'Where did Marx or Engels talk about the mass line? Where did Lenin (still less Stalin) talk about it? No such passage exists,' declared a leading theorist in 1981.[3] But, at the same time, this democratic impulse is regarded as having been abused when the loyalties thus gained were drawn on to involve the people in endless and ill-founded struggle movements against 'class enemies'.

That does not mean that Teng Hsiao-p'ing and his ideological spokes-

---

[2] *Resolution on CPC history (1949–81)*, 28. (Par. 17 of the Resolution.)
[3] Liao Kai-lung, talk of 8 October 1981 on the Resolution of 27 June on party history, *Yunnan she-hui k'o-hsueh* 2 (1982) 107.

men believe that Mao Tse-tung had come anywhere near to solving the problem of democracy under socialism. I have noted above, in Part 2, Mao's scant regard, in his later years, for any sort of formal and institutionalized democratic procedures. Teng Hsiao-p'ing himself, in perhaps the most remarkable speech he has made since 1978, declared in August 1980 that negative phenomena such as over-centralization and the excessive powers enjoyed by individual leaders, in particular by Mao, had resulted not only from the 'tradition of feudal despotism' inherited from the old China, but also from 'the tradition of concentrating power to a high degree in the hands of individual leaders in the work of parties in various countries in the days of the Communist International'. These influences, Teng argued, led to a bad system, and when the system is bad, even great figures may be encouraged in evildoing rather than restrained by it:

When Stalin gravely disrupted the socialist legal system, Comrade Mao Zedong said that this kind of thing could not have happened in Western countries such as England, France, and the United States. But although he himself recognized this point, because the problems of the system had not really been solved . . ., there none the less came about the ten years of calamity of the 'Cultural Revolution'.[4]

Teng therefore gave it as his goal 'to reform and perfect, in a practical way, the party and state systems, and to ensure, on the basis of these systems, the democratization of the political life of the party and the state, the democratization of economic management, and the democratization of the life of society as a whole'.[5] The clear implication of this approach is that, despite all the talk in the 1960s about breaking with the Soviet model, Mao Tse-tung's approach to political leadership remained to the end marked by Leninist authoritarianism.

As for the speed with which China could complete her revolution, whether or not Mao Tse-tung, as some have argued, regarded socialism as a mere way-station on the road to communism, he certainly believed that China, a decade or so after 1949, was already well launched on the process of creating a socialist society. Since 1978, on the other hand, the view has come to be accepted that China still has a long way to go to build socialism, let alone communism. In 1979, the term 'undeveloped socialism' (*pu-fa-ta ti she-hui-chu-i*) was introduced to characterize China's current stage of development. This concept was widely used for a year or two, and then rejected by the leadership because it appeared to cast too much doubt on whether socialism had taken root in China at all. Since June 1981, it has been said

---

[4] Teng Hsiao-p'ing, 'On the reform of the system of party and state leadership', speech of 18 August 1980 to the Politburo, in *Selected works of Deng Xiaoping (1975–1982)*, 311–12.
[5] *Ibid.* 319. (Translation modified on the basis of the Chinese text.)

rather that China is in the 'primary stage' of socialism, and still greater prominence has been given to this formulation since the Thirteenth Party Congress of October-November 1987.[6]

This assertion has both political and economic implications. It is argued that socialism will, in due course, bring not only greater abundance, but a higher level of democracy than any capitalist society can achieve. For the time being, however, because Chinese socialism is not highly developed, the capitalist countries may *appear* superior in many ways. Hence the threat of 'bourgeois liberalization'. Teng Hsiao-p'ing evoked the inter-relationship between these factors in a talk of April 1987, highlighting the need to move beyond a 'socialism marked by poverty', but stressing that this could not be achieved before the middle of the next century.[7] At the Thirteenth Congress, Chao Tzu-yang defined the parameters of the current line as follows:

> To believe that the Chinese people cannot take the socialist road without going through the stage of fully developed capitalism is to take a mechanistic position on the question of the development of revolution, and that is the major cognitive root of Right mistakes. On the other hand, to believe that it is possible to jump over the primary stage of socialism, in which the productive forces are to be highly developed, is to take a utopian position on this question, and that is the major cognitive root of Left mistakes.[8]

Chao has called for a new political structure to replace that 'which took shape during the revolutionary war years, was basically established in the period of socialist transformation' and 'developed in large-scale mass movements and in the process of constantly intensified mandatory planning'. In other words, Chao Tzu-yang wishes to adapt the political super-structure to the new era of the socialist commodity economy. But, at the same time, 'Great practice requires great theory,' declared Chao in his report, thus inverting Lenin's well-known axiom: 'Without revolutionary theory there can be no revolutionary movement.' This reversal is in fact characteristic of Chinese Marxism under Mao, as well as under Teng. But if theory must be grounded in practice, it defines goals, and asserts values, which are not simply immanent in reality.

Chao Tzu-yang refers to two (and only two) 'historic flying leaps' (*li-shih hsing fei-yao*) in the integration of Marxism with Chinese practice: the road to

---

[6] See Schram, *Ideology and policy*, 12–13, 35, and par.33 of the Resolution of 27 June 1981.

[7] 'We must continue to build socialism and eliminate poverty', in Teng Hsiao-p'ing, *Fundamental issues in present-day China*, 174–9. (Conversation of 26 April 1987 with Lubomir Strougal.) For a more detailed discussion of this line of thought in Teng Hsiao-p'ing's recent utterances, see my article 'China after the 13th Congress', *CQ* 114 (June 1988) 177–97.

[8] *Beijing Review*, 45 (1987) III—IV (insert). (Translation corrected on the basis of the Chinese text.)

power, and the reforms since the third plenum.[9] This plainly implies that the present leadership is carrying through an exercise in 'sinification' which Mao, after his earlier success, was unable to repeat after 1949. The current context Chao defines as follows:

Because our socialism has emerged from the womb of a semi-colonial, semi-feudal society, with the productive forces lagging far behind those of the developed capitalist countries, we are destined to go through a very long primary stage. During this stage, we shall accomplish industrialization and the commercialization, socialization, and modernization of production which many other countries have achieved under capitalist conditions.[10]

This whole theoretical framework, which envisages a social system designed to constitute the functional equivalent of the capitalist stage in the development of Western societies, while remaining somehow socialist in essence, might be seen as a return to the idea of an 'independent new-democratic stage' put forward by Mao Tse-tung in Yenan, and repudiated by him in 1953. At the same time, both theory and policy remain clearly directed toward the long-term goals of socialism and communism.

One author has recently concluded that today, the Chinese revolution is no longer 'continuous', as it was in the Maoist era.[11] In fact, though the mode and rationale of 'building socialism' have been transformed, a continuing process of radical change is still envisaged. Teng, like Mao, regards politics as central to socialist development, but in his case it is politics guiding and shaping the economic basis, rather than politics and ideology taking precedence over everything, and abrogating economic laws. A significantly different conception of Marxism is thus being applied today in China, but always with the same goal of making China rich and powerful, and building a new society which will be both socialist and distinctively Chinese.

I argued in Part 1 that Mao had devised the concept of the 'principal contradiction' because, unlike Marx, who was never in doubt as to the basic conflict underlying Western society in his own day (that between the proletariat and the bourgeoisie), Mao lived in a world characterized by a bewildering variety of social strata, deposited layer by layer in the course of a century of rapid change. Chinese and world society are not likely, in the coming decades, to grow less complex, nor is the interaction between countries and cultures likely to grow less intense. In this context, Mao's ideas about contradictions may provide, if not a map, then a compass, for charting the contours of a changing reality.

---

[9] *Ibid.* XXV–XXVI.   [10] *Ibid.* IV.
[11] See Lowell Dittmer, *China's continuous revolution. The post-liberation epoch 1949–1981*, especially pp. 257–69.

At the same time, Mao himself, as I have noted repeatedly (and as he remarked more than once), was full of contradictons. In an effort to sum these all up, let me conclude with what may appear to be nothing more than a bit of folklore, but has perhaps a deeper significance. I quoted above Mao's statements, and those of the Tsing-hua University Middle School Red Guards, regarding the Monkey King, Sun Wu-k'ung, at the beginning of the Cultural Revolution. Mao had repeatedly used Monkey as a political symbol in earlier years, and prior to the Great Leap, virtually all of these references were negative. Indeed, in May 1938 he went so far as to identify Monkey with the 'fascist aggressors' who would be buried in the end beneath the 'Mountain of the Five Elements' constituted by the peace front.[12] But suddenly, in 1958, the tone changed, and Mao declared:

Monkey paid no heed to the law or to Heaven (*wu-fa wu-t'ien*). Why don't we all learn from him? His anti-dogmatism [was manifested in] daring to do whatever he liked . . .[13]

Perhaps that sums up, better than any other single image, the essence of Mao's political role, and its profound ambiguity. Eternal rebel, refusing to be bound by the laws of God or man, nature or Marxism, he led his people for three decades in pursuit of a vision initially noble, which turned increasingly into a mirage, and then into a nightmare. Was he a Faust or Prometheus, attempting the impossible for the sake of humanity, or a despot of unbridled ambition, drunk with his own power and his own cleverness? More of the latter than used to be imagined, no doubt, and yet something of the former as well. Even today, the final verdict, both on the man and on his thought, must still remain open.

[12] Mao, *SW* 2.147.   [13] *Wan-sui* (1969) 185; *Miscellany*, 29.

BIBLIOGRAPHY

Ai Ssu-ch'i. *Che-hsueh yü sheng-huo* (Philosophy and life). Shanghai: Tu-shu sheng-huo ch'u-pan-she, 1937
Ai Ssu-ch'i. *Ta-chung che-hsueh* (Philosophy for the masses). Shanghai: Tu-shu sheng-huo ch'u-pan-she, 1936
Australian Journal of Chinese Affairs. Semi-annual. Canberra: Australian National University, Contemporary China Centre. 1979–
Baum, R. and Teiwes, F. C. *Ssu-ch'ing. The Socialist Education Movement of 1962–1966.* Berkeley: Center for Chinese Studies, 1968
Beijing Review. Peking: 1958– . (Prior to January 1979, *Peking Review.*)
Carrère d'Encausse, H. and Schram, S. *Marxism and Asia.* London: Allen Lane, The Penguin Press, 1969
Chang Ch'un-ch'iao. 'P'o-ch'u tzu-ch'an-chieh-chi ti fa-ch'üan ssu-hsiang' (Eliminate the ideology of bourgeois right). *Jen-min jih-pao,* 13 October 1958
Chang Wen-t'ien hsüan-chi (Selected works of Chang Wen-t'ien). Peking: Jen-min ch'u-pan-she, 1985
Chang Wen-t'ien, 'Lu-shan ti fa-yen' (Intervention at Lu-shan), in *Chang Wen-t'ien hsüan-chi,* 480–506
Chao Tzu-yang. Report of October 1987 to the Thirteenth Party Congress. *Beijing Review,* 45 (1987) inset
Che-hsueh yen-chiu (Philosophical research). Peking: 1955–66, 1978–
Ch'en, Jerome. *Mao papers.* London: Oxford University Press, 1970
Ch'en Pei-ou. *Jen-min hsüeh-hsi tzu-tien* (People's study dictionary). Shanghai: Kuang-i shu-chü, 2nd edn., 1953
Ch'en Po-chün. 'Lun k'ang-Jih yu-chi chan-cheng ti chi-pen chan-shu: hsi-chi' (On the basic tactic of the anti-Japanese guerrilla war: the surprise attack). *Chieh-fang,* 28 (11 January 1938) 14–19
Cheng-chih chou-pao (Political weekly). Peking: 1924–
Cheng Chih-piao. 'Mao Tse-tung chien-tang hsüeh-shuo ti li-shih fen-ch'i' (An historical periodization of Mao Tse-tung's thought on party-building). *Mao Tse-tung ssu-hsiang yen-chiu* (Chengtu), 2 (1985) 72–6, 93
Cheng, J. Chester. *The politics of the Chinese Red Army*: a translation of the *Bulletin of Activities* of the People's Liberation Army. Stanford: The Hoover Institution, 1966
Chieh-fang jih-pao (Liberation daily). Yenan: 1941–6
Chin Chih-pai. 'P'i-K'ung yü lu-hsien tou-cheng' (Criticizing Confucius and line struggle). *Hung-ch'i* 7 (1974) 23–34; translated in *Peking Review,* 32 (1974) 6–10, 12 and 33 (1974) 8–12
Chin, Steve S. K. *The thought of Mao Tse-tung. Form and content.* Hong Kong:

University of Hong Kong, Centre of Chinese Studies, 1979

China Quarterly, The. Quarterly. London: Congress for Cultural Freedom (Paris), 1960–1968; Contemporary China Institute, School of Oriental and African Studies, 1968– . Cited as *CQ*.

Chou Yang. 'The fighting task confronting workers in philosophy and the social sciences' (speech of 26 September 1963). *Peking Review*, 1 (1964) 10–27

Chou Yang. 'Kuan-yü Ma-k'o-ssu-chu-i ti chi-ko li-lun wen-t'i ti t'an-t'ao' (An exploration of some theoretical questions of Marxism). *Jen-min jih-pao*, 16 March 1983

Ch'üan-kuo Mao Tse-tung che-hsueh ssu-hsiang t'ao-lun hui lun-wen hsuan (Selected essays from the national conference to discuss Mao Tse-tung's philosophical thought). Nan-ning: Kwangsi jen-min ch'u-pan-she, 1982

Chung-kung yen-chiu (Research on Chinese Communism). Taipei

Chung-kuo jen-min chieh-fang chün cheng-chih hsueh-yuan hsun-lien pu t'u-shu tzu-liao kuan, *Mao Tse-tung chu-tso, yen-lun, wen-tien mu-lu* (A bibliography of Mao Tse-tung's writings, speeches, and telegrams). [Peking: February 1961]

Chung-kuo che-hsueh (Chinese philosophy). Peking: August 1979–

Chung-kuo Kuo-min-tang ch'üan-kuo tai-piao ta-hui hui-i-lu (Minutes of the National Congress of the Kuomintang of China). [Canton]: Chung-kuo Kuo-min-tang ch'üan-kuo ta-hui mi-shu-ch'u, [1924?]. Reprinted, Washington, DC, Center for Chinese Research Materials, 1971

Cohen, A. *The communism of Mao Tse-tung.* Chicago: University of Chicago Press, 1964

Compton, Boyd. *Mao's China: party reform documents, 1942–44.* Seattle: University of Washington Press, 1952

Day, M. Henri. *Máo Zédōng 1917–1927: documents* (Skriftserien för orientaliska studier 14). Stockholm, 1975

Dittmer, Lowell. *China's continuous revolution: the post-liberation epoch 1949–1981,* Berkeley: University of California Press 1987

Eighth National Congress of the Communist Party of China. Peking: Foreign Languages Press, 1956

Engels, Friedrich. 'Persia and China'. In *Karl Marx and Frederick Engels on colonialism*, 123–9

Esherick, Joseph W. 'On the "Restoration of capitalism": Mao and Marxist theory'. *Modern China*, 5.1 (January 1979) 41–77

Fairbank, John K. and Feuerwerker, Albert. *The Cambridge History of China* 13. Cambridge: Cambridge University Press, 1986

Fitzgerald, John. 'Mao in mufti: newly identified works by Mao Zedong'. *The Australian Journal of Chinese Affairs*, 9 (January 1983) 1–16

Garver, John. 'The origins of the Second United Front: the Comintern and the Chinese Communist Party', *CQ* 113 (March 1988) 29–59

Gernet, Jacques. 'Introduction', in S. Schram (ed.), *Foundations and limits of state power in China*, xv–xxvii

Glunin, V. I. 'The Comintern and the rise of the communist movement in China (1920–1927)'. In *The Comintern and the East* (ed. R. A. Ulyanovsky), 280–344

Goodman, David S. G. *Centre and province in the People's Republic of China: Sichuan and Guizhou, 1955–1965.* Cambridge: Cambridge University Press, 1986

Graham, Angus. *The book of Lieh-tzu*. London: John Murray, 1960
Graham, Angus. *Chuang-tzu*. The seven inner chapters and other writings from the book *Chuang-tzu*. London: Allen and Unwin, 1981
Grigoriev, A. M. 'The Comintern and the revolutionary movement in China under the slogan of the soviets (1927–1931)'. In *The Comintern and the East* (ed. R. A. Ulyanovsky). Moscow: Progress Publishers, 1979, 345–88
Harding, Harry. *Organizing China. The problem of bureaucracy 1949–1976*. Stanford: Stanford University Press, 1981
The historical experience of the dictatorship of the proletariat. Peking: Foreign Languages Press, 1959
History of the Communist Party of the Soviet Union (Bolsheviks). Moscow: Foreign Languages Publishing House, 1939
Hōgaku kenkyū (Legal research). Tokyo: Keiō University, founded *c*. 1925
Hsi-lo-k'e-fu [Shirokov] and others (translated by Li Ta and others). *Pien-cheng-fa wei-wu-lun chiao-ch'eng* (Course of instruction in dialectical materialism). Shanghai: Pi-keng-t'ang shu-tien, 15 May 1933
Hsiang-chiang p'ing-lun (Hsiang River review). Changsha: 14 July–18 August 1919
Hsiang-tao chou-pao (The guide weekly). Canton: Kuo-kuang shu-tien, Sept. 1922 – July 1927
Hsiao Sheng and Chiang Hua-hsuan. 'Ti-i-tz'u Kuo-Kung ho-tso t'ung-i chan-hsien ti hsing-ch'eng' (The formation of the first Kuomintang-Communist United Front). *Li-shih yen-chiu*, 2 (1981) 51–68
Hsin-hua yueh-pao wen-chai-pan (New China monthly digest). Monthly. Peking: 1979–1980. From 1981, retitled *Hsin-hua wen-chai* (New China Digest)
Hsin-min hsueh-hui tzu-liao (Materials on the New People's Study Society), ed. Chung-kuo ko-ming po-wu kuan, Hunan sheng po-wu-kuan. Peking: Jen-min ch'u-pan-she, 1980 (Chung-kuo hsien-tai ko-ming shih tzu-liao ts'ung-k'an)
Hsiung, James Chieh. *Ideology and practice. The evolution of Chinese communism*. New York: Praeger, 1970
Hsueh-hsi li-shih chueh-i chuan-chi (Specialized collection on the study of the resolution on [party] history. Peking: Publishing House of the Central Party School, 1982
Hsüeh-hsi wen-hsüan (Selected documents for study). n. p., n. d. [1967?]
Hu Hua, *Chung-kuo she-hui-chu-i ko-ming ho chien-she shih chiang-i* (Textbook on the history of China's socialist revolution and construction). Peking: Chung-kuo jen-min ta-hsueh ch'u-pan-she, 1985
Hu Hui-chang. 'Ta lien kang-t'ieh yun-tung chieh-k'uang' (A brief account of the campaign to make steel in a big way). *Tang-shih yen-chiu tzu-liao*, 4 (1983) 762–65
Huang, Philip. 'Mao Tse-tung and the middle peasants, 1925–1928'. *Modern China*, 1.3 (July 1975) 271–96
Hung-ch'i (Red flag). Peking: 1 June 1958–16 June 1988. (From July 1988, replaced by *Ch'iu-shih* (Seeking the truth).)
Issues and studies. Taipei
I-ta ch'ien-hou (Before and after the First Congress). ed. Chung-kuo she-hui k'o-hsueh yuan hsien-tai shih yen-chiu-shih, Chung-kuo ko-ming po-wu-kuan

tang-shih yen-chiu-shih. Peking: Jen-min ch'u-pan-she, 1980. (Chung-kuo hsien-tai ko-ming shih tzu-liao ts'ung k'an).

Jen-min jih-pao (People's Daily). Peking: 1949– . Cited as *JMJP*

Jen-min ta hsien-chang hsueh-hsi shou-ts'e (Handbook for the study of the people's Constitution). Shanghai: Chan-wan chou-k'an, November 1949

Jen-min ta hsien-chang hsueh-hsi tzu-liao (Materials for the study of the people's Constitution). Tientsin: Lien-ho t'u-shu ch'u-pan-she, October 1949

K'ang-chan ta-hsueh (The War of Resistance University), 6–8, April–June 1938

Knight, Nick. *Mao Zedong's 'On contradiction'. An annotated translation of the pre-liberation text.* Nathan, Queensland: Griffith University, 1981. (Griffith Asian Papers Series 2.)

Knight, Nick. 'Mao Zedong's *On contradiction* and *On practice*: pre-liberation texts'. *CQ* 84 (December 1980) 641–68

Kraus, Richard. *Class conflict in Chinese socialism.* New York: Columbia University Press, 1981

Kuan-yü chien-kuo i-lai tang ti jo-kan li-shih wen-t'i chueh-i chu-shih pen (hsiu-ting). (Annotated edition of the Resolution (of 27 June 1981) on some questions of party history since 1949. Revised). Peking: Jen-min ch'u-pan-she, 1985

Kung Yü-chih. 'Fa-chan k'o-hsüeh pi-yu chih lu – chieh-shao Mao Tse-tung t'ung-chih wei chuan-tai "Ts'ung i-ch'uan hsüeh t'an pai-chia cheng ming" i wen hsieh ti hsin ho an-yü' (The way which the development of science must follow – presenting Comrade Mao Tse-tung's letter and annotation relating to the re-publication of 'Let a hundred schools of thought contend viewed from the perspective of genetics'). *Kuang-ming jih-pao*, 28 December 1983

Kung Yü-chih. 'Mao Tse-tung yü tzu-jan k'o-hsüeh' (Mao Tse-tung and the natural sciences), in *Mao Tse-tung ti tu-shu sheng-huo*, 83–114

Kung Yü-chih. '"Shih-chien lun" san t'i' (Three points regarding 'On practice'), in *Lun Mao Tse-tung che-hsüeh ssu-hsiang* (On Mao Tse-tung's philosophical thought). Peking: Jen-min ch'u-pan-she, 1983, 66–86

Kung Yü-chih, P'ang Hsien-chih and Shih Chung-chüan. *Mao Tse-tung ti tu-shu sheng-huo* (Mao Tse-tung's reading activities). Peking: San-lien shu-tien, 1986

Kuo Hua-jo. 'Mao chu-hsi k'ang-chan ch'u-ch'i kuang-hui ti che-hsueh huo-tung' (Chairman Mao's brilliant philosophical activity during the early period of the anti-Japanese war). *Chung-kuo che-hsueh*, 1 (1979) 31–7

Kyōto Daigaku Jimbun Kagaku Kenkyūsho. *Mō Takutō chosaku nenpyō* (Chronological table of Mao Tse-tung's works), Vol. 2. *Goi sakuin* (Glossary and Index) Kyoto: Kyōto Daigaku Jimbun Kagaku Kenkyūsho, 1980

Lardy, N. and K. Lieberthal (eds.) *Ch'en Yun's strategy for China's development.* Armonk: M. E. Sharpe, 1983

Le Gros Clark, Cyril Drummond. *The prose-poetry of Su Tung-p'o.* Shanghai: Kelly and Walsh, 1935

Legge, James. *The Chinese classics.* 5 vols. Reprinted Hong Kong: Hong Kong University Press, 1960

Lenin, V. I. 'Conspectus of Hegel's *Science of logic'. Collected works* 38. Moscow: Foreign Languages Publishing House, 1961, 85–238

Lewis, John Wilson (ed.) *Party leadership and revolutionary power in China.* Cambridge: Cambridge University Press, 1970

Li Hsin. 'Kuan-yü Chung-kuo chin-hsien-tai li-shih fen-ch'i wen-t'i' (On problems of periodization of Chinese modern and contemporary history). *Li-shih yen-chiu*, 4 (1983) 3–6

Li Jui. *Mao Tse-tung t'ung-chih ti ch'u-ch'i ko-ming huo-tung* (The early revolutionary activities of Comrade Mao Tse-tung). Peking: Chung-kuo ch'ing-nien ch'u-pan-she, 1957

Li Jui. *The early revolutionary activities of Comrade Mao Tse-tung.* Translated by Anthony W. Sariti, edited by James C. Hsiung, introduction by Stuart R. Schram. White Plains, N. Y.: M. E. Sharpe, 1977. (Translation of Li Jui, 1957.)

Li Jui. 'Hsueh-sheng shih-tai ti Mao Tse-tung' (Mao Tse-tung during his student years). *Hsin-hua wen-chai*, 1 (1984) 175–81

Li Jui. *Lun San-hsia kung-ch'eng* (On the three gorges project). Changsha: Hunan chi-shu ch'u-pan-she, 1985

Li Jui. *Mao Tse-tung ti tsao-ch'i ko-ming huo-tung.* Changsha: Hunan jen-min ch'u-pan-she, 1980 (Revised edition of Li Jui, 1957)

Li Jui. 'Ch'ung tu Chang Wen-t'ien ti "Lushan ti fa-yen"' (On re-reading Chang Wen-t'ien's intervention on Lushan). *Tu-shu*, 8 (1985) 28–38

Li-shih yen-chiu (Historical research). Monthly. Peking: 1954–66, 1975–

Li Ta-chao. *Li Ta-chao hsuan-chi* (Selected works of Li Ta-chao). Peking: Jen-min, 1962

Li Ta-chao. 'Ya-hsi-ya ch'ing-nien ti kuang-ming yun-tung' (The luminous Asiatic youth movement). In *Li Ta-chao hsuan-chi* 327–29

Liang Hsiao. 'Yen-chiu Ju-Fa tou-cheng ti li-shih ching-yen' (Study the historical experience of the struggle between the Confucian and Legalist schools). *Hung-ch'i*, 10 (1974) 56–70

Liao Kai-lung. 'Ch'üan-mien chien-she she-hui-chu-i ti tao-lu' (The road to building socialism in an all-round way). *Yün-nan she-hui k'o-hsüeh*, 2 (1982) 1–8

Liao Kai-lung. *Ch'üan-mien chien-she she-hui-chu-i ti tao-lu* (The road to building socialism in an all-round way). Peking: Chung-kung chung-yang tang-hsiao ch'u-pan-she, 1983

Liao Kai-lung. 'Kuan-yü hsueh-hsi "chueh-i" chung t'i-ch'u ti i-hsieh wen-t'i chieh-ta' (Answers and explanations regarding some questions which have been posed in connection with the study of the 'Resolution [of 27 June 1981]'). *Yun-nan she-hui k'o-hsueh*, 2 (March 1982) 101–10

Liao Kai-lung. 'Kuan-yü Mao Tse-tung kung-kuo p'ing-chia ho she-hui-chu-i kao-tu min-chu – tui Shih-la-mu chiao-shou lun Mao Tse-tung ti chi p'ien wen-chang ti p'ing-shu' (Regarding the evaluation of Mao Tse-tung's merits and faults, and high-level socialist democracy – a commentary and evaluation on several articles by Professor Schram on Mao Tse-tung), in Liao, *Ch'üan-mien . . .*, 319–37

Liao Kai-lung. 'Li-shih ti ching-yen ho wo-men ti fa-chan tao-lu' (The experience of history and the path of our development), *Chung-kung yen-chiu* (Taipei), (September 1981) 107–77

Liao Kai-lung. 'She-hui-chu-i she-hui chung ti chieh-chi tou-cheng ho jen-min nei-pu mao-tun wen-t'i' (The problem of class struggle and of contradictions among the people in socialist society), in Liao, *Ch'üan-mien. . .*, 229–83

Liao Kai-lung. *Tang-shih t'an-so* (Explorations in party history). Peking: Chung-kung chung-yang tang-hsiao ch'u-pan-she, 1983

Lin Yun-hui. 'Lueh lun Mao Tse-tung t'ung-chih tui Li-san lu-hsien ti jen-shih ho ti-chih' (A brief account of Mao Tse-tung's understanding of, and resistance to, the Li Li-san line). *Tang-shih yen-chiu*, 4 (1980) 51–9

Ling Yü. 'Mao Tse-tung t'ung-chih ho Li-san lu-hsien ti kuan-hsi t'ao-lun tsung-shu' (A summary of the discussion regarding Comrade Mao Tse-tung's relationship to the Li Li-san line). *Tang-shih yen-chiu*, 3 (1982) 78–80

Liu Shao-ch'i. 'Letter to Comrade Sung Liang [Sun Yeh-fang]'. *Hung-ch'i*, 7 (1980) 2–4

Liu Shao-ch'i. *Lun tang* (On the party). Dairen: Ta-chung shu-tien, 1947

Lun Mao Tse-tung ti che-hsueh ssu-hsiang (On Mao Tse-tung's philosophical thought). Peking: Jen-min ch'u-pan-she, 1983

McDonald, Angus. *The urban origins of rural revolution. Elites and masses in Hunan Province, China, 1911–1927*. Berkeley: University of California Press, 1978

MacFarquhar, Roderick. *The origins of the Cultural Revolution. 1. Contradictions among the people, 1956–1957. 2. The Great Leap Forward, 1958–1960*. London: Oxford University Press, 1974, 1983

MacFarquhar, Roderick, and Fairbank, John K., *The Cambridge History of China* 14. Cambridge: Cambridge University Press, 1987

Mantici, Giorgio. *Pensieri del fiume Xiang*. Rome: Editori Riuniti, 1981

Mao Chu-hsi kuan-yü kuo-nei min-tsu wen-t'i ti lun-shu hsüan-pien (Selections from Chairman Mao's expositions regarding problems of nationalities within the country). [Peking]: Kuo-chia min-tsu shih-wu wei-yuan-hui ti-san ssu (Third Department of the State Commission on Minority Affairs), October 1978

Mao Chu-hsi tui P'eng, Huang, Chang, Chou fan-tang chi-t'uan ti p'i-p'ang (Chairman Mao's criticism and repudiation of the P'eng, Huang, Chang, Chou anti-party clique). [Peking: 1967]

Mao Chu-hsi wen-hsuan (Selected writings by Chairman Mao). n.p., n.d. [Peking, 1969?]

Mao Tse-tung. *Basic tactics* (edited and translated by Stuart R. Schram). New York: Praeger, 1966. (Although the Chinese original used for this translation, *Chi-ch'u chan-shu* (Hankow: Tzu-ch'iang ch'u-pan-she, 1938) has Mao's name on the title page as author, it is, as indicated above, almost certainly not by him.)

Mao Tse-tung che-hsüeh p'i-chu-chi (Mao Tse-tung's collected annotations on philosophy). Peking: Chung-yang wen-hsien yen-chiu-shih, 1988

Mao Tse-tung che-hsüeh ssu-hsiang (chai-lu) (Mao Tse-tung's philosophical thought (Extracts)). Compiled by the Department of Philosophy of Peking University. [Peking]: 1960

Mao Tse-tung chu-tso hsuan-tu (Selected readings from Mao Tse-tung's writings). 2 vols. Peking: Jen-min ch'u-pan-she, 1986

Mao Tsetung. *A critique of Soviet economics*. Translated by Moss Roberts. New York: Monthly Review Press, 1977

Mao Tse-tung. *Pien-cheng wei-wu-lun. Chiang-shou t'i-kang*. (Dialectical materialism. Lecture notes). Dairen: Ta-chung shu-tien, n. d. [*c.* 1946]

Mao Tse-tung. *Quotations from Chairman Mao Tse-tung*. Peking: People's Publishing House, 1966

Mao Tse-tung. *Selected readings*. Peking: Foreign Languages Press, 1967. (Translation of an earlier, and substantially different, version of *Mao Tse-tung chu-tso hsuan-tu.*)

Mao Tse-tung. *Selected works of Mao Tse-tung.* 5 vols. Peking: 1960–5 and 1977

Mao Tse-tung shu-hsin hsuan-chi (Selected letters of Mao Tse-tung). Peking: Jen-min ch'u-pan-she, 1983

Mao Tse-tung ssu-hsiang wan-sui (Long live Mao Tse-tung thought). [Peking: 1967]

Mao Tse-tung ssu-hsiang wan-sui (Long live Mao Tse-tung thought). [Peking: 1967], supplement

Mao Tse-tung ssu-hsiang wan-sui! (Long live Mao Tse-tung thought!) [Peking: 1969]

Mao Tse-tung ssu-hsiang yen-chiu (Research on Mao Tse-tung's thought). Quarterly. Chengtu: 1983–

Mao Tse-tung t'ung-chih lun Ma-k'o-ssu-chu-i che-hsüeh (chai-lu) (Comrade Mao Tse-tung on Marxist philosophy – extracts). Urumchi: Hsin-chiang ch'ing-nien ch'u-pan-she, 1960. (Compiled by the Office for Teaching and Research in Philosophy of the Party School under the Chinese Communist Party Committee, Sinkiang Uighur Autonomous District.)

Mao Tse-tung ssu-hsiang yen-chiu (Research on Mao Tse-tung's thought). Quarterly. Chengtu: 1983–

Mao Zedong. Une étude de l'éducation physique (edited and translated by Stuart R. Schram). Paris: Mouton, 1962

Marx, Karl. 'Critique of the Gotha programme'. In Karl Marx and Frederick Engels, *Selected works.* London: Laurence and Wishart, 1970, 311–31

Marx, Karl. 'Revolution in China and in Europe', in *Marx and Engels on colonialism*, 15–23

Marx, K. and Engels, F. *On colonialism.* Moscow: Foreign Languages Publishing House, n.d.

Mei-chou p'ing-lun (Weekly review). Peking: 22 Dec. 1918–31 Aug. 1919

Meisner, Maurice. *Li Ta-chao and the origins of Chinese Marxism.* Cambridge, Mass.: Harvard University Press, 1967

Miscellany of Mao Tse-tung thought. Arlington, Virginia: Joint Publications Research Service, 1974 (JPRS no. 61269). (Translation of materials from *Mao Tse-tung ssu-hsiang wan-sui.*)

Mi-ting (M. Mitin) and others. Translated by Ai Ssu-ch'i and others. *Hsin che-hsüeh ta-kang* (Outline of the new philosophy). Shanghai: Tu-shu sheng-huo ch'u-pan-she, 1936

Modern China. Los Angeles: 1975–

'More on the historical experience of the dictatorship of the proletariat'. *Jen-min jih-pao*, 29 December 1956

'On the historical experience of the dictatorship of the proletariat'. *Jen-min jih-pao*, 5 April 1956

Pai-chia cheng-ming – fa-chan k'o-hsüeh ti pi-yu chih lu. 1956 nien 8 yueh Tsingtao i-ch'uan hsüeh tso-t'an hui chi-shu (Let a hundred schools contend – the way which the development of science must follow. The record of the August 1956 Tsingtao conference on genetics). Peking: Commercial Press, 1985

Pan Ku. *The History of the Former Han Dynasty* (translated by Homer H. Dubs). 3 volumes. Baltimore: Waverly Press, 1938, 1944, 1955

P'eng Te-huai. 'Letter of opinion'. In *The Case of P'eng Teh-huai. 1959–1968.* Hong Kong: Union Research Institute, 1969, 7–13

Resolution on CPC history (1949–1981). Peking: Foreign Languages Press, 1981

Rōnin. English-language periodical, Tokyo, founded *c*. 1970

Saich, Tony. *The origins of the First United Front in China: the role of Sneevliet alias Maring*. Leiden: Brill, forthcoming

Scalopino, Robert. 'The evolution of a young revolutionary – Mao Zedong in 1919–1921'. *JAS* 42.1 (Nov. 1982) 29–61

Schram, Stuart. 'Chairman Hua edits Mao's literary heritage: "On the ten great relationships"'. *CQ* 69 (March 1977) 126–35

Schram, Stuart. 'China after the Thirteenth Congress', *CQ* 114 (June 1988) 177–97

Schram, Stuart. 'Decentralization in a unitary state: theory and practice 1940–1984'. In S. Schram (ed.), *The scope of state power in China*, 81–125

Schram, Stuart. *Documents sur la théorie de la 'révolution permanente' en Chine*. Paris: Mouton, 1963

Schram, Stuart (ed.). *Foundations and limits of state power in China*. London: SOAS and Hong Kong: The Chinese University Press, 1987

Schram, Stuart. *Ideology and policy in China since the Third Plenum, 1978–84*. London: SOAS, 1984

Schram, Stuart. 'The limits of cataclysmic change: reflections on the place of the "Great Proletarian Cultural Revolution" in the political development of the People's Republic of China'. *CQ* 108 (Dec. 1986) 613–24

Schram, Stuart. *Mao Tse-tung*. Revised edn. Harmondsworth: Penguin, 1967

Schram, Stuart. 'Mao Tse-tung and the theory of the permanent revolution, 1958–1969'. *CQ* 46 (April–June 1971) 221–44

Schram, Stuart (ed.). *Mao Tse-tung unrehearsed*. Harmondsworth: Penguin, 1974

Schram, Stuart. *Mao Zedong: a preliminary reassessment*. Hong Kong: The Chinese University Press, 1983

Schram, Stuart. 'Mao Zedong and the role of the various classes in the Chinese revolution, 1923–1927', in *Chūgoku no seiji to keizai* (The polity and economy of China). Tokyo: Tōyō Keizai Shinpōsha, 1975 ('The late Professor Yuji Muramatsu commemoration volume') 227–39

Schram, Stuart. 'The Marxist'. In Dick Wilson (ed.), *Mao Tse-tung in the scales of history*. Cambridge: Cambridge University Press, 1977, 35–69

Schram, Stuart. 'New texts by Mao Zedong, 1921–1966'. *Communist Affairs* 2 (2) (1983) 143–65

Schram, Stuart. 'On the nature of Mao Tse-tung's "deviation" in 1927'. *CQ* 27 (April–June 1964) 55–66

Schram, Stuart. 'The party in Chinese communist ideology'. In J. W. Lewis (ed.), *Party leadership and revolutionary power in China*, 170–202

Schram, Stuart. 'Party leader or true ruler? Foundations and significance of Mao Zedong's personal power'. In S. Schram (ed.), *Foundations and limits of state power*, 203–56

Schram, Stuart. *The political thought of Mao Tse-tung*. Revised edition. New York: Praeger, 1969

Schram, Stuart (ed.). *The scope of state power in China*. London: SOAS and Hong Kong: The Chinese University Press, 1984

Schurmann, H. Franz. *Ideology and organization in Communist China*. Berkeley: University of California Press, 1966

Schwartz, Benjamin I. 'The primacy of the political order in East Asian societies'. In S. Schram (ed.), *Foundations and limits of state power*, 1–10

Shaffer, Lynda. *Mao and the workers: the Hunan labor movement, 1920–1923*. Armonk, N. Y.: M. E. Sharpe, 1982

Shaffer, Lynda. 'Mao Ze-dong and the October 1922 Changsha construction workers' strike'. *Modern China*, 4.4 (October 1978) 374–418

Shih Chung-ch'üan. 'Tu Su-lien "Cheng-chih ching-chi hsüeh chiao-k'o shu" ti t'an-hua' (Talks on reading the Soviet textbook of political economy). In *Mao Tse-tung ti tu-shu sheng-huo*, 148–78

Shih Chung-chüan, 'Ma-k'o-ssu so shuo ti "tzu-ch'an chieh-chi fa-ch'üan" ho Mao Tse-tung t'ung-chih tui t'a ti wu-chieh' (The 'bourgeois right' referred to by Marx, and Comrade Mao Tse-tung's misunderstanding of it). *Wen-hsien ho yen-chiu* (1983) 405–17

Shih Chung-chüan. Review of *Mao Tse-tung che-hsüeh p'i-chu-chi*. *Che-hsüeh yen-chiu*, 10 (1987) 3–9, 40

Snow, Edgar. *The long revolution*. London: Hutchinson, 1973

Snow, Edgar. *Red star over China*. London: Gollancz, 1937

Socialist upsurge in China's countryside. Peking: Foreign Languages Press, 1957

Stalin, Joseph. *Economic problems of socialism in the USSR*. Peking: Foreign Languages Press, 1972

Stalin, Joseph. *Marxism and questions of linguistics*. Peking: Foreign Languages Press, 1972

Starr, John Bryan. *Continuing the revolution: the political thought of Mao*. Princeton: Princeton University Press, 1979

Strong, Anna Louise. 'Three interviews with Chairman Mao Zedong'. *CQ* 103 (Sept. 1985) 489–509

Studies in Soviet Thought. Quarterly. Dordrecht: D. Reidel (for the Institute of East-European Studies at the University of Fribourg, Switzerland), 1961–

Su Shao-chih. *Tentative views on the class situation and class struggle in China at the present stage*. Peking: Institute of Marxism-Leninism Mao Zedong Thought, Chinese Academy of Social Sciences, 1981

Su-wei-ai Chung-kuo (Soviet China). Moscow: Izdatel'stvo Inostrannykh Rabochikh, 1934

Sun Tzu. *The Art of war*. Translated and with an introduction by Samuel B. Griffith. Oxford: Clarendon Press, 1963

Takeuchi Minoru (ed.). *Mao Tse-tung chi* (Collected writings of Mao Tse-tung). 10 vols. Tokyo: Hokubōsha, 1970–2. Second edition, Tokyo: Sōsōsha, 1983. *Mao Tse-tung chi, pu chüan* (Supplements to the collected writings of Mao Tse-tung). 10 vols. Tokyo: Sōsōsha, 1983–6

Tang-shih hui-i pao-kao chi (Collection of reports from the meeting on party history). Peking: Chung-kung chung-yang tang-hsiao ch'u-pan-she, 1982

Tang-shih yen-chiu. Peking: Central Party School, 1980–

Tang-shih yen-chiu tzu-liao (Research materials on party history). Chengtu: Szechwan jen-min ch'u-pan-she (for the Museum of the History of the Chinese Revolution), 1980–

Teng Hsiao-p'ing. 'Conversation of 26 April 1987 with Lubomir Strougal'. In Teng Hsiao-p'ing, *Fundamental issues in present-day China*, 174–9

Teng Hsiao-p'ing. *Fundamental issues in present-day China*. Peking: Foreign Languages Press, 1987

Teng Hsiao-p'ing. 'On the reform of the system of party and state leadership', in Teng Hsiao-p'ing, *Selected works*, 302–25

Teng Hsiao-p'ing. *Selected works of Deng Xiaoping (1975–1982)*. Peking: Foreign Languages Publishing House, 1983

Teng Li-ch'ün. Comments of 11–12 August 1981 on the Resolution of 27 June 1981. In *Tang-shih hui-i pao-kao chi*, 74–174

T'ien Yuan. 'Tsai lun Mao Tse-tung t'ung-chih tui Li-san lu-hsien ti jen-shih ho ti-chih' (More on Comrade Mao Tse-tung's understanding of and resistance to the Li Li-san line). *Tang-shih yen-chiu*, 1 (1981) 65–71

Ting Wei-chih and Shih Chung-ch'üan. 'Ch'ün-chung lu-hsien shi wo-men tang ti li-shih ching-yen ti tsung-chieh' (The mass line is the summation of our historical experience). *Wen-hsien ho yen-chiu* (1983) 420–28

Ts'ai Ho-sen wen-chi (Collected writings of Ts'ai Ho-sen). Peking: Jen-min ch'u-pan-she, 1980

Tso-chuan. See Legge's translation, *The Ch'un Tseu* with *The Tso Chuen*, in *The Chinese Classics*, V

Tsou, Tang. 'Marxism, the Leninist party, the masses and the citizens in the re-building of the Chinese state'. In S. Schram (ed.), *Foundations and limits of state power*, 257–89

Tu-shu (Reading). Peking: 1979–

Tung T'ai. 'Tui-tai "wai-lun" ti ching-yen chiao-hsun' (The lessons to be learned from our experience in dealing with "foreign theories" [about China]'. *Jen-min jih-pao*, 9 March 1979

Tzu-liao hsuan-pien (Selected materials). [Peking]: January 1967

Ulyanovsky, R. A., ed. *The Comintern and the East*. Moscow: Progress Publishers, 1979

Wakeman, Frederic. *History and will*. Berkeley: University of California Press, 1973

Wang Nien-i. 'Mao Tse-tung t'ung-chih fa-tung "wen-hua ta ko-ming" shih tui hsing-shih ti ku-chi' (Comrade Mao Tse-tung's estimate of the situation at the time when he launched the 'Great Cultural Revolution'), in *Tang-shih yen-chiu tzu-liao*, 4 (1983) 766–74

Wang Shu-pai and Chang Shen-heng. 'Ch'ing-nien Mao Tse-tung shih-chieh-kuan ti chuan-pien' (The transformation in the world view of the young Mao Tse-tung). *Li-shih yen-chiu*, 5 (1980) 47–64

Watson, Andrew. *Mao Zedong and the political economy of the border region*. Cambridge: Cambridge University Press, 1980

'Wei shih-mo yao cheng-feng?' (Why do we want to rectify?). *Jen-min jih-pao*, 2 May 1956

Wen Chi-tse. 'Mao Tse-tung t'ung-chih tsai Yenan shih-ch'i shih tsen-yang chiao-tao wo-men hsüeh che-hsüeh ti?' (How did Comrade Mao Tse-tung teach us to study philosophy during the Yenan period?). In *Ch'üan-kuo Mao Tse-tung che-hsüeh ssu-hsiang t'ao-lun hui lun-wen hsüan*, 68–82

Wen-hsien ho yen-chiu (Documents and research). Peking: Chung-yang wen-hsien yen-chiu-shih, 1983–

Wilson, Dick (ed.) *Mao Tse-tung in the scales of history*. Cambridge: Cambridge University Press, 1977

Wittfogel, Karl A. 'Some remarks on Mao's handling of concepts and problems of dialectics'. *Studies in Soviet thought* 3.4 (December 1963) 251–77

Womack, Brantly. *The foundations of Mao Tse-tung's political thought*. Honolulu: The University Press of Hawaii, 1982

Wu Chiang. 'Pu-tuan ko-ming lun-che shih ch'e-ti wei-wu lun-che' (A partisan of the theory of the permanent revolution is a thoroughgoing dialectical materialist). *Che-hsüeh yen-chiu*, 8 (1958) 25–8

Wylie, Raymond F. *The emergence of Maoism: Mao Tse-tung, Ch'en Po-ta, and the search for Chinese theory, 1935–1945*. Stanford: Stanford University Press, 1980

Yang, Benjamin. 'The Zunyi Conference as one step in Mao's rise to power', *CQ* 106 (June 1986) 235–71

Yang Ch'ao. *Lun Mao Chu-hsi che-hsüeh t'i-hsi* (On Chairman Mao's philosophical system). Hsi-yang ti-ch'ü yin-shua-so. 2 vols. 1978

Yang Ch'ao. *Wei-wu pien-cheng-fa ti jo-kan li-lun wen-t'i* (Some theoretical problems of materialist dialectics). Chengtu: Szechwan jen-min ch'u-pan-she, 1980. (Revised edition of the previous entry.)

Yao K'ai. 'K'ai-shih ch'üan-mien chien-she she-hui-chu-i ti shih-nien' (The ten years which saw the beginning of the all-round construction of socialism). *Hsueh-hsi li-shih chüeh-i chuan-chi*

Yao Wenyuan. *On the social basis of the Lin Piao anti-party clique*. Peking: Foreign Languages Press, 1975

Yen Yuan. 'Ts'un hsueh', in Yen Yuan, *Ssu ts'un pien*. Peking: Ku-chi ch'u-pan-she, 1957, 40–106

INDEX